Mittie and Thee
An 1853 Roosevelt Romance

Martha "Mittie" Bulloch Roosevelt, at age 22, about 1856,
Courtesy of the Theodore Roosevelt Collection, Houghton Library, Harvard University

Theodore Roosevelt, at age 31, in 1862,
Courtesy of the Theodore Roosevelt Collection, Houghton Library, Harvard University

Mittie & Thee
An 1853 Roosevelt Romance

Connie M. Huddleston
&
Gwendolyn I. Koehler

The Bulloch Letters
Volume I
Friends of Bulloch, Inc.
Roswell, Georgia

Mittie & Thee: An 1853 Roosevelt Romance

Published by:
Friends of Bulloch, Inc.
Roswell, Georgia

Text and cover design copyright © 2015 by Connie M. Huddleston and Gwendolyn I. Koehler.
All rights reserved. No part of this book may be used or reproduced in any manner whatsoever without written permission except in the case of brief quotations embodied in critical articles and reviews. For information, please address Connie Huddleston at Interpreting Time's Past, LLC, 450 Old Richmond Road, South, Crab Orchard, KY 40419.

Cover design by Interpreting Time's Past, LLC

ISBN- 13:978-0-692-52031-4

Images of Martha "Mittie" Bulloch and Theodore Roosevelt courtesy of the Theodore Roosevelt Collection, Houghton Library, Harvard University.

Table of Contents

List of Figures vii
Dedication viii
Acknowledgements. ix
Preface xi
Introduction: Setting the Stage 1
   The Bulloch Family 1
   The Roosevelt Family 15
   Beginnings of the Romance 18
   America in 1853 20
Chapter I: May and June 23
Chapter II: July 43
Chapter III: August 55
Chapter IV: September 103
Chapter V: October 139
Chapter VI: November 183
Chapter VII: December 201
   The Wedding 205
End Notes 209
Bibliography 217
List of Persons 221
Appendix A: The Chronicles of Roswell 233
Appendix B: The Spectre Cow 239
Index 243

List of Figures

Martha "Mittie" Bulloch Roosevelt,
    at age 22, about 1856 ii
Theodore Roosevelt, at age 31, in 1862 ii
1853 Map of Roswell. xv
Roosevelt Family Tree by 1853 xvi
Bulloch Family Tree by 1853 xvii
Franconi's Hippodrome (New York City) 27
New York's Crystal Palace 70
Croton River Dam, 1843 Engraving 86
Croton Reservoir in Manhattan, erected in 1842 86
Uncomfortable Position of Mr. Jones During a
    Table-Turning Experiment 110
Singer Sewing Company Advertisement, 1851 129
The Death of Virginia
    by Guillaume-Guillon Lethière 134
Harper's New Monthly Magazine's Bridal Fashion 179
Interior of Opera House at Niblo's Garden 187
Daniel Elliott's Sprectre Cow illustration 242

Dedication

I dedicate this book to
my dear friend Bonnie Glendening
in appreciation for
her unfailing support and enthusiasm.

Gwendolyn I. Koehler

and

To the Bulloch Hall docents,
who tell this story every day,
and the visitors who listen.

Connie M. Huddleston

Acknowledgements

Without the interest and support of many individuals and groups, publication of these letters would never have been possible. The project began with the collection of historian Clarece Martin, now held in the Bulloch Hall Archives. We deeply appreciate her family's donation of the materials and her initial work on the letters.

The generous monetary donation from the Magnolia Sampler Guild of Bulloch Hall, who fell in love with the charm of Mittie and Thee's story, and the Friends of Bulloch, Inc., who matched their donation, made possible our research at the Houghton Library, Harvard University. Others who contributed to funding this endeavor are chapters of the Daughters of the American Revolution, the Children of the American Revolution, and the Daughters of the Confederacy.

The archivists, curators, and staff of the Houghton Library, Harvard University, graciously assisted our research in the Theodore Roosevelt Collection. In particular, Heather Cole, Curator of the Theodore Roosevelt Collection, guided our access to the letters and provided suggestions of additional materials, many of which proved extremely valuable.

We wish to sincerely thank the remarkable and diligent interns from Kennesaw State University and other universities who enabled us to speed up the lengthy transcription process. Their dedication to cataloging the letters and to assisting with accurate transcription has allowed us to proceed way beyond what we could have accomplished on our own. Included in this part of the work were several of Bulloch Hall's volunteers and docents. Bulloch Hall's staff, Pam Billingsley, Site Coordinator, and Janice Metzler, Assistant Site Coordinator, enthusiastically encouraged us on.

Walt Wilson, valued friend and first reader, checked our facts and injected humor into the process. Our professional editors from Warneke Reading, Natalie and Ed Warneke, read our manuscript as totally objective readers who knew nothing of the story. Their insights and corrections gave us a helpful perspective of our work. Warneke Reading's grammatical suggestions smoothed out our typos and crazy language. Sherron Lawson, kept our feet on the ground, stepped up and read the almost completed manuscript, gave us worthwhile comments, and checked our every dot and dash. For all their input into this labor of love, we thank them from the bottom of our hearts.

Finally, Gwen and Connie have to thank their long-suffering husbands, Arthur Koehler and Charlie Huddleston who have endured five years of our obsession and will continue to suffer as we finish the remaining letters and books. We appreciate their love, their humor, and their sacrificial financial support.

Preface

Bulloch Hall, Roswell, Georgia, is the antebellum home of James Stephens Bulloch and Martha Bulloch. Built in the late 1830s, this Greek Revival town home served as one of the Bulloch children's many homes and was their last in the South. Today, Bulloch Hall is operated as a house museum and is owned and administered by the City of Roswell. The Friends of Bulloch, Inc., (501(c)3) actively work to assure Bulloch Hall is well cared for and funded. The site contains, a reproduction farmhouse entrance center and gift shop, Bulloch Hall, a summer house, two reproduction slave quarters (one of which holds administrative offices), a reproduction carriage house, two reproduction privies, two restored well houses, and a large pavilion used for events.

In 2008, Bulloch Hall's archives received forty-eight boxes from the estate of a local historian filled with miscellaneous papers, memorabilia, print clippings, and copies of newspaper articles covering a wide variety of topics related to Roswell's history. Copies of Bulloch and Roosevelt family letters, some complete and others simply random pages, lay scattered throughout the boxes. After reading through a few of the pages, we (the authors) realized we possessed a treasure trove of family information and stories. Initially we did not have a clear idea of the source of the letters. Later in our search, we found partial lists of letters that had been obtained from the Theodore Roosevelt Collection housed in the Houghton Library, at Harvard University.

In 2014, we (the authors) traveled to Harvard to examine that collection and locate additional letters and/or find missing pages. Curator Heather Cole provided invaluable assistance as we explored the entire Bulloch family-related collection and found additional letters and documents that helped complete the story.

At Bulloch Hall, university interns, volunteers, docents, and staff, helped sort the contents of each box. They matched pages whenever possible, and the arduous four-year-long task of transcribing began. Letters were written on small, often transparent paper with pen and ink, so, the transcriber had to determine if a mark on the page was intentional punctuation or merely an ink blot. Copies of some letters were faint and high intensity lighting and computer enhancement aided in their interpretation. Some words simply remained indecipherable, and some letters were incomplete. We came to every new letter with feelings of anticipation and delight, as each revealed new insights about the family members.

Transcribing letters written in the 19th century poses a fascinating set of problems. There were no standard rules of punctuation or capitalization, and alternate word spellings and meanings were often used. For example Mittie referred to her fiancé as *Thee, Thee-a-te, Thee-ate, Thee a te,* and *Theeate. Myown, atlast,* and *atall* were almost always written as one word, an indication of personal style. Some individuals used hyphens inconsistently. *Grand-mother* would also be written as *grand mother* or *grandmother.* Letter formation varied greatly from writer to writer (if you can't read cursive you can't read old letters). Individual handwriting changed with age, stress, and circumstance. Writers often inserted words above the text (These words are presented as superscript.), and did not capitalize days of the week. It took each transcriber considerable time and patience to become comfortable with individual writing styles. Some writers commonly used dashes between sentences. We found unfamiliar vocabulary words, *quondam* and *philopena*, for instance, which sent us to the dictionary. We thought the word *waitor* was a misspelling of waiter, as it sometimes was, but learned it was "a tray on which something was carried." Our writers did not use periods after Mr, Mrs, or Dr. We have maintained the original spelling of all words as written as well as the original punctuation.

Letters writers of the 19th century used a variety of stationary. Sometimes the writer folded a sheet of paper in half. They might begin writing on page one, then on page three, next on page two, and finally on the left side of page one. When the writers ran out of room, they often turned the paper to one side and continued writing in the margin or even perpendicular over the previously written first page.

Three different individuals interpreted each letter. The first interpreter transcribed by hand. Then a second set of eyes proofed the results. The letter was then typed, compared to the original, and proofed again. Gwen reviewed all work and performed the fourth and final proofing.

Transcribing many letters from a particular individual is a deeply personal experience. The transcribers came to know the correspondents intimately, imagining each writer was watching to ensure accuracy in content and tone. These Bulloch and Roosevelt letters from 1853 provide a singular window into personal lives of the 19th century and a pivotal moment in American history. The courtship letters are the focus of this book.

Additional Bulloch and Roosevelt letters included in the collection have been and are still (2015) being transcribed. We plan to publish the letters from 1854 until the beginning of the Civil War in the next volume. A final volume of letters will encompass all those from the beginning of the War until the War's end.

To increase reader enjoyment and understanding of these letters, we have researched those individuals mentioned and discussed within each letter. Within the letters, we simply inserted last or full names where necessary for understanding. In order to not interrupt the flow of the original letters, a glossary of individuals is provided at the end of the book. Our intent being to provide the reader with basic birth and death dates, family relationships, and the person's status in the year 1853. When we could not identify an individual with great accuracy, we provide no further info than did Mittie and Thee. It should be noted that some individuals did not have middle names, such as Martha "Mittie" Bulloch and Theodore Roosevelt. Middle names are present when applicable.

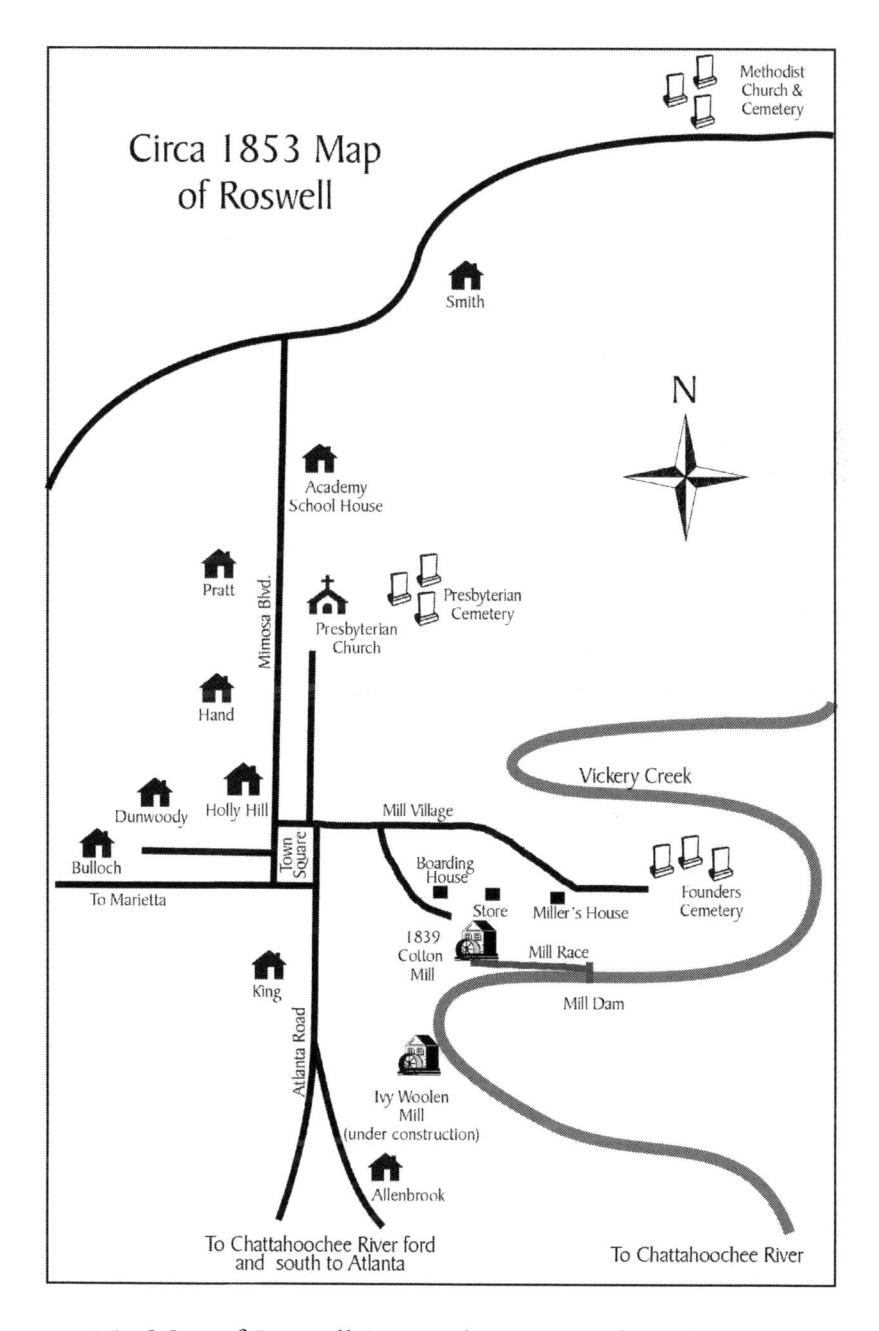

1853 Map of Roswell (original courtesy of Michael Hitt)

xv

Roosevelt Family
by 1853
(relevant persons only)

James Jacobus Roosevelt
1759-1840
married
Maria Helena Van Schaack
1773-1845

Nicholas Roosevelt
1767-1854
married
Lydia Marie Latrobe

→ Henry Latrobe Roosevelt
1812-1884

Isaac Roosevelt
1790-1863

Cornelius Van Schaak Roosevelt
1794-1871
married
Margaret Barnhill
1799-1861

James John Roosevelt
1795-1875
married
Caroline Van Ness
1810-1876

→ James Nicholas Roosevelt
1836-1856

Catherine Angelica Roosevelt
1802-1844

William Henry Roosevelt
1811-1823

Silas Weir Roosevelt
1823-1870
married in 1845
Mary West
1823-1877

James Alfred Roosevelt
1825-1890
married in 1847
Elizabeth Norris Emlen
1825-1912

Cornelius Van Schaak Roosevelt, Jr.
1827-1887

Robert Barnhill Roosevelt
1829-1908
married in 1850
Elizabeth Thorne Ellis
1833-1877

Theodore Roosevelt
1831-1878

→ Margaret Barnhill Roosevelt
1851-1927

John Ellis Roosevelt
1853-1939

Archibald Bulloch
1730-1777
married
Mary DeVeaux
1745-1818

↕

James Bulloch
1765-1806
married
Ann Irvine
1770-1833

Daniel Stewart
1761-1829
married
Sarah Susannah Oswald
1770-1807

↕

Martha "Patsy" Stewart
1799-1864

| John Whitehead Elliott
1818-1820
| Susan AnnElliott
1820-1905
married
Hilborne West
1818-1907
| Georgia Amanda Elliott
1822-1848
| Charles William Elliott
1824-1827
| Daniel Stewart Elliott
1826-1862

married in 1818

married in 1832

James Stephens Bulloch
1793-1849

↕

Anna Louise Bulloch
1833-1893

Martha "Mittie" Bulloch
1835-1884

Charles Irvine Bulloch
1838-1841

Irvine Stephens Bulloch
1842-1898

John Elliott
1773-1827
married
Esther Dunwody
1775-1815

↕

Hester "Hettie" Elliott
1797-1831

married in 1817

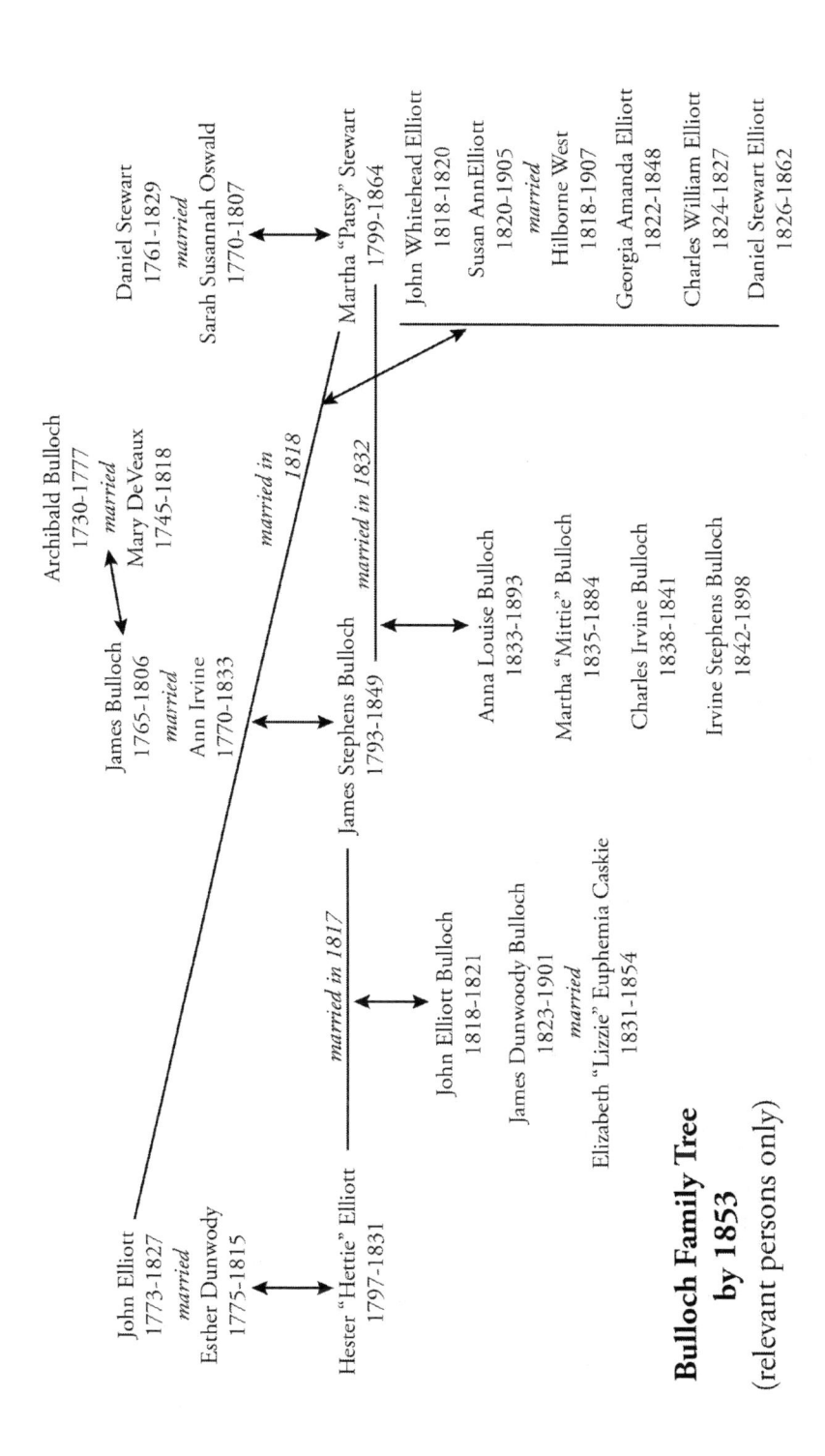

John Elliott Bulloch
1818-1821

James Dunwoody Bulloch
1823-1901
married
Elizabeth "Lizzie" Euphemia Caskie
1831-1854

Bulloch Family Tree
by 1853
(relevant persons only)

xvii

Introduction
Setting the Stage

The Bulloch Family

The year 1853 began just like all those since 1849 for the James Stephens Bulloch family of Roswell, Georgia. Martha "Patsy" Stewart Elliott Bulloch, matriarch and widow, who lost her daughter Georgia Amanda Elliott in 1848 and her husband James Bulloch in February 1849, still dressed each day in the total black of deep mourning. Her eldest daughter Susan Ann Elliott had married Hilborne West of Philadelphia in January 1849 and now resided in that city with her husband's family. Martha's son from her first marriage, Daniel Stewart Elliott, traveled in Europe with her former step-son-in-law and family friend Robert Hutchison. Poor Robert tragically lost his wife, Martha's step-daughter, Corinne Louisa Elliott and their two small daughters in the June 1838 boiler explosion and sinking of the Steamship *Pulaski* off the coast of Palmetto Bluff, South Carolina.[1] Robert survived, one of only 59 souls to do so, while approximately 100 men, women, and children perished. One other young man called Martha *mother*, the son of James Stephens Bulloch and his first wife Hester. James Dunwoody Bulloch served as Lieutenant on the SS *Georgia*, a ship of the United States Mail Steamship Company while on furlough from the United States Navy.[2]

[List of Persons, p.223, provides more information on various people mentioned in book.]

1

Introduction: Setting the Stage

By the beginning of May, spring resided in all its southern glory. Trees and flowers bloomed as the days warmed easily to the mid-70s. The hustle and bustle of life could be heard in this small, upcountry mill village. Each day the large white-columned Greek Revival home at the end of Bulloch Avenue filled with the sounds of her children's gaiety and the subdued noises made by their enslaved African-Americans as they carried out their chores. Martha enjoyed the company of her two daughters still at home, Anna Louise, age 20, and Mittie, age 18, and son Irvine Stephens, a boy of only 11, the remaining children of her marriage to James Bulloch.

It was here that our story of an enduring love and the birth of a future president truly began. To understand the many characters in this story, one must travel a bit further back in time and examine the intertwining roots of the family tree that brought about the events of 1853.

Mittie's story began with the complicated tale of her parent's romance, oft told, yet undocumented. According to family lore, in 1817, in Liberty County, Georgia, twenty-four-year-old James Stephens Bulloch, business man, planter, and veteran of the War of 1812 proposed to eighteen-year-old Martha "Patsy" Stewart, daughter of Revolutionary War General Daniel Stewart. Despite her reputed love for this man she had known since early childhood, she did as the fashion of the time dictated and refused his offer. Tradition indicated she could expect another offer. However, much to her dismay, James instead proposed to her friend, Hester Elliott (1797-1831), daughter of neighbor John Elliott. Hester readily accepted his offer and made wedding plans. Meanwhile, Martha, a noted beauty, received an offer of marriage from that same John Elliot, age 44, a Yale graduate, some 26 years her senior.

James and Hester (Hettie) married on 31 December 1817, followed quickly by the marriage of Martha and John on 6 January. Both weddings took place in the Midway Congregational Church in Liberty County. Thus Martha became James' stepmother-in-law. The community saw Martha's marriage as one of prestige and advantage for the couple. As one local resident remarked:

> Mr. Elliott was a remarkably handsome man of high order of intellect and education and most courtly manners. During his senatorial term, he located his family in Philadelphia; a few years before the date of this note, he had married his second wife, Miss Patsy Stewart of Liberty County, daughter of General Stewart, leaving out in the cold many younger aspirants for the hand of the truly beautiful and accomplished lady.[3]

History has not revealed the nature of James and Hettie's relationship; however, it was not uncommon for young women to marry for status instead of love. James was quite a catch. The residents of Liberty County and Savannah (Chatham County) already recognized this young man for his family connections. His grandfather was the first *president* of Georgia, Archibald Bulloch, the man who first read the Declaration of Independence to the citizens of the state. Additionally, James had by this time established himself as a gentleman investor, public servant, and factor in Savannah.

James and Hettie resided in Savannah on Broughton Street. Hettie bore James at least two children, of whom sadly only one lived to maturity, James Dunwoody Bulloch (1823-1901). Their first son, named John Elliott for her father, died at age two years and 10 months in Burke County, Georgia, in late September 1821.[4]

Though marrying a man old enough to be her father, Martha embraced the role of stepmother to John's three daughters who remained at home, Caroline Matilda (a 22 year-old spinster, who died before 1827), Jane Elizabeth (age 9), and Corinne Louisa (age 5). Perhaps an added attraction was the anticipation that John Elliott was a likely candidate for the United States Senate. Martha's first child, John Whitehead Elliott, was born on 7 November 1818. Her life changed greatly when the Georgia legislature elected John to the U.S. Senate in 1819. John took his young wife to Washington where she charmed residents with her stylish and gracious ways. Tragedy struck the family in November 1820 when her first-born son died. Another son, Charles William, born in 1824, would survive a mere three years. The infant mortality rate was high in the 1820. Only three children from this union would live to maturity; Susan Ann (1820-1895), Georgia Amanda (1822-1848), and Daniel Stewart (1826-1862).[5]

Historical records show that the two families were much entwined, with James, John, and their wives often traveling together for business and pleasure. Years passed with James and Hettie residing in Savannah, while John and Martha split their time between his Liberty County plantation, their new expansive Savannah home, and Washington, D.C. and Philadelphia.

In 1824 with John's term of office completed, they returned south and rejoiced at the birth of son Daniel Stewart (1826). Unexpectedly, on 9 August 1827, John Elliott died in Savannah. His obituary in the *Savannah Georgian* stated:

> On Thursday morning the 9th inst. the Hon, JOHN ELLIOTT, late a Senator in the Congress of the U. S. from the State of Georgia.

> This estimable man had but recently determined to make this city [Savannah] his future home; his friends were about realizing the pleasures they had promised themselves from this agreeable society, when alas! he has been summoned hence, possessed of every thing calculated to attach him to the world, and the world to him.
>
> Mr. Elliott had received intelligence from his plantation situated about 40 miles from this place, of uncommon sickness and mortality among his negroes, by the prevalence of the Dysentery - he visited them to administer to their comforts and extend to them all the assistance which an enlightened and humane master could afford in their distress; but unfortunately, he remained there too long, and contracted the disease, of which he died, on his return to Savannah after an illness about ten days.[6]

John's death left a grieving 28-year-old Martha with four small children from their union, including nine-month-old Daniel, and two stepdaughters, Jane Elizabeth, age 18, and Corinne Louisa, age 14, to raise. Compounding the family's grief was the death of three-year-old Charles in early September.[7]

It seems this shared grief brought James, Hettie, and Martha even closer together. At age 55 and in robust health, no doubt expecting to live many more years, John Elliott died intestate. James became the executor of John's estate. Managing John's extensive plantation and other business holdings occupied a tremendous amount of his time in the coming years. That first year, both families lived in *full mourning*. Then, for half a year, the families continued in *half mourning*, attending only small social events and traveling little.

Introduction: Setting the Stage

On 1 May 1828 following her father's death by not quite nine months, Jane Elizabeth Elliott married John Stevens Law, a physician from Liberty County.[8] Sadly, Jane enjoyed only eleven months of marital bliss. The *Savannah Georgian* on 18 April 1829 carried the following notice:

> A Card: Dr. Jno. S. Law tenders his warmest thanks to his friends and fellow citizens for their unremitted exertions for his welfare during the fire of yesterday April 17.

On 30 April, the *Georgian* posted Jane's death notice, documenting her death only three days after the fire. Jane's death, falling so soon after the fire, presumably at their home, leaves the nature of her death to speculation.

It seemed Martha's period of mourning would never end, as one month later on 27 May 1829, Martha's father General Daniel Stewart died at his plantation in Liberty County. Within a two year period, Martha lost her husband and young son, her stepdaughter, and her father. Daniel's obituary in the *Daily Georgian* read:

> Obituary. General Daniel Stewart, a Patriot of 1776, died at his residence in Liberty County on the 27th ult. aged 69 years. In the Revolutionary War, although but 16 years of age, such was his love of country and military ardor, increased by the aggressions of Great Britain, and the depreciations of the tories in his neighborhood, he joined the standard of his country and was frequently in the battle under Generals Sumpter, Marion, and Col. Wm. Harden, at Pocotaligo, was taken prisoner near Charleston, and put on board the English Prison Ship in that harbor: and probably no man suffered more or went

through more perils and hardships during the whole war and the different Indian deprecations afterwards, on the Georgia frontier. General Stewart enjoyed the confidence and esteem of his fellow citizens, to a great degree. He filled in his native county every public office in the gift of the people, and to his death was honored and respected by them, and from his retiring and unostentatious manners and love of the society of his family and friends, refused many offices tendered him. We have indeed few such men to spare![9]

Life went on. Martha inherited a substantial amount from her father's estate. Her personal wealth increased with her inheritance from her husband's estate insuring a comfortable life style. Steamship records of the times show that Martha traveled, sometimes with only her children and a few servants, to the North during the South's hottest months of summer and often to Charleston, South Carolina. At other times she was accompanied by James, Hettie, and their small son, Martha's stepgrandson.

Hettie's health deteriorated, and at some point in 1830, James, Hettie, and their seven-year-old son moved in with Martha at her Savannah home. On 21 February 1831, Hettie died of what was described as a "protracted and painful" illness.[10] Life now found Martha and James, living as *brother and sister*[11] while raising children from three marriages. On 12 January 1832, her stepdaughter Corinne Elliott married family friend Robert Hutchison.

One year and two months after Hettie's death, on 8 May 1832, James and Martha married. Savannah resident Mary Telfair wrote to her friend Mary Few of Virginia that a good deal of buzzing was taking place over a match among members of the church. It was said that "the church would weep over such a marriage." She described Mrs. John Elliott as a woman of exalted piety. But clearly she had misgivings about this upcoming marriage:

> . . . she married in the first instance a Man old enough to be her father and no doubt sacrificed feeling to ambition. She made a most exemplary Wife & (hardest of all duties) an excellent Step Mother. For four years she has acted the part of a dignified Widow which of all characters (Step Mother excepted) is the most difficult to support, and now she is about marrying her husband's daughter's husband — he has been living in the house with her ever since the death of his wife and I thought viewed by her with sisterly regard. I begin to think with Miss Edgeworth that propinquity is dangerous and beyond the relationship of Brother and Sister mutual dependence is apt to create sentiment more tender than platonic. . . It does not strike me as a criminal connection, but one highly revolting to delicacy. . .[12]

Mary Telfair went on to expound that the late Mr. Elliott's surviving daughter's feelings "were very much enraged." Telfair stated that this daughter, Corinne Louisa, was devotedly attached to her stepmother, but now refused to have any interaction with her brother-in-law.[13] Mary Telfair ended with "I feel sorry for Mrs. Elliott, she had in her first marriage to practice an Apprenticeship to self denial, in order to conciliate the good will of daughters as old as herself — by a noble and disinterested course of conduct she received their confidence and affection and fulfilled her duties as a wife as faithfully as if she had married from Love."[14]

This marriage brought about Mittie's birth, then the move to Roswell, and finally to the year 1853. In the intervening years, Martha and James lived in Savannah, on Liberty County plantations, and in Hartford, Connecticut. Their first child Anna, born in 1833, joined the family while in one of their southern residences. It was during their extended stay in Hartford, where James Dunwoody Bulloch, age 14, Susan Elliott, age 15, Georgia Elliott, age 13, and Daniel Elliott, age 9, were attending school that Mittie was born on 8 July 1835.

In the spring of 1838, Martha, James, and four of their children (Susan, Georgia, Anna, and Mittie) left Savannah for the "colony" at Roswell, Georgia.[15] Fifteen-year-old, James Dunwody Bulloch and eleven-year-old Daniel did not make the trip with the rest of the family, as both still attended boarding school in Middletown, Connecticut. James Bulloch had invested in the Roswell Manufacturing Company, newly established in the town, and had received acreage for a home as part of the deal. Located in Georgia's Piedmont region, Roswell sprang into being due to the efforts of Roswell King and his son Barrington. In the early 1830s, Roswell King had initiated a plan to build a cotton mill on Vickery Creek in what was then Cherokee land. He and his son purchased land lots, started recruiting investors, and began building the mill and other business concerns. James Bulloch invested in the company early in its conception.

It is believed that six slaves joined James and Martha and the children on the journey. These were most likely *Daddy* Luke Moumar, the butler and handyman whom Martha had taught to read and write, and his wife *Maum* Charlotte, the housekeeper, along with *Daddy* Stephen, the coachman, *Maum* Rose, the cook, *Daddy* William, and *Maum* Grace the nursemaid.[16] Taking along oxcarts of belongings, the family traveled first by sloop or steamship to Augusta, and then

Introduction: Setting the Stage

across eastern Georgia to the Chattahoochee River, and finally on to Roswell.

At first, the family lived in a small cabin, called Clifton Farm, while their new home was under construction. Located approximately four miles east from their new home site, this cabin had likely recently housed a Cherokee family. Willis Ball, a Connecticut skilled builder, designed and built their new Roswell house. Historic architects agree he based his work on the widely-used Asher Benjamin books such as *The Architect, or Practical House Carpenter* and *The American Builder's Companion.* With Tuscan columns across its wide verandah, the lovely home sat at the end of a long lane leading to the town square. At one time a captain's or widow's walk may have graced the roof.[17]

In late 1838 or early 1839, their family expanded with the birth of Charles Irvine. He was baptized by the visiting Reverend Nathaniel A. Pratt during his first visit to the colony on 20 October 1839, the same day the Roswell Presbyterian Church was organized. Two years later, in 1841, Charles Irvine Bulloch died at age two years and nine months. The family buried him in the new town cemetery, now known as Founders Cemetery. In 1842, Martha delivered her ninth and last child Irvine Stephens Bulloch.

The family worshiped at the Presbyterian Church, only a short walk down present day Mimosa Boulevard. Anna, Mittie, and Irvine attended the Academy, Roswell's school, built directly north of the church. They socialized with the Colony's other prominent founders, the Barrington King family, the Archibald Smith family, the Reverend Nathaniel A. Pratt family, and their cousins, the family of John Dunwoody. John had married James Stephens Bulloch's sister Jane in 1808. They raised five sons and one daughter. The

Dunwoodys occupied Phoenix Hall (now called Mimosa[18]) directly adjoining the Bulloch property. The family frequently traveled to the coast to visit friends and relatives. The Bullochs were wealthy, well educated, and well traveled.

As Anna and Mittie grew to be young women, Martha sent them to Barhamville, South Carolina, to Dr. Marks' South Carolina Female Academy to further their education. Dr. Marks located his academy near Columbia, South Carolina, and named the area Barhamville. A physician by training but educator by choice, Dr. Humphrey Marks opened the academy on 1 October 1828. His original idea was a place with "scale of economy" that would be make it affordable to those of moderate circumstances.[19] The school offered four years of studies built on a collegiate basis and soon attracted the daughters of many of central South Carolina's wealthiest planters. The girls studied the ornamental arts, the Classics, music, dancing, and languages such as French, Italian, Spanish, and Latin. Marks and his wife, fellow educator Jane Barham (1788-1827), the school's namesake, thought studying these subjects would make an so called *accomplished lady*. After the death of Jane Barham, Marks hired and later married Julia Pierpont Warne, head of the flourishing girls' school at Sparta, Georgia.[20]

Mittie and Anna lived at the school for two terms each year. They were well attended with servants to draw baths, tend fires, and see to their needs.[21] School rules required them to write home on the first day of each month. The staff inspected all incoming letters, and those deemed of a "trifling nature" were frowned upon. The girls were not even permitted to converse with a young man without the written permission of their parents. By the early 1850s, the school had well over 100 young ladies in attendance and bookkeeping had been added as a new course.[22] It is not clear how long the girls

Introduction: Setting the Stage

attended the Academy; however, the girls were in attendance in the fall of 1849.

On 11 July 1849, their half-brother, James Dunwoody Bulloch, "Brother Jimmie," a midshipman in the United States Navy, wrote of his stepmother and half-sisters:

> Mother bears her weight of years most stoutly & with the meekness woman only knows, regards her cares & sorrows as the will of her maker. With my two little sisters I am delighted. They have grown up fine full graceful girls, intelligent & full of loving kindness. Though differing in many respects, they are each quite perfect in their peculiar style. "Mitty" as we call the younger is a black haired bright eyed lassie lively in her disposition with a ready tongue, she does everything by impulse and with an air of perfect self confidence, but she is a warm hearted little darling. Annie is a sensitive confiding little creature, all heart & soul with large soft slowly winking eyes & great long lashes. She does every thing with gentleness & has a way of nestling by her brothers side which is truly touching.

Another glimpse of Mittie's character can be seen in her correspondence with Miss Sarah Green of nearby Marietta. Although neither the writer or recipient noted the year, Sarah Elizabeth Green likely wrote this letter in 1848 as the accompanying envelope is postmarked 24 July, a Monday. Sarah notes on the bottom of her letter that she wrote it on a Monday and would send it by "return mail." Sarah attended the Kennesaw Institute (Kennesaw Female Seminary).[23]

My dearest Mittie
  Thank you for your affectionate and most welcome note. I received it late Saturday night and I answer it early

this morning and will send my letter by return of mail as I promised. I fear you have already thought me guilty of breach of promise for I hear Carrie [Shackleford] returned from Roswell last Wednesday but you see I am entirely free from that offense.

It was indeed tantalizing to be with you only for a few moments, after a separation for years indeed - it seems as a dream that I have seen you at all. I can scarcely believe that tall, dignified, young lady, the same little, mischievous Mittie, who I knew in "days of yore." My companion in all fun and mischief and the sharer of my escapades into which I was led by my wild thoughtlessness in "the merry days, which <u>my childhood</u> knew." I love to recall the memories of "bygone days." I am <u>very old</u> now. Eh Mittie! But indeed I do feel <u>very ancient</u>, do you? Have you changed at all? And has Anna? Kiss dear Anna for me, and tell her she must write to me. Sister says you may call her anything you fancy, so you do not put a <u>Miss</u> on to it. She hopes never to be so much a young lady, as to forget her old friends and among that precious few, we are too happy to remember yourself and Anna.

It would give us both, much pleasure, dear Mitt to visit you in Roswell, but I do not think we shall be able to do so. We have set our hearts on having you with us. Ma [Martha E. Marvin Green] expects to go up to Murray County, this week to see Aunt Esther. She will "remain till she comes back," during which time Sister will be left Mistress of the mansion. Her principal duties will be to preside over the family wide, and keep me out of mischief. You and Anna must positively come over, and help me laugh at her dignity. I will hear of no excuses take no denial. You will come, won't you my darling? You have spent about ten days with Carrie, and I will <u>be jealous</u> if you do not spend two weeks at least with me. You know very well I love you

Introduction: Setting the Stage

twice as much as Carrie does. To which of the Northern schools do you and Anna think of going? How long do you expect to remain?

I saw Carrie when she was spending the summer here, two years ago. Don't you think she has changed a great deal since then? I don't mean in her looks. Do tell me, was she not dreadfully smitten with Horace Pratt at that time. I am sure she talked and seemed to think of no one else. When I saw her this Summer, I commenced quizzing her about him, but she denied any sort of partiality for him. At that I was not at all surprised for I knew and told her that her fancy for him was to sudden to last - "too like the lightning, which is come and gone er we can say it lightens." But she was wounded at my doubts of her, and evaded <u>by the shades of all former loves</u>. A____ constancy to this most excellent ____ (as I thought, <u>most ugly</u>) being. But "____ light as ____, was never meant to last. I was a moments phantasy, and as such it has passed."

She says she <u>never loved</u> him (I believe it, though I am sure she <u>thought</u> she did) and ridiculed me for being so green as to believe her. I thank her most sincerely for the compliment and hope <u>even to be as green</u>. I should not like to become so much of the world, as to doubt what a friend in all seriousness told me. Should you? How miserable life would be, if there was no one whom we could trust - <u>how more than miserable</u> if there was no one whom we <u>would</u> trust. I would not have mentioned this affair de coeur of Carrie's if I did not know that you knew all about it. Ma and Sister desire their love to you. Do dear Mittie write me soon and frequently. If you thought it needful to apologize for your writing, what must you think of mine? I have no excuse to offer, but Mittie dear please

"Don't view it with a contrite eye,
But pass its imperfections by."

What day shall we expect you? Ma and Sister unite with me in much love to yourself, your Mother, and Anna, and also to Miss Matilda.

Be sure, now, and let me hear from you <u>very</u> <u>soon</u>, and you will find a prompt correspondent in your devotedly attached friend.

S. E. G.

Kennesaw Institute -
Miss Marthy Bulloch -
Monday -

The Roosevelt Family

Now that we have set the scene in Roswell, the much less confusing New York side of this love story needs to be told. Wealthy New York businessman, Cornelius Van Schaak Roosevelt (1794-1871) and his wife Margaret Barnhill (1790-1861) raised five sons, Silas Weir (1823-1870), James Alfred (1825-1898), Cornelius Van Schaak, Jr. (1827-1887), Robert Barnwell (1829-1906), and Theodore (1831-1878). By 1853, James, Robert, and Silas had married, however, only Robert had children. Theodore, who had just returned from the *Grand Tour of Europe* on the United States Mail Steam Ship *Arctic* on 19 April 1852, worked for Roosevelt & Son, the family business.

The Roosevelts lived on the corner of 14th Street and Broadway in Manhattan. Theodore's father, Cornelius, was a glass merchant, an ultraconservative abolitionist, and a Quaker by birth. Cornelius' forefather, Claes Martenszen van Rosenvelt arrived in the New York area in 1644. Claes' son Nicholas' two sons established the two branches of the family. Johannes (1689-1750) established the Oyster Bay Roosevelts while Jacobus (1692-1776) established the line known as the Hyde Park Roosevelts.[24] Each line would later produce an American president. During the intervening years, family members married into Welsh, English Quaker, Scottish, Irish, and even German families, creating an all-American blood line by the time of the American Revolution.

Two historic texts detail Theodore's character. The first is from his son, President Theodore Roosevelt, and was taken from his personal letters:

> I was fortunate enough in having a father whom I have always been able to regard as an ideal man. It sounds a little like cant to say what I am going to say, but he really did combine the strength and courage and will and energy of the strongest man with the tenderness, cleanness and purity of a woman. I was a sickly and timid boy. He not only took great and untiring care of me—some of my earliest remembrances are of nights when he would walk up and down with me for an hour at a time in his arms when I was a wretched mite suffering acutely with asthma—but he also most wisely refused to coddle me, and made me feel that I must force myself to hold my own with other boys and prepare to do the rough work of the world. I cannot say that he ever put it into words, but he certainly gave me the feeling that I was always to be both decent and manly, and that if I were manly nobody would laugh at my being decent. In all my childhood he never laid hand on me but once, but I always knew perfectly well that in case it became necessary he would not have the slightest hesitancy in doing so again, and alike from my love and respect, and in a certain sense, my fear of him, I would have hated and dreaded beyond measure to have him know that I had been guilty of a

lie, or of cruelty, or of bullying, or of uncleanness or of cowardice. Gradually I grew to have the feeling on my own account, and not merely on his.[25]

The second character assessment is from his daughter Corinne Roosevelt Robinson in *My Brother Theodore Roosevelt*. This family story also demonstrates the frugal nature of Cornelius and Margaret despite their wealth:

> The youngest, my father, Theodore Roosevelt, often told us himself how he deplored the fate of being the "fifth wheel to the coach," and how many a mortification he had to endure by wearing clothes cut down from the different shapes of his older brother, and much depleted shoes about which, once, on overhearing his mother say, "These were Robert's, but will be a good change for Theodore," he protested vigorously, crying out that he was "tired of changes."

> As the first Theodore grew older he developed into one of the most enchanting characters with whom I, personally, have ever come in contact; sunny, gay, dominant, unselfish, forceful, and versatile, he yet had the extraordinary power of being a focused individual, although an "all-round" man.[26]

Theodore's 1851 passport application gave an accurate description of him as a 19-year-old man. The description stated he stood 6 feet tall, had a high forehead, blue eyes, and a thick nose on a long face. His mouth and chin are listed as large with lighter hair and a light complexion.[27]

Introduction: Setting the Stage

Beginnings of the Romance

How these two such different people came to meet is an intriguing story of nineteenth century connections. Two early twentieth century books give us what may be conflicting stories. Yet, like many oft repeated tales, they may just be variations of one story. Corinne, their daughter wrote:

> [speaking of Roswell] . . . There the beautiful half-sister of my mother, Susan Elliott, brought her Northern lover, Hilborne West, of Philadelphia, whose sister, Mary West, had shortly before married Weir Roosevelt, of New York, the older brother of my father, Theodore Roosevelt. This same Hilborne West, a young physician, of brilliant promise, adored the informal, fascinating plantation life, and loved the companionship of the two dainty, pretty girls of fourteen and sixteen, Martha and Anna Bulloch, his fiancée's young half-sisters.
>
> Many were the private theatricals and riding-parties, and during that first gay visit Doctor West constantly spoke of his young connection by marriage, Theodore Roosevelt, who he felt would love Roswell as he did.
>
> A year afterward, inspired by the stories of Doctor West, my father, a young man of nineteen, asked if he might pay a visit at the old plantation, and there began the love-affair with a black-haired girl of fifteen which later was to develop into so deep a devotion that when the young Roosevelt, two years later, returned from a trip abroad and found this same young girl visiting her sister in Philadelphia, he succumbed at once to the fascination from which he had never fully recovered,

and later travelled [sp] once more to the old pillared house on the sandhills of Georgia to carry Martha Bulloch away from her Southern-home forever.[28]

Silas Weir Roosevelt and Mary West married in 1845. Susan Elliott and Hilborne West married in January of 1849. If as Corinne stated, Theodore was 19 when he met Mittie, then this would have been in 1850. Historic records show that Theodore visited Roswell in February of 1851 and was introduced as a friend of Mr. West.[29] Yet in *The Boys' Life of Theodore Roosevelt*, Hermann Hagedorn stated that Mittie and Theodore met at the wedding of Susan and Hilborne.[30] Despite this discrepancy over their initial meeting, it seems that Mittie and Thee met several times between their first meeting and the winter of 1852 in Philadelphia. The story continued in early 1853 with Anna Bulloch returning South while Mittie visited Thee's family in New York.

Savannah February 9th 1853

My Own Dear Mittie

I have been away from Savannah for a week paying a visit in Carolina to Mrs Hugers. This is the reason I have not answered your letter before. Mother sends me the description of your reception. How very splendid it must have been. I also think Mrs. McAllister as a ridiculous woman. The idea of being now so devoted to you. On yesterday the boy with my band and Thee's beautiful present arrived. You cannot think how much obliged I am to you both. Tell Thee I rather think he won the philoprena – I think the handkerchief perfectly lovely, it is so fine. I went round to the Pavilion to a small party on last evening. Mr Noble Hander sent his carriage around for Lila and me. We had a very lovely time. Miss Fannie Livingstone asked me all about you said she knew Mr and Mrs James Hodge are in Savannah on their way to visit Roswell. Tell Thee I think he would like to write to one sometime to remind him of his Roswell correspondents. Love and remembrances to all.

Good bye my darling sister –

Yours truly
Anna.

Philopena is a game in which a man and woman who have shared the twin kernels of a nut each try to claim a gift from the other as a forfeit at their next meeting by fulfilling certain conditions such as being the first to exclaim "philopena." Another tidbit from the letter showed Anna spending time with the "Hugers" in Carolina. This was possibly Daniel Elliott (1778-1854) and Isabella Huger (1780-1865). Daniel served as a Senator for South Carolina from 1843 to 1845. None of the other individuals mentioned in Anna's letter have been identified.

In the spring of 1853, Mittie and Thee began eight months of correspondence before their wedding, interrupted by Thee's visit to Roswell in July. Interspersed, as appropriate, are letters from other family correspondence.

America in 1853

In 1853, Roswell was a small but growing mill village with a few significant Greek Revival style homes, a church and school, and residences for the mill workers. The Roswell Manufacturing Company (RMC), a cotton mill, provided a place of employment and fueled the growth of the community. The RMC also ran a company store which contained the Roswell post office. The Roswell Presbyterian Church served as the physical center of the village and the focus of much of the community's social life. Children whose parents could afford the tuition attended the Academy.

The Bullochs traveled to Marietta, a village about fourteen miles away, for more detailed shopping than the local shops offered. Trips to Savannah and Charleston kept the Roswell's women and girls in the height of fashion. Fashion dictated floor-length, full-skirted dresses with tight bodices. Ladies wore corsets, never showed their bare arms during the day, and covered their heads with hats or bonnets while outdoors. Up to fourteen pounds of petticoats might be worn to achieve the style of the day. Corded petticoats helped support the weight of the skirts as hoops were not yet in fashion.

Everyone eagerly awaited the next issue of *Harper's Monthly Magazine* with its serialized novels such as *Bleak House* by Charles Dickens. By 1853, *David Copperfield, House of Seven Gables,* and *Moby Dick* had been published along with the controversial *Uncle Tom's Cabin.* Women read *Godey's Ladies Book* a primary reference for fashion of the day. Popular music of the day included *Farewell My Lilly Dear* and *My Old Kentucky Home* by Stephen Foster. Brahms published his *Piano Sonatas No. 1*.

The family's social life centered around the church and family entertainments held at the house. The youth of the village enjoyed tableaux, theatricals, musicals, picnics, bowling, and horseback riding. Letter writing, reading aloud, returning calls, and afternoon teas occupied much of a lady's afternoon. Correspondence dwelt heavily on health and family issues.

In New York City, Thee lived in a world of mansions versus tenements. The city held little available housing for the

Introduction: Setting the Stage

middle class. More than one half of New York's residents were foreign born. Dance halls, bars, gambling, and prostitutes made the nearby Five Points district of lower Manhattan dangerous and infamous. Transportation proved chaotic in New York City, with streets choked with wagons and carriages. City leaders considered both pedestrian bridges and elevated trains as solutions, but improvements were costly.

The financially successfully members of the Roosevelt family occupied a brownstone in Manhattan, suiting their social standing and income. The women of the family could afford the luxuries and goods available in A.T. Steward's Emporium and Lord & Taylor's Department stores. They moved among the elite and wealthy of the city, spent holidays in the country. They traveled to Europe.

The United States Stars and Stripes held 31 stars, and Franklin Pierce served as President. The approval of the United States Congress for the survey for the Continental Railroad was well received. The Treaty of Guadaloupe Hildage in 1848 greatly increased the size of the country and when rail connections to Chicago were completed, westward expansion increased. Many in the country strongly disapproved of the 4th National Women's Rights Convention held in Cleveland, Ohio, which focused on gaining the right to vote for women. The issue of abolition loomed over the country.

People greatly feared outbreaks of yellow fever and malaria, diseases spread by the bite of the female mosquito. Little could be done to prevent outbreaks of these and other contagious diseases, such as tuberculosis (consumption), cholera, whooping cough, scarlet and typhoid fever.

Chapter I
May and June

The romance between Miss Mittie Bulloch and Mr. Theodore Roosevelt reignited in the winter of 1852 and into 1853, carried on through correspondence over the next eight months. The first letter however, was not from either Mittie or Thee, but Martha Bulloch. This letter presented a clear view of Martha's ideas about love and marriage.

Roswell May 21st/ 1853

Mr. Roosevelt
  Dear Sir,
Your letter of 13th inst, I received yesterday, and reply by return of mail. Your visit to Roswell I recollect with much pleasure. During so short a visit, of course I had but little opportunity of becoming personally acquainted with you. But that little impressed me favourably. My son & daughter Mr. and Mrs. West [Hilborne and Susan] have also ever spoken of you in terms of unqualified respect and esteem. I have never interfered with the matrimonial designs of my children, and never will when the object chosen is a worthy one. The choice I leave entirely to themselves - Therefore, I refer the matter back to Mittie & yourself.

Yours sincerely
M Bulloch-

With Martha's permission to wed, Thee responded directly to Mittie. At least one intervening letter passed between the two but was not retained in the collection.

Chapter I

New York May 31st 53

Dearest Mittie

    A week will have passed tomorrow since I last wrote or spoke to you; one third of the time to be passed by me in purgatory is concluded, and I am beginning to calculate how many hours will be required after leaving here to reach Roswell via Savannah, as Mr Bulloch [James Dunwoody] decidedly advises me to take that route.

    Of course I have received no letter from you although this evening I try to persuade myself that you are composing one to me. Your mother's reached me tonight, having been ten days on the road; fortunately its contents were already received from "sister" [Susan West or Mary West Roosevelt] through Lizzie [Elizabeth "Lizzie" Ellis Roosevelt] who returned from Philadelphia yesterday. Your mother seems determined not to help me any and, if you had not already consented, three weeks would not pass without seeing me in Roswell; as it is "my fortune is made," and I suppose I must obey orders. Do thank your mother for her kind letter and tell Anna I do not intend to bring it South with me as even she could not improve it.

    When you write (which I particularly request will be immediately) it might be as well to direct to the care of Roosevelt & Son, although it is merely rendered advisable by a change of clerks and consequently present confusion in our Post Office.

    I paid Mrs Bulloch [Elizabeth "Lizzie" Caskie Bulloch] quite a long visit last night and have seen your brother several times; of course you, as the cord of sympathy between us, are frequently spoken of. Mr Hutchison [Robert Hutchison] speaks in very high terms of you, likes you all the better for having so much spirit and ascribes numerous other pretty speeches, all of which I would keep to myself did I not think you would fully appreciate them, and that they would not change your feelings toward him. He has just presented a fine horse to Mrs Bulloch's sister [Nannie Euphemia Caskie Harrison], which he has sent to the south, to which place she has returned. He is talking of going to Europe, but does not think he will get off. Mrs Bulloch has determined to accompany her husband on his next cruise, she seems much better and sends her best love. Mr Bulloch passed last saturday evening with me, or rather I suppose I ought to say with the family, but to own the truth I monopolized him as much as possible in myown quiet room.

Mr Rockhill left me this morning, I went with him one night to the Hippodrome; of the six women who raced thru fell, their horses slipping on a wet part of the tan; one was carried out a good deal hurt, the others remounted and continued the race with but little spirit. The whole of the performances seemed to border on the cruel. Rockhill is an exceedingly clever person, a very good disposition and indeed has all that one could desire in a friend except – a red nose. This will seem to you I know an insurmountable objection and so I will drop him for the present, assuring you that; although not an intimate friend, I esteem him very highly.

Mrs Hull and sister are still with Mary [Roosevelt], apparently in about the same state as ever; one very strong, the other very weak and neither of them very attractive. Mary must be painfully sensible of the change from her previous guests; as I was, last sunday evening at tea. There was the welsh rabbit, there was everything just as it had been those Sundays before except – I scarce know how to describe the change. It was not formal, that was impossible but I found myself really conversing, and thinking what I ought to do for the sake of politeness, instead of doing, as in days gone by, just as I pleased.

Chapter I

Mother's right hand is disabled by a slight attack of (apparently) rheumatism, we hope it will prove nothing, but she wanted me to inform you of it as it had prevented her from writing to you as she has so long desired to. I think I have told you already Mittie all that she would say, as it could be much more than an expression of her feelings of affection for you, but I know as soon as she is well enough she will write and then you can judge for yourself.

Remember your promise to tell me exactly all about your health and I will rely fully upon what you say and save myself. I assure you a great deal of uneasiness by being able to do so.

I have laid aside a new novel by the author of "the initials" to read loud in case we get time, it is named "Cyrilla;" also the Putnam of this month for fear you may not get it, it contains an exceedingly good piece on New York society styled "Paul Potiphas's Meditation," I have already read it aloud once down stairs.

And now Mittie requesting you once more to write as often as you possibly can make up your mind to, I remain

Yours only
Thee

Located at Madison Square on Fifth Avenue between 23rd and 24th Streets, Franconi's Hippodrome (hippodrome from the Greek words for horse, hippos, and course or track, dromos) opened on 2 May 1853 in a replica of a Roman arena. The show featured chariot races, gymnastic exercises, ostrich races, and performing animals. The wood and brick arena, covered with a red, white, and blue canvas roof, seated 10,000 in a two-story amphitheater with a 700 foot circumference. The performing company of Sands' Circus along with a group of French equestrians led by Henri Narcisse Franconi entertained in a very elegant and resplendent style.[31]

THE HIPPODROME, Madison Square, New York, 1853.

Franconi's Hippodrome (New York City)

Thee laid aside two literary works for Mittie. The first was *Cyrilla: A Tale* by Baroness Jemima Montgomery Tautphoeus, an Irish novelist married to the chamberlain to the King of Bavaria. Her first novel, *The Initials* (published in 1850), enjoyed wide readership. *Cyrilla* was based on a true-life murder trial.[32] The second reading was the latest volume of "Putnam's Magazine." George William Curtis (1824) wrote *Paul Potiphas's Meditation* which was a portion of the *Potiphar Papers* serialized in the magazine in 1853. Curtis, a Transcendentalist, helped found the magazine with George Palmer Putnam. *The Potiphar Papers*, a satire on the fashionable society of the day, were widely read and later published as a volume in 1856.[33]

Mittie suffered from what the family called "heart palpitations" most of her life. This term refers to the heart beating too fast or too hard or skipping beats. Most sufferers feel this in their chest or throat. It was and is not considered a serious problem and often resulted from stress or anxiety. While Thee was composing his letter to Mittie, she traveled home from New York. Upon her return home she penned her

Chapter I

first surviving letter to Thee. Based on letter dates, postmarks, and comments about when letters were received, the post between New York City and Roswell took on average from seven to ten days.

Roswell June 1st 1853

Your letter gave me so much heartfelt pleasure, I find myself immediately replying tho I have only received it some few minutes since. I am sure even Thee will not complain of my want of punctuality in this case.

We traveled unceasingly, night and day, arriving in Marietta on sunday morning completely used up. Wishing to avoid shocking the good people of Roswell by a drive on sunday, and being very much fatigued we did not come on home until monday morning, surprising and delighting Mother by a much sooner arrival than she had anticipated. Mother seems to have a general idea that she has been slightly imposed upon, owing to my returning home not quite so free as when I left in the fall. I did not have to employ my persuasive powers, as I found a letter had been sent, enclosed in one to Sister.

I suppose ere this you have seen that our engagement is approved of. I can assure you Mother is predisposed in your favor, and since my predilection now will welcome you in Roswell more cordially (I will not say more lovingly) than she.

The first day from Mittie was rather lonely, was it? I cannot tell you for fear of flattering you, how much I thought of you that day. I will say this much, you were ever nearest my heart.

(As you finished my letter I am not still jealous of Mr Rockhill.) I am very glad you concluded to be polite. I should much rather have a shorter letter than have you neglectful of your friends.

I wish to keep my engagement secret till after you have visited me, so of course I have told none but my immediate family. You would really be amused to hear how I have to evade the different attacks made. My ring has caused quite an excitement, but Anna in order to confuse is wearing a diamond ring also, the same ring whose history I told you, a memorial of the rise and fall of love in my brother.

I will not write you anything "disagreeable about delays." Come your appointed time allowing me three weeks at home, only be sure and tell me positively on what day to expect you, the uncertainty would be so unpleasant. I feel quite impatient to see you, but you must not come any sooner than the time we agreed upon.

It gratifys me exceedingly that you have been to see brother Jimmie and Lizzie [Bulloch] I do hope you saw her. I was so anxious that you should meet, I think I told you how very much we love each other. I know you will feel interested in her on that account. Will you not dear Thee?

Anna is waiting for me to go to walk so I must come to a conclusion. In my next I hope to be a little more interesting, for altho I feel perfectly well I have not quite yet recovered from my fatigue.

Please give my love to your Mother. Anna sends hers to you.

Yours and yours only
Mittie Bulloch

New York June 5 1853

Dearest Mittie

It is a quiet sunday afternoon, my window is open and looking down upon the garden (which now looks prettier than at any other season of the year with all the

Chapter I

roses in bloom, the vines fresh and green and wrens making spasmodic efforts to sing); I almost imagine myself miles away in the quiet country.

Add to this the influence of a small daguerreotype which I have borrowed and after looking at frequently am persuaded reminds me very much of the original, and I gradually find myself sinking into a dreamy state and building a castle with one other inmate besides myself.

There is no further need of a ride out of town to obtain flowers, our own garden is overflowing; I picked one moss rose bud, which is now in a glass of water on my desk, intending to see if it could be enclosed in this letter, but it seems hopeless. It does mean "confession" according to the floral interpretation, which I have obtained to bring to your place with me as I promised.

We are all preparing for the country, having determined to leave for Staten Island in two or three days; all are delighted at the prospect and otherwise following out their old habits, except Mrs James (Lizzie) who has once again gone to Philadelphia for a few days. Her brother's health is about the same.

I paid another visit to Mrs Bulloch the night before last and had an exceedingly pleasant talk with her, she told me about a monday night you had passed with her, when you may remember that Mr West accompanied us to the door. I knew that you would not desire to have anything that concerned you a secret from me now, particularly when it would only, if such a thing could be, increase my love towards you.—Today I have been made quite melancholy by hearing that the same evening that I was there, after I left Mrs Bulloch had another hemorrhage. Mr Bulloch does not seem to think it a severe one and still expects her I believe, to go in the Georgia with him tomorrow, I intend to desert Mary's for a part of this evening and pay him a visit. I will return at the same time your mother's daguerreotype which I brought over to show my mother; your own I intend to keep until you give me a better one or let me possess the original. I did not dream that whatever you had been connected in my mind with, would have such a charm for me when you were away; that ring, that you rather despised, I have learnt to prize very highly, and those sofas up at Mary's seem almost sacred.

This letter is composed as ladies' letters generally are, having the important item for the latter part. It is that your answer to this will be the last letter you need write me before I depart for Roswell, and even that one ought to be written as soon as possible after the receipt of this in order to allow me to receive it. This will be a little sooner than your week but I know you too well to doubt that you will grant so slight a request, when you know how great a disappointment it would be to me not to receive it. This is the third I have written without receiving one answer; it is a proof of my entire confidence in Mittie.

Night. I brought your moss rose bud together with some other flowers over to Mrs. Bulloch's, but was sorry to hear that the bleeding continued and that she was very weak indeed. The doctor insists upon it she must go tomorrow, considering a voyage apparently almost her last hopes; it seems sad that one who had so many loveable qualities about her should be intended apparently to be with us for so short a time.

I had just begun to feel acquainted with her, and that I would like her exceedingly; she seemed to take such a genuine interest in all that concerned you and consequently some in me.

The tea at Mary's was more like old times than for several sundays past, all the party were so relieved by the

Chapter I

departure of guests who had not one feeling in common nor one sympathy with any of us or our plans.

Mother has a country friend who has just come as everything is in disorder preparatory to moving to the country, but mother of course is as calm as a summer day and you would think it was not the slightest inconvenience; she even wanted to put off her departure several days, but fortunately the lady is a really pleasant person and would not allow anything of the kind.

Mrs Judge Roosevelt [Caroline] spent last night with us in a very delightful frame of mind; mother asked her if she had heard any more about herself from her previous informant, but she appeared to have entirely forgotten the conversation to which you were a witness.

I will write you certainly once, probably oftener before I leave for the south, informing you of my time of sailing and when you may expect me there; it seems a long time to wait yet, and you can apply a portion of the sad tenor of this letter to not having received any news from you, and feeling a little of the pain of "hope deferred." I would like to persuade you to write oftener when we will be separated, after my visit, for so great a length of time that I shudder when I think of it.

Remember me to your family and believe me
Yours only
Thee

Thee had borrowed Martha Bulloch's daguerreotype of Mittie. When Louis Daguerre's photography equipment arrived on the *British Queen* in New York in 1839, hundreds of applicants or budding photographers began setting up shop. Within two to three years, photography shops became common place even in small towns. By the 1850s, approximately three million daguerreotypes were produced annually in the United States as the price had dropped drastically.[34] Daguerreotypes, produced mainly between the late 1830s and 1855, were images on polished silver so they are very reflective, like a mirror. As the image was placed on silver, which is subject to tarnish, daguerreotypes had to be placed behind glass and sealed with paper tape so air could not tarnish the plate. This plate was then inserted into a small hinged case. To see the image on a daguerreotype, it is often necessary to tilt the case back and forth.

In late 1852, James Dunwoody Bulloch, "Brother Jimmie," due to the lack of opportunities for advancement in the United States Navy and his wife Lizzie's [Elizabeth Euphemia Caskie] failing health, requested transfer to the New York and Alabama Steamship Company. Although he remained in the Navy on furlough, James was assigned to the United States Mail Ship *Georgia* in early 1853. James became a close and valued friend of Theodore Roosevelt, often sharing his concerns about Lizzie's health as she suffered with tuberculosis most of her adult life. By June of 1853, her health had deteriorated and taking a sea voyage on her husband's next sailing came highly recommended from her physician. At this time James served as captain of the United States Mail Steam Ship *Georgia*. James held the position of captain of the *Georgia* for only one run.[35]

Roswell, June 9th
I am afraid my friends will tire of my correspondence before I have sufficiently used them. I expect you are amused at the trip this letter has taken to first, it did not go to be revised and corrected, but really I was afraid Mrs Weir Roosevelt would think me an intolerable bore and after wondering who I should enclose it to, I concluded Sister [Susan West] would be the best person, and the letter would be only one day late when it reached you.

Chapter I

Your second letter I have received. I will not thank you for it, That would be merely as [...] expressions of feeling, when you are perfectly well aware how much pleasure it gives me to think I am constantly in your thoughts. Your letters are in evidence of this last assertion I am sure.

I have just received a letter from Brother Jimmie and Lizzie [Bulloch]. It was written after they had seen you. I cannot tell you how glad I am that you have made mutually pleasant impressions. They speak in the most enthusiastic terms of you. I wish to show you the letter when you come South, some time when we are by ourselves when "redicious" people choose to leave us alone

Mr Hutchison [Robert] has experienced a remarkable change of feeling since our last combat, what he now denominates Spirit he then termed temper and pride. What change has come o'er the spirit of his dreams I cannot imagine, of one thing however, I am certain. I shall never change the opinion I have of him at present, I have no feeling of ill will, but I understand him perfectly, and consequently have a great contempt for him.

I have been a great deal bored lately, by the attentions of an old beau of school memory. however, as he left Roswell this morning, I begin to experience quite a feeling of relief. it seemed so ridiculous to be driving out with him, and receiving visits, when I knew so perfectly well that if he was aware of my engagement how immediately all his attentions would be wanting in enthusiasm.

I am afraid you will think me very foolish for what I have written, but I thought it might amuse you dearest - brother Jimmie & Lizzie think you are very much attached to me. I wonder if they can be mistaken. I think I only write this because I wish to elicit a fresh assertion of your love for me, not that I doubt you in the smallest degree -

Does it not seem strange to think we should have met and become engaged, after having only known each other time enough to create a passing interest, and then to be separated for almost three years - Some times when I think of it all I feel as ' tho it were ordered by some higher power. I expect you will term this last one of my "<u>sensible remarks</u>."

Anna and I are just getting through the usual amount of village attentions. After having been away you are a great deal noticed for a short time till the novelty dies away. Tomorrow we dine with the Smiths, the same family to whom Miss Smith (the young lady who fascinated you when you were here last) belongs - I really anticipate it in comparison with the others, they are so much the most refined people in the place, and if you do not shock their various prejudices, they are really quite agreeable.

I hope by this time your Mother's hand is quite well. I am a little timid about her letter, tho I am so afraid I am not really deserving of her good opinion and then she will be disappointed in me, I have one consolation, you will always be my refuge if I fail to please. and if ever you should fail, I might persuade Tom King to retire with me in the far West. I will not be able to write you again so I will have to tell you good bye till we meet in Roswell.

Your own
Mittie

I had a very slight palpitation the other evening. It passed away immediately, & I took only <u>one</u> glass of wine. I would not mention it if I had not made the foolish promise. I feel perfectly well now. We anticipate the books you are going to bring with you.

Mittie

Chapter I

New York June 10th 53

<u>Dearest</u> Mittie

 Although your letter seemed intended to show me that I ought not to address in such strong language, I do not find any other expletive that would half express my feelings and so I must use this one until you suggest another; as for pretending not to consider you superlatively "dear" Mittie I know you would, with reason, not believe it any more than I believe that you do not really return as strongly my feelings, although you may not express them in quite the same language.

 One week from tomorrow and I hope to be the "mighty deep" (something I never before looked forward to with pleasure) making the space less and less which divides us. I will start on Saturday the 18th, unless prevented by necessity, and hope to reach your house some time the ensuing wednesday.

 I am trying to school myself to coolly shaking hands with you when we meet before the family; don't let anybody out of the house know when I am coming as I am afraid my visits of welcome then would give you a very disagreeable impression of my temper; I hope you look forward to the meeting as I do and will not love me the "most" when others are by and I cannot express my feelings toward you.

 I have stayed in town tonight and am the only occupant of our whole house, it seems a little dreary, and still there is a luxury in being left with one's own thoughts as companions occasionally.

 All but James & Lizzie [Roosevelt] will be on Staten Island tomorrow, Rob & his wife being the last installment. The death of Mr George Emlen who has been so long sick has obliged Lizzie and James to spend the last week in Philadelphia; although not unexpected it seems to have been a great shock to them all and of course we feel a sympathy with them, Lizzie of course particularly.

James' absence and the sickness of two clerks has given me full occupation, but still I find that, without interfering with business, a thought of Mittie will occasionally creep in and brighten up my feelings, even at 14 Maiden Lane where such a thing as a sentiment would be laughed at as a humbug worthy of Mr Barnum's collection.

Mr Morris [Dr. George Morris] whom you may have heard me speak of as a companion in Europe and friend of mine is in town at present and after dining with him this afternoon he asked me to come and see his family; I promised but told him that I would be detained at the house for a few minutes first, so that you see this letter is literally written in time which I cannot call my own. I knew however I would be out of town for a day or two and really have wanted to answer your letter ever since the first moment I received it, and was merely prevented by the feeling that you might not care to hear from me so often, according to the views with regard to writing which you expressed in your note to Mary; which by the bye I did not believe at all, and am fully convinced you have proved was not meant by answering both my letters immediately.

My literature for Roswell is increasing, but I think it would be best to give Anna the literature to read first, so that she may advise us which is best worth reading, in the meanwhile I know we will be fully occupied talking, to make up for the last month - it is half past nine and I must close remaining

Your own
Thee

11 PM   P.S. I have returned from the Morris' where I received a severe lecture and some melted ice-cream as recompense for my delay; I think you would like some

Chapter I

members of the family while George who I know so well and think very highly of you would consider slow, but I will try to explain his character to you some day. He is one of the few people I know intimately.

All are well; mother would send her love if she was anywhere in the neighborhood. Give any that you can spare of any love to Anna and your mother and "do don't" give away too much, I feel as if I would be very miserly and like to keep all yours.

Thee

New York June 15th 53

Dearest Mittie

Although I will be with you almost as soon as this note I could not resist the desire to write to you after receiving your letter this morning, if it was only to tell you positively when I hoped to be with you. I will leave on saturday the 18th by way of Charleston as it seems probable that will let me reach your house next wednesday _morning_; if I should not arrive you must not be astonished however as I am basing my calculation upon connecting everywhere.

I am spending this evening again in town, indeed I find there are so many at Staten Island that it is impossible for me to be alone there, and I don't feel as if I could write as I want to, (without any constraint) in a crowd.

Lizzie [Roosevelt] has just returned from Philadelphia after the death of her brother and I have spent a large part of the evening with her; she has been packing too and seems really almost sick. My visit seemed to brighten her up and I hope when she gets into the country with the others of the family she will recover her spirits. She was very glad she had seen you before you went away and sends a great deal of love.

Mother has just got settled and seems to have recovered almost from everything and says, as I will reach you almost as soon as a letter from her could, she is going to send it by me as she thinks I would be able to explain her feelings also, in case she should not do them justice upon paper. As for her not loving you Mittie, that is entirely out of the question and no I will not use up any more of this valuable little piece of paper on the doubt.

I will not say I was sorry to hear of the "palpitation" as of course they would not leave you in a moment and its being a light one is a proof that they are gradually disappearing with "youth." Don't forget your promise however.

You pay us both rather a poor compliment in thinking that it would "bore" Mary [West Roosevelt] to be the medium of our correspondence, but I think the course you took in directing to me direct was much the wisest; indeed I would a little prefer no concealment with regard to what we might acknowledge without shame on either side, but of course you are the best judge. It is no secret here.

It is midnight but I still hear Cornel's voice [Cornelius Roosevelt, Jr.] at intervals proclaiming that he "trumps," from which I judge that he is enjoying himself as much as if he had gone to West Point, as he came down to do with a young lady to day. He is consoling himself I suppose.

I have just finished packing my trunk and have that feeling that something is forgotten which is induced by the thought that nothing can be replaced in Roswell, a mistaken idea but one which I cannot divest myself of. Wouldn't Tom King feel insulted?

June 16th. I find by day light that I must take your precaution unless I wish others to read what I have not written for their benefit.

Chapter I

I will not commence another sheet but will retain a little for that meeting which I look forward to as I never looked forward to anything before.
Your own
Thee

With Thee now on his way to visit with Mittie and her family in Roswell, Margaret Roosevelt took the time to pen the following letter to her son's prospective bride.

Airfield June 17th [1853]

Dear Mittie   I cannot allow Theodore to leave me, without writing you a few lines, if it is only to express to you what I have not had an opportunity of doing before my pleasure in the prospect of our future connection, I am fully prepared to love you Mittie. I feel as if I shall realy gain <u>another daughter</u> and you know how particularly fortunate I have been in this respect — We are altogether at present on Staten Island enjoying the green fields, and pure air. Just at this present moment a severe thunder shower is passing over us, and as rain has been much wanted we feel it quite a blessing, though some nervous ladies would probably object to the vivid flashes of lightning. I feel glad that your little sister in law was able at last to accompany your brother when he sailed through. I fear her situation is very precarious. I suppose Anna continues to make the hearts of the poor young men sore, and to retain her own in all its freshness, but her day will come yet, - she will be obliged to succumb some time, give her much love from us all. She can scarcely realize how often she is spoken of, and how kindly, Weir and Mary are both positively in love with her. Please dear Mittie present the kind regards of Mr Roosevelt and myself to your Mother. I hope sometime to have the pleasure of making her personal acquaintance. I have long known her intimately by reputation, with much love to you from us both, I remain yours

very truly
M Roosevelt

Chapter II
July

Thee arrived in Roswell in late June and departed sometime in late July. Letters penned between him and Mittie after this date shed some light on their activities during this brief visit.

Roswell, July 26th, 1853

Thee-a-te, dearest Thee-a-te

I promised to tell you if I cried when you left me, I had determined not to do so if possible, but when the dreadful feeling came over me that you were indeed gone, that I could no more look into those loving eyes, I could not feel myself pressed against the manly heart which beat so truly for me. I could not help my tears from springing and had to rush to myself – how I wished again and again for my own dearest one. I have wandered alone disconsolatry all day, everything now seems associated with you, if I go into the parlor I almost expect to hear your voice, if I run up the staircase to my our rooms, I feel as if you were near, and turn involuntarily to kiss my hand to you. When I see everything as usual except one dreadful blank which none but one could ever fill. A few minutes after you left I went back onto the parlour, there on the sofa was the cushion all mashed just as we left it before we went into lunch, I took my seat but there was no one now, to refuse to move just one quarter of an inch. I should not have minded if you had been ever so near me there – such a flood of recollections the sofa brought up to my mind. Thee I feel as tho you were part

Chapter II

of my existence, and that I only lived in your being. Was it more pleasant for us to be together for a month? I love you now so entirely. I mean I am so confident of my deep love. Did not those few hours after breakfast pass rapidly? There was a painful harm about them, happy but oh how short lived, I felt all the time as tho they were going, Time always flew with us, but those hours rivaled its former flight, and after that short parting how heavily it has hung. Darling I was so excited when we parted I do not remember if you kissed me, I only felt we were to be separated. Thee-a-te if I could only be with you for one short hour, just to have from you a fresh assurance of your love I would not tire of hearing it repeated over and over again. How foolish I am my letter is a perfect rhapsody, excuse, and think only of the love that prompted such a mild effusion. Tom King has just been here to persuade us to join the "Brush Mountain Pic-Nic" to morrow. We had refused decidedly about dinner time giving as our reason that Mother was afraid to have us exposed to the heat, but Tom represented it in such a light, and said we would be missed so very much that Anna and I have concluded to go. We are to leave at six oclock tomorrow morning. It is quite late so I shall stop till after my return. July 27th We have just returned after having had a most delightful time. I wished again and again that you were of the party. Anna drove there in a buggy with Mr Clapp (I did not envy her) and I went in Mr Smiths carriage with Dr McGill, Miss Beman and Lizzie Smith. When we arrived at the foot of the mountain we all wandered off in parties picking the same beautiful wild flowers after a while Tom called us all up and gave orders for the ascent – saying at the same time that he had determined that Mrs Habersham and myself were to ride up on horse back as it would be to fatiguing. Nat led up my horse - and Tom Mrs Habershams. We did look so queenly riding up just as much as we could to keep on holding to anything within reach. The mountain is so very steep. We rode until we reached the last peak, here twas impossible for the horses to have a foot hold so we dismounted and went the rest of the way on foot. Only a short distance and we were fully repaid by the beautiful extended view from the top. We remained some time and then began our descent. When we reached the foot the gentlemen had blankets spread, and the carriage cushions put upon them, then they all left us to lie down and rest. About four oclock we had our dinner – such appetites – sand wiches chicken wings legs and breast disappeared. We had a delightful dinner. Tom had a fire built and we had nice hot tea, about six oclock we commenced our return. I had promised to ride back with Henry Stiles. So I did so and you cannot imagine what a picturesque effect our riding party had – not having my habit – I fixed a bright red shawl as a skirt and a long red mantle on my head turban fashion with long ends streaming. Lizzie Smith and Anna dressed in the same way. Anna was relieved from Mrs Clapp by returning by Nat Pratt. We were all perfectly wild with spirits and created quite an excitement in Roswell by such a gay cavalcade I was joked all day by the different people. Dr McGill wished to know what was the matter with my eyes. They were all swollen he supposed I had been crying a great deal lately. Then Henry Stiles asked if we had not missed the Roosevelts very much. I said "oh dreadfully – that we felt perfectly lost without you. There is to be a riding party tomorrow afternoon. I am going with Henry Stiles. Dearest Thee I am anxiously expecting your letter. I hope and yet I am almost afraid so that I will hear from you from Richmond. It seems like two months instead of two days that I have not been with you. Do you think of me often? I was standing at the back door this evening. Monroe was out there he spoke to me of you and said "Miss Mittie I do love

Chapter II

that Mr Roosevelt, he is such a gentleman, why he let me hold his watch and chain as long as I pleased." I am afraid I have tired you by my long Brush Mountain account, I thought you might be interested. I must close, I ought to be in bed for I have taken so much exercise to day. Do give my best love to your Mother and all who would like to have it. Thee-a-te good night yours devotedly

                              Mittie Bulloch.

While Brush Mountain has not been identified, there is a steep hill in Cobb County, near Kennesaw, named Brushy Mountain that may indeed be the destination for this adventure. However, given its distance from Roswell, it is more likely that their trip was to the area around what is now called Mountain Park, just northwest of Roswell. Typically, at a walk or trot horses can cover from four to nine miles in an hour. A carriage on a decent road averaged between seven and ten miles per hour. These estimates make a nearby mountain more likely as their destination.

                          Richmond July 29th 53

Before Breakfast
        Dearest Little Mittie

My letter, if letter it could be called, from Charleston must have frightened you. I would apologize did I not know that you would appreciate the feelings which prompted it, and would excuse all its faults did you know the circumstances under which it was written; a pen discarded by some one else, ink thicker than the water of Richmond, through which one cannot see the bottom of his basin, paper not too good, a hand less steady than usual after twenty four hours rail road travel, and half an hour allowed to dinner, during which it was composed; add to this a desire to express my love to you

July

and a want of words to do so and I think even its failings are explained away.

I have not seen a piece of blue sky since leaving you and it is now pouring down in torrents; going from Washington Charleston to Wilmington we had quite a severe storm and about the middle of the night I heard the man who had boasted that he had secured the berth above me lamenting that he was whet through and must sleep on the floor. I felt that I ought to laugh but it only produced a groan as I felt that the umbrella which, I was too weak to take from under me made a still deeper incision into my back. I comforted myself with a comparison of myself and the aligator with firewood inside, and followed his (the aligator's) example.

Through some mismanagement, cause unknown, we got on shore and lay there seven hours, of course thus losing our express train; while there we had breakfast and there I discovered that your doctrine of courses has not spread among the masses; on analyzing the remains on one plate I discovered fish, ham & eggs, chicken and musk melon. I thought of you and had my plate changed four times, which piece for devotion did not seem to be appreciated by the waitors [sic].

One unfortunate young man created with reason much commiseration among the passengers he left his parents and family last winter in Pennsylvania and went to Florida from which place he was now returning under the charge of a keeper, insane.

The climate was presumed to be the principal cause although it was rumored that maltreatment had something to do with it also. He showed a disposition to jump over board and had done so in coming from Savannah, but the instinct to preserve life when once in danger was too strong for him and he swam until picked up.

Chapter II

The accommodation train arrives here in the morning and thus the delay has enabled me to execute my original plan. After three nights and two days in a rail-road car the first thing ordered was water in profusion, this was the color of blood but otherwise refreshing, then an entire change of dress and an effort (very much needed) to <u>part my hair</u> and I sit down to refresh myself by communicating my thoughts and feelings to one who while she laughs at my petty annoyances will in her heart regret them too. As yet, I have discovered nothing about the Caskys (is it spelt right?) but after breakfast I intend devoting myself to discovering them if in town; I will devote the remainder of this sheet to chronicling my good or evil success this afternoon, in the meanwhile farewell, O! would I could say it in person. I am so sorry that I did not ask you to write sooner, it seems an eternity not to hear from you till tomorrow week, do think of how anxiously I will expect your letters.

Afternoon. I feel fully repaid for any inconvenience I may be put to by the thought that I really have been the means of giving Mrs Bulloch [Lizzie Caskie Bulloch] a little pleasure. She seemed very glad to see me and had just received your mother's letter this morning announcing my probable visit. I spent an hour and a half with her talking of course a good deal about you. She sends much love to "little Mittie" and is expecting a letter from her now, since she will have time to write. The Dr gives her strong hopes, but he is newly employed; one thing is certain she has had no bleeding at the lungs since June.

Miss Casky [Ellen Laura] has promised to give her love to the others and I am only charged with it to you.

Do take a great deal of care of yourself, indeed remember all your promises to me.

I have been during this trip making my calculations of how we would come (in Nov.) and find the Branchville

July

RR proposes to be done by the 1st of Oct, indeed my plan is complete if thirty six hours Rail R travelling would not tire you out. If so we can change it. And now I will promise to try not to allude to the subject again and would prefer that you would not answer this but unless favorably but I find that it would be more convenient for business also could I reach home by Dec 1st. Don't look sad but just skip it if not agreeable -I saw my attempt at waking you reversed last night in the Rail R car. A lady tried to wake her husband who was yelling with night mare only he took decided measures and knocked her over on the next seat. It reminded me forcibly of your room, indeed his feelings seemed similar to your own when I tried to wake yours, only I would have much preferred receiving the blow to hearing your scream. Tell Anna that James Bulloch is expected about the 18th of next month and to write a week before that and I will see that it reaches him.

    Do tell me about your mother's health, tell me everything; above all do tell me how much you love me, that it is not diminished by seperation, that you still regard us as, as fully bound to each other as though joined by the clergyman, do write your feelings as you said you would.
Mrs. Bulloch [Lizzie] says she thinks my visit has improved me and made me stouter, so you see, three nights and two days have not worn me out. In a few minutes I expect the carriage to bring me to the cemetery as I saw Washington's monument and the church in which Patrick Henry spoke "treason," this morning; the letter is exceedingly interesting to me as carrying one's feelings back to the times which "tried men's souls."

    With love to Anna and your mother and thanks to Tom which I [...tted].

                         I am Yours Theodore Roosevelt

Chapter II

P.S. I leave tonight and read it probably tomorrow night.

Roswell, July 31st, 1853

Dear Thee-a-te,

 Anna has just left for Sunday school. This is the time we used to spend together in the parlour, as it would be rather foolish to imagine you by my side, when in reality you are far far away from me, I have determined to commence a letter to you as the only substitute for your presence. Yesterday afternoon between five and six I thought of you as in the boat for Staten Island on your way to Airfield, and how glad they all would be to see you. I am almost confident you would have been as glad to see me <u>then</u> as any of them, even 'tho Nellie Lathrop had been expecting you also. I could not help feeling a little tinge of regret and a kind of longing to be with you for a little while, had I been asked why, my only answer would have been <u>just so</u>

 Anna and I walked up and down the piazza thinking and talking over the saturday before how very differently the time had been employed, when we were all riding so gaily <u>before</u> Anna and Mr. Clapp [Nathaniel Bowditch Clapp]. We recalled many little incidents of your visit with a great deal of pleasure, and a shadowy feeling of sadness to think they had all passed away. Darling, I thought of many things she could not, things only connected with ourselves, their identity lost, if heard of by others, and only enjoyed silently, yet there was a sympathy that could have shared them, only that was far away and could only be cherished in thoughts. I suppose this quiet sunday morning you are about preparing for a drive over to church, you would not go to the Methodist with your Mother for anything. Oh no. <u>bigoted</u> Thee must go to the "Dutch Reformed." I wish I could take the drive

July

with you, bye-the-way how did you find your horse? I hope better. I should advise him in future to bite his nails. Mine are becoming perfect talons, with the exception of one poor finger which I forgot entirely about and lacerated fearfully. Sunday afternoon. I do not dislike teaching my sunday school class but when Mr. Pratt [Rev. Nathaniel] after service this morning announced that there was to be no school this afternoon, a strange feeling came over me, I cannot say it was one of <u>joy</u> but something very nearly related to it, first cousin (although you think nothing of them, I do.) Only think not to be obliged to take that warm walk. I have been quite good to day, committed to memory a hymn that I have always admired very much. Thee, Mother told me last night that the next time I wrote you I must with her love ask you if you continued to get the one hundred and third psalm, and that when you had finished, please to get the twenty-third- she wishes to hear them perfectly the next time you may happen to pay us a visit. If Weir or Jim [Roosevelt brothers] should hear this, they would think you had become a convert to the Roswell "Prayer Meetings."

Do you remember the long talk we had last sunday night when they had all gone to church? it seems a short time, and yet I have gone through such a dreadful time of missing you, that it must be a very long one. It seems ages since I last spoke to you. I wish I could "despise distance" (Dr. Kinloch's expression) and just find myself seated on some little bench at Airfield by Theeate's side - Would it be a pleasure for you to have me there? You cannot imagine what a pleasure it has been to me to have your gold pen, 'tho I never saw you use it, yet you said it had been constantly with you, and I think it is so pleasant, when one that we love dearly is absent to have some little thing, they had used or had been connected personally with them. The pen itself does not equal my expectations, I will finish tomorrow.

Chapter II

August 1st   We leave tomorrow morning for the Springs consequently I have been almost exterminated with the effort of packing. Anna intends writing you the latter part of this week, principally because I may be prevented from writing my regular time. we do not reach the Springs till late wednesday afternoon. Last Friday I was engaged to ride with Mr Clapp. but fortunately a thunder shower coming up prevented. was it not a happy release? I am afraid we shall meet him at the Springs, or Falls.
Cousin Charlie [Dunwoody] and I think of leaving Mother and Ellen [Dunwoody], and going off for a few days to "Talulah" & "Tacoa" but I will write you from there. I have not heard from you yet, and my first letter will have to be forwarded - making it some days later when I receive it. (see little piece of paper) Today when Cousin Charlie came and told us he had sent for our letters, and when the person returned not one from you, I know a letter from you has reached Roswell long before this, 'tis so tantalizing, this will be the third letter I will have written without receiving one, with the exception of the one from Charleston*. Dearest Thee how delightful 'twould be, to be with you this afternoon. we would have so much to say. Would you like to be with your own Mittie just so .. good bye. I can say nothing but that I love you more and more. Yours. Mittie Bulloch

---

Airfield July 31st 53

Dearest Little Mittie
     Last night saw me reach home and receive a most hearty welcome from each member of the family. All surrounded me and I was immediately overwhelmed with questions about Roswell, Mittie, Annie, and Mrs Bulloch. The latter seemed to be if anything the one of whom a

July

description was most desired and I could think of no other means than comparing her with myown mother; I then found to my astonishment that "sister" [either Lizzie or Mary Roosevelt] and some others of this family had already instituted the same comparison. You know as far as myown views are concerned I could not pay a higher compliment.

Weir's first request as he shook hands with me was that I would take a lantern and help him look for the little red chicken which was hid, in a state of health, somewhere. I presumed [...] was the one whose battles he had [rec'd] and his sickness the effect of injuries received [...] was agreeably surprised to find that it [...] one of a number brought from China by Lew West who has just returned and is now lying out in the grass.

After having a long talk with the family; Lizzie Ellis, Weir and myself carrying candles started out to discover the chicken as well as on their part to show me the numerous young ducks, chickens and one goose which have made their appearance during my absence. I included Charley, my horse, in the survey and had a very pleasant time, particularly as I discovered that this latter animal had entirely recovered; and now Mittie whenever you will pay me the visit you proposed I will promise as pleasant a drive as Staten Island can produce the - sooner the better.

Mother's room adjoins myown and just as I was finishing dressing this morning she knocked at the door & said she must have a quiet talk with me. I opened it of course and the first words she spoke as she came in, her eyes sparkling with pleasure, were "Well Thee I suppose the you found Mittie the dear little think we all thought her." I could not withstand the temptation and settled any doubts if she had any by giving the kiss from you. I know you would forgive me if you had seen the pleasure it gave; she insisted upon having another from myself.

53

Chapter II

    Then ensued quite a long talk about our future; as you said it might make a little difference in your arrangements it would be as well to tell you that we will have a reception for my friends in New York. This will take away from the necessity of sending any invitations here except to members of the family and some near relations, of whom I will send a list at some future day.

    Lizzie Ellis' note emanated from her own heart, indeed I find that each one looks forward to having you as a companion, as though you were all-ready a most intimate friend.

    I drove over to church this morning alone and it recalled to my mind the last time we went to church together under Bachus' care, also our last drive, with everything in such bad order; and still I enjoyed that drive so incomparably more than this one with fine horse fine harness and an exceedingly comfortable wagon, vulgarly called buggy.

    O Mittie: how much I wish I had you here, everything around convinces me more and more that we could be happy together. As they all gathered round by twos last night I could not help looking forward to the time when I would have one, who I do love as sincerely as they love each other, as my companion; and then I thought how long I would be seperated from you and I am afraid I [letter is incomplete/ missing pages]

    Thee had traveled to join his family at Airfield, most likely the name of their country home on Staten Island. Despite the best efforts of the authors and historians at the Theodore Roosevelt Birthplace in New York City, the exact location of Airfield has not been determined.

Chapter III
August

The beginning of August 1853 found Mittie and her mother [Martha] with cousin Charlie Dunwoody and his wife Ellen at the White Sulphur Spring resort. Established in the early 1840, the town of White Sulphur Springs, located about six miles north of Gainesville, in Hall County, Georgia, was known for its medicinal spring. Also known as Oconee White Sulphur Springs, the hotel featured wide porches, double parlors, and a dining room that could accommodate 100 guests. The hotel continued to operate until 1929 and burned in 1933.[36]

Beginning in the mid-eighteenth century, English aristocracy began "taking the waters" at various spas and seaside resorts where "wading" was encouraged. Although it began as health movement, life at the spa or resort soon evolved into time of leisurely pleasure for most. It has been said of the early nineteenth century establishments:

> . . . the last of the new spas, small establishments more like public pleasure gardens, offering a glass of sparkling water as an excuse for pure entertainment. The spa age was a unique period in social history, fascinating for its contrasts between artificial languishings and cultivated fragility on the one hand and, on the other, those mortifications of the flesh imposed in health's name.[37]

Chapter III

Part of the experience often included drinking sulphur or mineral waters from local springs. Many patrons sipped the water twice daily, while some bathed in the water, morning and night to relieve arthritis, rheumatism, gout, stomach complaints, and even sexually-transmitted diseases. Women and men did not bathe together, but at separate times of the day while clothed in lightweight "bathing" garments.

Like many English customs, taking the waters and visiting spas and resorts became popular in the United States as well. Spas and resorts in the mountains of New York, New Hampshire, and even the southern states were quite common. Most had "seasons" and were frequented by wealthy clientele.

New York   Aug 2nd 53

Dearest Mittie

How can I express to you the pleasure which I received today in reading your letter? I felt, as you recalled so vividly to my mind the last morning of our parting, the blood rush to my temples and I had, as it was in the store, to lay it ^(the letter) down for a few moments to regain command over myself. I had been hoping against hope to receive a letter from you - but such a letter. 'O Mittie how deeply how devotedly I love you; do continue to return my love as ardently as you do now, if possible learn to love me more; I know my love for you merits such a return. And do dear little Mittie continue to write (when you feel moved to) just such "rhapsodies" as you excuse yourself for writing in this letter. I never before received a letter which gave me any proportion of the pleasure; and now when I read it over quietly in myown room in town and no one to disturb me that pleasure is doubled.

I had blamed myself a good deal for not having urged you to go to the Brush Mountain (taking care not to fatigue yourself) and I was consequently very glad to hear you had gone, doubly so as it proved pleasant. Of course I felt interested in hearing all about it, and always intend to feel interested in forwarding your pleasures (except perhaps polking [polka]) and hearing about them. —

Lizzie Ellis asked me if I was "homesick" and this probably expresses better than anything else my feelings. I have fallen quietly into my old habits and work at the store all day apparently unchanged in any particular. The book keeper, who I told you had given me advice about not marrying a southern lady after I was engaged to you, was terribly horrified when it was announced. Of course I laughed at it, for I knew perfectly well that if he knew the southern lady I was going to marry neither he nor anyone else could object. Lew West is delighted and paid you some compliments which if they alluded to your fine points of character, I would repeat, but Lew's and my estimate of you differ materially.

I went to see about your Harper [*Harper's New Monthly Magazine*] and found that it had been sent regularly; it would be best to inquire at the post office and make them examine into the cause of its non-arrival. I think Bucket's character is developing nobly and reminds one of Dicken's old style. The scene with Mr Chadband and Sir Liecester struck me as very good.

Whose life was it that your mother recommended for our sunday reading?

I left your ear-rings to be mended and ordered a pair of cuff buttons to have T.R. engraved on them. If they do not suit which is highly probable, lay them aside somewhere. They will probably take the change from getting the ear-rings mended so I will have nothing to return to you. I will direct them to Anna as it will save the necessity of forwarding them twice merely for you to have them where I suppose they will not be needed.

Chapter III

    I quite long to hear how you enjoy the springs, but if above all things that they are making you as strong as a youthful amazon. Above all your promises to me remember that one, that you will take care of yourself for <u>my sake</u>. When I think of the probability of your being sick and me far away my feelings are not such as perhaps they ought to be, trusting as I hope I do in one who can guard and protect you.

    Several of my friends have nominally had their feelings hurt at not being told of my engagement; of course everyone knows of it now and scarce a day passes that I do not receive a congratulation. No one of course knows you, and their surmises are very amusing about you; I hear some of them through friends.

    Give my love to your mother, and write to me just as often dearest as your feelings prompt you to, besides the letters which I look forward to regularly; my longing to hear from you seems to be insatiable. You ask me a question that I am tempted from its self evidence not to answer. "Do I think of you often?" as though the thought of you did not pervade my whole being. O Mittie! do write about your love to me, and I will try, as you I believe object to them, not to make my letters in future quite so entirely "love letters," I will not promise for I am very apt to write what if is uppermost in my heart and this is a feeling that I can confide to no other.

    I would write more Mittie, but it is very late and I have to try mother's horse to morrow morning before breakfast, so I must close remaining

    Yours if possible more entirely than when at Roswell
                           Theodore Roosevelt

    Thee and Mittie were reading *Bleak House* by Charles Dickens which was serialized in *Harper's New Monthly*

Magazine from March 1852 to September 1853. Notable characters included Mr. Chadband, an oily evangelical clergyman, Sir Leicester Dedlock, a fuddy-duddy hereditary knight, and the perceptive Police Inspector Budget.

New York Aug 4th 1853

As I am staying in town for the purpose of quietly reading over dear little Mittie's letters again I find it impossible to prevent myself from expressing feelings which are apparently strengthened every day more and more, and seem to be somewhat relieved by imparting, although not lessened. I would not like to say how often I had read the only letter I have received from you since my return; I looked anxiously for another to day but in vain. This is my third letter to you this week, but what can I put on paper to express feelings which even when we were together words could not give utterance to. Sometimes I look over a letter think it cold, that it will not interest you at all, then I think of the <u>intense</u> pleasure a letter from you gives me and I send it in the hope that it may give you only a moiety of that pleasure.

You say you do not remember whether I kissed you at parting it seems to me as though I could recall each one that I had received during the visit. The last one was given Mittie as she leaned against the piano in the parlour; but when I was looking at the buggy from the piazza Mittie came up and held my hand so confidingly that it gave me more pleasure than a kiss would have before so many. How well I remember that last sunday evening when even little Mittie's fears seemed to render her if possible more love able.

How changed my life is now, here I am tonight with no one in the house but servants; my tea, which used to be so social a meal with us, sitting on two chairs by my side, consisting of dry toast and tea, "claava" being out of

Chapter III

the question and I knowing no substitute for so excessively warm an evening.

Yesterday I hired a saddle horse for mother and was leading him up and driving myown when a little boy asked if he could not have a ride. I of course consented and we reached the house successfully he took tea with us and as a return I offered to drive him back about two miles to his grand mothers. He then told me his mother lived in New York would be anxious about him and he was going to walk six miles over to the other ferry. It was dark and raining hard and although not an agreeable night for a drive I thought I would, in such a cause, drive him part of the way. I eventually drove him to within about a half mile of the ferry when the road became impossible to drive further without the ability to see an inch and I told the boy he must walk the rest of the way, thinking that as he had intended walking six miles this would be no hardship. He, to my astonishment, then commenced weeping most bitterly. He had two alternatives either to return with me to his grandmother's or walk to the boat and relieve his mother's mind. Either one seemed to make him miserable but fear at length conquered affection and he drove back with me, thus having given me three hours driving for nothing. In the mean while the family at home were in considerable excitement about my disappearance. Mother had determined I was upset, indeed at one time when I came in contact on a full trot with another wagon going equally fast I expected to be, this occurred in the darkest part of the road. Mother gave me some black berry brandy really very weak but which she imagined strong enough to prevent the ducking from killing me. I then retired (after reading over Mittie's letter) for the night.

I paid Lew [West] a visit on board his ship yesterday, he showed me his bunk, I believe he calls it, which I had to say was very comfortable also to make sage remarks about the qualities of the ship, which I fear did not increase his respect for me. At length I changed the subject by buying some Java sparrows for Lizzie [Roosevelt] that I found there. They are pretty little birds but strike me as particularly dumb; she don't seem to object to this quality however, indeed how can she when it extends to a little infant which as Rob semi occasionally holds it by the hands I suppose must be hers.

I told you I would enclose those ear-rings to Annie I will write to her at the same time. You must take my part if she objects to my addressing her as "Dear Annie." I can't see any impropriety in it and I have always made myown feelings my criterion of action.

There is a clasp button in the shape of a horse's head which I picked up and send on for you to give to the youth that you wanted one for if you think it will answer for him. Do think of me often and believe me <u>always</u>

Yours
Theodore Roosevelt

Sulphur Springs Aug 7th

I received you letter from Charleston my dearest Theeate, only a short time before we left Roswell, and have been here ever since last Thursday the fourth - without hearing another word, Anna is to send all my letters to me, but I very much doubt if I get them, there is no mail arrangement whatever, either receiving or sending letters depending entirely upon any private opportunity to Gains Ville, a little village about seven miles from the springs. We left home on the second and had gotten about eight miles from home, when we found that "the recent rains had swollen the creeks so very much, as to render them impassable in

Chapter III

a carriage, and a bridge had been washed away." Nothing was left for us but to return home which we did, much to Annas amazement. she was just in the act of going over to Cousin Marions. As we drove up to the door Sarah came running out, cousin Charlie said to her - "Make home quick Miss Mittie has left her ear-rings and we have come back for them." Sarah rushed up stairs and made frantic searches for them, after we had all come in for some time, she entered the room and with a bland smile said she could find none, Think of our returning for my ear-rings. The next day we made a more successful start, and reached Cumming that evening. There we staid all night and positively live to tell it, <u>filth</u> was <u>the</u> predominant feature of every thing. The land-lady was a combination of dirt, lace, and disease, and presided with an air of the greatest complacency, as 'tho every thing was the best possible and served in a princely style - Our chambermaid was a <u>boy</u> of fourteen years of age!

The next day we reached the Springs. There is scarcely any company at all, consisting almost entirely of yellow old ladies and gentlemen (very much in need of sulphur water, evidently) who return to their rooms immediately after meals. To day the coach arrived full, some young ladies and gentlemen, and next week they say will bring a great many. The table is delightfully kept, the accommodations good, extremely plain but perfectly clean, the furniture consists of Bed, Table, & chair, these three items being completely used up with various things, (leaves) my lap as the only thing to write upon, ink-stand being on the floor, occasions quite a fearful stretch of the arm, to be done very cautiously or else the ballance of the port-folio is lost. Frequently every thing is in danger of being completely anihilated. The spring is about a quarter of a mile from the Hotel, and you have to descend quite a steep hill. I go down every morning at <u>six or half past</u> before breakfast, then we all three take a drink of

August

the water, and bring up a glass for Mother, about an hour after breakfast we go down again- after this second trip we do not go till in the afternoon late, but all during the day drink the water, even take it at meals. I never drink the free-stone water at all now, I have become so accustomed to the other, The country is beautifully romantic and wild, and there are a great many pretty walks. I have brought a great many books, and have to read to amuse myself. there is a Bowling Alley but we have not been able to bowl on account of a poor man, who has been very sick ever since we arrived, and died this morning, such a melancholy event for his friends. Mother and I are reading aloud, she had to leave a while ago. and while she was gone I read the last part to see how every thing terminated, When she came back and found what I had done, she said she wished you had been here to prevent it, and I must be sure and tell you as it would amuse you, so I have done so. Was it right? I have just come from dinner, I wish you could see the girls their mother and brothers who have just arrived. greately dressed up crackers, great fat bare arms at a two o'clock dinner! Mr. [Bendon] the artist visited Roswell after we left. so I missed that pleasure - There is an old lady here who has taken quite a fancy to me, she told me to day that she expected her son shortly, and she was going to give him to me! how little she knows about my dearest Thee, and that he was the only person who <u>ever would</u> or <u>ever could</u> suit me I was so disappointed, the mails are so irregular. I dare say I shall not hear from you for a week - yet. Anna is going to pay a visit to Carrie Shackelford while we are away. I wish you could see a note I have just received from Tom King. I should say smell it, for that is the point, highly embossed and so scented that it is perfectly sickening. Do give my love to your Mother. Did you give her the kiss, with the message - I send a note to Lizzie [West], enclosed. My love to all who ask after me. and believe me dearest Thee

Chapter III

only yours.
Mittie Bulloch

Do give my love to your Mother, and to all of them. I have promised to read to Mother, or I could write more, I think I have tired you already.

yours only.
Mittie

August 9th   This is the first opportunity I have had to send my letter. and will have none again 'till next week. So dearest Thee will have to be satisfied with one a week till I get home, I am perfectly well.

Airfield Aug 7th 53

Dearest Mittie

    I received your second letter yesterday. Had it not come I fear this one would have given strong evidence that my spirits were not quite so lively as in days gone by. I have applied this to the weather which is miserable, but I am afraid a good deal more is owing to thinking continually of one who is far away and from whom it takes so very long for me to hear.

    You will see from my previous letters that we have both recalled the same scenes, indeed it is one of my greatest pleasures to recall to myself all that we did together and those numerous proofs of love that you gave me, none of which I think Mittie would recall now, would she? I was very sorry that my letter written at Charleston (although a miserable composition) did not reach you as it was written particularly not to disappoint you in hearing from me as you had expected. I left it in charge of the hotel to be sent to the post-office and suppose it was neglected. The one

August

from Richmond I mailed myself and suppose you will have received that long ago, this is my sixth letter, it seems as though it gave me more pleasure to write to you than to talk to any one else "except mother"! – I will obey your mother's request the first quiet evening when it will not interfere with my correspondence, to which I now generally devote all my leisure evenings; although I had fully determined to have your assistance in committing them to memory.

I am so glad that you wrote that one of your nails was not grown, as it gave me a faith in the rest of an announcement that I was disposed to regard as a poetical license.

Do continue to leave them undisturbed, you know how fond I am of seeing a pretty hand and how much I think that disfigures it.

To prove that I am not "bigoted" I drove down this morning to the episcopal church at Brighton where a little boy bored me and himself all the service by insisting upon finding the places in the prayer book. I know a great many in the church and received one or two invitations to dinner which of course I did not accept. I only drive the horse now so as to have him in good order for our driving next summer, he is quite well, and seemed by an immense display of spirits to show an appreciation of the compliment which you paid him in enquiring after his health. Do not do it again or I know he will be perfectly unmanagable.

My efforts to obtain mother a saddle horse proved very futile, I brought one up with me which appeared during the ride that I took on it to be all that could be desired. The next ^{day} the family rode it in the lane with equal pleasure, then next mother went out alone to ride behind the carriage with it. After going quietly for half a mile it suddenly began to kick and never stopped until mother nominally had jumped off, in other words had landed on the road,

65

Chapter III

fortunately unhurt. She was going to make another trial but it kicked again and she gave it up. In the evening I put on a lady's saddle and found that it went as quietly as ever until I thought it was probably because I always ride with an easy rein. As soon as I tightened it the horse balked (is it spelt right?) then kicked and really gave me some as good practice in riding as I have had in some time.

Atlast after a severe whipping he started on a run and I soon had him under command again. Of course he would not answer for the ladies, and I must make another effort; mother is so discouraged that she does not want to have one got for her at all, but I have determined to try once more.

This is the only day during which I see the family and the entire change from old times sometimes fairly startles me. Each one wanders out with one or more children, some by the hand some being drawn in little wagons, the older ones threatened with whippings when they almost kill any of the pets and the next moment performing the same operation to hear the same threat repeated, occasionally though very rarely diversified by the reality. I enjoy very much myself seeing all the pets; it gives so entirely a country look to the place, the pigeons all fly down on the piazza to be fed, the ducks will not allow themselves to be kicked out of your way and an ancient rooster of Lizzie Ellis' [Roosevelt] and Turveydrop the chinese goose (so called from his noble carriage) both come in the evening to be put to bed.

Lizzie Ellis was very much pleased with your note, she seems to be a greater favorite with the family this summer than heretofore, and I know is determined if possible to make you like her, which I think indeed each member of the family will do. It seems absurd Mittie but I really seem to miss the care you used to take of me, no one would care here if I should wear a green coat to church and as for the rest of my dress or hair Chrysties' [tightly rolled curls] is of

August

much more consequence as want of care in him would look disrespectful. I don't know what the charm was about the way in which you did it but what I miss from you, I would consider meddling or bordering on it from any one here.

Sometimes I try to philosophise and believe that your theory is much the most correct one of enjoying myself just as I used to before we met; but Mittie can't you feel now that is a little more difficult for you to enjoy as much the same pleasures that you used to? Don't you see now the difference which you wanted me once to explain to you but which can only be truly felt?

I have already a dozen times answered your question of would it be a pleasure to have you by my side here, every moment that I am here seems so very much longer than it would were you here. Sometimes I almost wonder when there is so little certainty of pleasure here, if my proposition to have you here this summer was so very wild a one. Do tell me as you promised about your health and let the springs have every chance to make you strong.

Mother sent her best love to you when we were talking of you yesterday evening she is almost the only one to whom I ever speak of you at all freely and even then you know there is much that cannot be told to anyone.

      Yours Devotedly
      Theodore Roosevelt

"Turveydrop," a character in Dicken's *Bleak House*, was described as a perfect model of deportment.

      New York Aug 10th 1853

Myown Dearest Mittie

How I wish I could hear from your own lips just three words, each one to be separated by a "<u>period</u>." I received a letter to day from Anna which she carefully informs me was

Chapter III

not a willing offering, but owing to a promise exacted by you, so instead of answering it tonight I have written to you; although I must try to bring my letters down a little more in accordance with the number I receive lest you may think them rather <u>numerous</u>.

My life has been varied pain and pleasure since my last; mother was attacked in an unaccountable manner and not seeming much better the Dr. was sent for and decided that it was internal injuries caused by the fall from the horse. We passed one very sad evening, last night however she was better and I executed a plan which I had formed immediately on my arrival. It was of paying a visit to the Misses Morris of whom you have heard me speak as very kind to me in Europe, cousins of George Morris. I started at six in the evening, drove out fifteen miles to their place, spent over two hours there discussing all that had transpired since we parted (eighteen months ago) and reached home about half past twelve at night! So you see in this one case I followed your advice and have been fully repaid by the pleasure I received in both the drive and the visit. I have promised to spend some sunday there if possible; the road passes by Mrs Lawrences' and as I passed there my mind would wander back to the last ^{time} I had traversed that road, so that my companion found me exceedingly abstracted for some time. I wondered if we would have the same pair of horses to take the drive when we should at some future day go out together. How very long it seems to look forward to, only two weeks ^{yesterday} have passed since we last sat on the sofa together and promised - O Mittie do you ever think of all that we promised each other then and do you still feel as fully willing to fulfill those promises? You know I do not doubt it, but there is something so delightful in hearing repeated over and over again that you love me. Do remember this and never think a letter can be uninteresting to me which contains a renewed assurance of your love; on the other hand Mittie if you would rather I should write more sensible (as you would term them) letters do tell me so, as I know they could be easily improved in that particular.

Mary has been troubled with a slight attack of fever and ague; Lizzie (Jim's wife) was rather unwell and altogether we have had quite a sick household, none however, mother included, at all dangerously ill, merely enough to depress them all.

There is but one bright side to the story of my life at present - that I have prevailed upon a restaurant ^{keeper} to cook <u>Egg-plant</u> so that it is eatable. Imagine the amount that I devour daily.

I have not been in to see the Chrystal Palace yet but passed it last night when entirely lighted up. The effect was beautiful much more so of course than by daylight, it looked like one mass of moon - like light. I know no other expression to convey an idea of the effect of the ground glass. Otherwise New York is exceedingly quiet and when once home I never move out of the house. My first effort is a bath then I come up into myown room put on a dressing gown (must I give that up?) and sit down to write. You may know that my letters dated New York are all written under similar circumstances. Mr Kermit has been sick to night and I have sent in word that I was here in case they wanted me, which may necessitate me to put on something warmer. The weather has taken a suddenly clear and warm turn, which we all feel doubly from being so long unaccustomed to it.

And now dear little Mittie I must leave you and write a short epistle to George Morris, remaining as ever
                    Yours Devotedly
                    Theodore Roosevelt

Chapter III

In 1853 in Reservoir Square, New York's Crystal Palace opened its *Exhibition of the Industry of All Nations*. Located between Fifth and Sixth Avenues on 42nd Street, Georg Carstensen and German architect Charles Gildemeister designed the exhibition building based directly on London's Crystal Palace. President Franklin Pierce spoke at the dedication on 14 July 1853. Adjoining the main iron and glass building constructed in the shape of a Greek cross, and crowned by a dome 100 feet in diameter, stood the Latting Observatory, a wood tower 315 feet high which allowed visitors a view of Queens, Staten Island, and New Jersey as well as Trinity Church.[38]

New York's Crystal Palace

On 12 July, Anna penned a letter to her sister at Sulphur Springs, Georgia.

Roswell 12th, 1853

My dear Mittie

I hope you will receive all of your letters. I have been very careful about sending them. This is the fourth. I have not heard a word from you since the note Henry [Dunwoody] brought. It is so strange no letters have come at all but yours since you left. Don't forget to tell me something of them they look so interesting. Cousin Mammie and I have been so amused lately, "Barbaree Scriven" has been in Marietta and Uncle John and Aunt Jane [Dunwoody] have written such dear old Liberty Co letters and sent the carriage up for her. They expected her yesterday evening but "Barbaree" was sick and could not come, so "Sophy" has written to ["Janery"] to go up there and they can both enjoy their "dear friend Barbaree together." The whole proceeding has been a most amusing one. Nothing happens in Roswell. While I think of it I must tell you dear Mittie just think now how sweet it will seem to Mr Blunt when he hears it, if you will give your ring to one of his sisters and I know the other will accept of your bracelet. Thee will understand it if you only explain the case. You know everything is in the way you do such things- All of the servants are quite well. <u>Sally</u> says I must tell you that she has pinned up her tail carefully but this damp weather has made it grow so that it will fall down and drag all of the time. She wishes you would give her some advice upon the subject. She asks how the Sulphur water agrees with your tail. Tell <u>darling</u>, Henry was busy all day yesterday planting turnips. I sent for Irvine [Bulloch] and got him to come to see me for a few moments yesterday. He looked quite well and was dressed remarkably well. Do tell me exactly how Mother is. Give much love to <u>Ellen</u> and Cousin <u>Charlie</u> [Dunwoody]. Tell them their little baby [Rosaline] is really a most lovely child. It has improved so much just since I first came over to Aunt Jane's. It sleeps nearly all day so quietly that we hardly know she is in the house, and only wakes at night to take the bottle. Cousin Marion sends much love to you all. Uncle John sent Ellen's box on Monday- Cousin Marion [Dunwoody] had a nice letter from Mrs Rice [Rosaline M. Jackson] on Monday-

Chapter III

Irvine sends his best love to dear Mother [Martha Bulloch] and his little [wife]. An invitation came to us yesterday to attend the fancy ball at Catoosa on the twelfth. Can you imagine who sent it? That blot has just dropped since I have finished.

I long to see you and my darling Mother, but I hope you will stay as long as the water will benefit you both. Does the Blessed walk down to the spring? How does she like it? Goodbye

Your affectionate
Sister Anna

As Mittie reminds Thee at the end of this letter, she continued to write him but was often unable to post the letters due to limited postal service in upcountry Georgia. Receiving letters seemed difficult at Sulphur Springs as Mittie had just received several from Thee at one time. Imagine their frustrations at trying to answer questions and carry on meaningful correspondence with letters arriving weeks after they were sent.

Sulphur Springs Aug 13th

After waiting for two weeks still hoping yet almost despairing three letters came from you my dearest Thee, one day the letter from Richmond, the next two from New York, we were all in the parlour when a gentle man handed me the two last, a good many others received letters at the same time and as they commenced reading theirs, I did ^{mine} also - a young gentleman came up to me, and asked if I had heard from "him," I said, "oh yes and he sends a great deal of love to you," after this I was left in quiet to read and enjoy - when I came to the "Theodore Roosevelt" of the last, I had almost forgotten where I was, so completely had I lost my presence in the letters, They gave me a great deal of pleasure, and if it gives you any comfort to think that your own "little Mittie" loves and thinks of you always. let me tell you it is so. Scarcely an hour passes I do not have your memory some where very near my heart of hearts. at times more vividly than others, but never forgotten entirely - you know you have always said I am difficult at times — having courses of love - one thing is certain 'tho you may be some times decidedly in the foreground, you always occupy a prominent position - I am enjoying my self very much at the springs 'tho Mother and I are quite home sick and are wanting to see Anna and Irvine dreadfully - In this warm weather (I never felt any thing to compare to the heat here 'altho we are just among the mountains and the nights decidedly cool) we sigh so for the range of a large airy house, instead of the cramped confines of one small room for two. Mother I hope and think is better - they say it takes sometime for the waters to produce a decided change particularly when a case is of such long standing as hers is, time is required - and she will perhaps feel better after we return. I am perfectly well, every body says to me "well surely you have not come for your health, your are looking as bright as possible" Thee-a-te---possibly you may be disappointed since you expect in me a "youthful Amazon," but the water has really done me a world of good, the change also has been very good. If we only had wholsome food 'twould be a great deal altho, I wrote you at first that the table was good - but since that time a change has come o'er the spirit of its dreams - and every thing is awful, to make a meal impossible, Ellen Dunwody and I have been about half starved, Mother and Cousin Charlie who are less fastidious survive - We have written to Anna to have large supplies sent by Henry when he comes in the carriage for us - in order that we may make one good meal before reaching Roswell, so they will not imagine the Springs have done us evil instead of good and also that we

Chapter III

may meet them with some affection instead of immediately rushing to the pantry and frantically making a sandwitch - Do you remember our lunches? but I wander. My mind runs on some thing to eat - you perhaps have never been in this condition, but I would like even a clean piece of bread. Thee dearest you will not complain of this being a "love letter" it is almost a heart rending appeal from a member of a half famished garrison. Through all I have never felt better my own dear Thee a te, and to make up for it Ellen and I have determined to have lunches, suppers & dinners in one continued round when we reach home. I went out driving with a gentleman, (quite a pleasant widower) a few evenings since in company with another buggie (vulgarly called wag gon lady & gentleman, to a beautiful limestone spring - about six miles. had a delightful drive, the wag gon light and new, with a splendid pair of bay horses - and the harness all new - not interesting from anticquity and fit to be put in a glass case for show as a relic of the olden times. The fact is, I must confess I rather missed not stopping to tie the tongue to the buggie, and confine with a sleigh string the traces to some important part. I feel strangely out of a dilapidated vehicle where every drive is a hairbreadth escape. We got delightful peaches one consolation in times of adversity. I am glad Lew West had returned. I know his Mother was so perfectly charmed to see him, I cannot imagine what he could have said of me, surely he does not think I have <u>no mind</u> at all. I think Weir will eventually go deranged upon the subject of little <u>red chickens</u>. You said nothing upon the subject of Jim and Lizzie. I am very familiar imagine Mr and Mistress put before their names. I am glad your Mother took so much interest in me, I really love her, but you must not tire her by talking of me. I am conceited enough to think I interest you but doubt ful about other people. I mean to any extent - I hope you told your Mother I only

<u>sent</u> the kiss, I did not give it to you for her - if this was not impressed upon her. I think I shall have to scold you a great deal both by letter, and if I should ever meet with you again - please give a great deal of love to her this time I see you cannot be trusted with any thing else Thank you Thee, for your trouble about the ear-rings - how thoughtful 'twas in you to think about the cuff buttons at one time I thought of commissioning you with them but was afraid it might be asking too much and my passion for ear-rings was too great to give them up - I hope I shall hear from you soon my dearest dearest Thee I delight in your letters - but I am afraid after hearing so lately I will not for some time again. Give my love to all, Have you received the letter with the one enclosed to Lizzie Ellis?

ever your affectionate
Mittie Bulloch

I cannot write with regularity here, so you will only get letters at random, till we go home. I could write but cannot have them mailed

Mittie

    Due to the remote location of the resort, mail delivery and pickup probably occurred once or twice a week. It is also possible that Mittie was unable to "purchase" postage at that remote location.

Airfield Aug 14th 53

Myown Little Mittie
    It has been over a week since I have heard from <u>you</u>, which I try to account for by delays in the mail; but it requires all my stoicism and the numerous arguments which I can address, to convince me of the absurdity of feeling any uneasiness.

Chapter III

I have just answered Annie's letter and the twilight is becoming too dark to advise of writing, so that this will have to be short; as I only write to you from myown room and a light there would attract mosquitoes and make it ever after unbearable.

So many are sick that the sunday would have been rather slow had not we all exerted ourselves, this however had rather the effect of making it particularly lively.

Lizzie Ellis [Roosevelt] has just returned from town with two sick children [Margaret and John], which were cause of much uneasiness. Rob is away sporting and of course we all feel a double sympathy for her on account of her loneliness.

Mother and Mary are better but as they were both used up on the same day that William our man servant ran away everything that day devolved upon Lizzie Emlen [Jim Roosevelt's wife] and to our utter astonishment she acquitted herself nobly; it has shown her in quite a new light.

Fever and ague is the cause of all the sickness, not at all dangerous but so disagreeable that all our castles with regard to Airfield are blown to pieces. -

I am reduced to sitting before my room on the piazza ^{for the light}; indeed I would give this up was it not that I knew you would expect to hear from me and that I can no longer leave them all sick here and write to you quietly in town. Do not fear however but that I will find a means to answer all letters which may come from myown loved one. It is perfectly dark and I must finish this before breakfast tomorrow, -

All have gone to bed or at least disappeared from the parlour and I take advantage of their absence to add a few last words. Annie's letter contains all the family news and this would but be a duplicate which I don't approve of, particularly when I have so much ^{to say to you} that it would be impossible to speak to any other about. I do so often wish once more to hear Mittie's voice and I am not sure but that the apearance of love which it will contain is one of the greatest causes of my anxiety to receive her letters, although I am not so selfish as not to think of Mittie's health too.

Cornel [Roosevelt] is at Schooley's Mt and as he sent a request down to forward him a fancy costume we presume must be enjoying himself. His note contained no information and only these few words required as directions.

Rob has been gone about four days, since which time poor Lizzie has had to sit up pretty much all night with her infants who have become sick since his departure, she of course has not written him to return, indeed is glad he is not here to be disturbed. -

Weir has just wandered in with a bottle of blackberry brandy in his hand which as we are advised to live high to avoid the fever he proposes that we should indulge in, it is mother's manufacture and of course utterly harmless as a stimulant. The bottle giving out we, according the ancient habit of our youth, carefully cork it up and put it in the place now occupied by a full one. It serves to amuse us where there is scarce more excitement now than in Roswell. Driving now at night on the island is prohibited on all sides and one is even abused if he sits out to enjoy the moonlight.

Although contained in Anna's letter as you may not see it I must give you a little account of William's flight. It is so exactly like a slave. He had married the cook and engaged to spend the summer with us; when mother was sick in bed however his wife got his clothes in a bundle and William disappeared mysteriously. She professed utter ignorance and great sorrow but her duplicity was discovered through the other servants. He will be longing to come back in the fall when of course we will not take him. He was a slave and this will probably account for his mode of departure.

Chapter III

    I read your favorite psalm loud to mother this afternoon as she lay in bed and find that it is a great favorite of hers.

    Give my love to your mother and respects to Charley [Dunwoody] and his wife.

    Tell me all about your acquaintances and amusements and believe me

                      always yours devotedly
                      Theodore Roosevelt

Lizzie's infant is crying up stairs.

    Cornel wrote from Schooley's Mountain asking for a fancy costume. No doubt he was staying at the area's famous resort. Schooley's Mountain, located in northern New Jersey along Lake Hopatcong, is near Hackettstown. The town served as the station for the famous Schooley's Mountain Springs, which was once recognized as the most fashionable watering place in America. New York and Philadelphia's elite residents flocked to the resort for the healthful mountain air, the mineral waters, and the comparative ease of access.[39]

    Thee's report of their man William's departure tells an all too common story of the period. As Thee relates that William was a runaway slave, William's position in the household and even the city was tenuous. He could have at any time been picked up and returned to the South for the reward. The Fugitive Slave Law or Fugitive Slave Act, passed by the U. S. Congress on 18 September 1850, was considered part of the Compromise of 1850 between Southern slave-holding interests and Northern Free-Soilers. This law required that all escaped slaves be returned to their masters and that officials and citizens of the free states had to cooperate with this law. Throughout the north, bounty hunters and regular citizens could lawfully capture escaped slaves, using little more than an affidavit, and return them to the slave's master for the reward. William's only hope was to escape over the border into Canada. The Roosevelts' hiring of William despite his status as an escaped slave and their legal responsibility to turn him over to authorities demonstrates their strong abolitionist views.

Anna wrote to Mittie during her extended stay at Sulphur Springs to bring her up to date on the news from Roswell. Anna stayed with the Dunwoody's during her Mother's absence. She mentioned several people in her letter including the unidentified *Tudie*, Charles Dunwoody and his parents Jane and John, *Mammie* (also unidentified), and Rosa, the infant daughter of Charles and Ellen.

Roswell Monday 15th

My dearest Mittie

By to days mail your letter to me and this one to you arrived. I have only changed this one of yours to another enveloppe because I did not redirect it properly. I have not even unfolded it. I hope you have received all of the letters I sent you. I have written to you and darling Mother constantly. And this is the fifth one of dear Thee's I have sent since you have been at the Springs – I wrote the Blessed by the last mail and sent her a long one from Tudie [probably Susan West] to us, which she begged me to enclose to you. I send in this letter a letter Thee enclosed to Cousin Charlie in one to me. I hope you have gotten my last letter it gave you a long account of our errings etc. etc. Yes I have written Thee a long before this one came to me – I told him not to think of hearing from you as the mail did not seem inclined to leave the Springs Aunt Jane and Uncle have gone to Marietta so Cousin Mammie, Rosa and I are monarch of all we survey – We have had two pleasant riding parties since you left the

Chapter III

last one on Saturday. A cousin of the Smiths is now visiting them and is even taller and slimmer than the leanest Smith but exceedingly pleasant. I have just come over from a game at the alley – This morning Mr Pratt gave holliday so Henry Stiles and Willie Smith came over for me to join Lizzie and Mrs Barnwell. We had a very pleasant time I am to take tea with Lizzie this evening and after tea Mrs Habersham and Lizzy and Tom King will meet us at their gate and we are all going to by moonlight You ought to see how very pleasantly Cousin Marion, Rosa and I get along in this big house or have quite room enough. Yesterday morning it was warm that Cousin Mammie sent Rosa into Cousin Ruth's room, she went into Ellen's and left me hers, so that each of the ladies had a nice large room and dressing room at their service. I do really think Rosa has improved astonishingly. I think she is so dear and fat. I can easily see she is a tall and delicately formed child but she is so plump. Irvine was here to see me yesterday. He went to ride with me on Saturday in our riding party. The little fellow is quite happy and always looks very clean and behaves well. All of the servants are well & Send much love to you Sally says if your tail is green do don't come home for she might catch it from you – Cousin Marion does not write because it tires her so and I will give her messages for her – she sends much love to all – Longs to see the Blessed Ellen Mittie and Cousin Charlie

 Good bye – I am quite excited to see into Thee's letter it looks so interesting.

 In the previous letter, Anna had written on two full pages and then a few additional lines perpendicular to the first across the first page, a practice popular at the time. At this point Anna ran out of room and failed to sign her letter. Of course, Mittie would have been quite aware of the letter's author. Thee begins his next letter with a little *pointed* note to Mittie.

Thee feels just as if he could
make himself very interesting.
New York Aug 18th 53
Myown Little Mittie

How I would like to have you here now not only for my sake but (excuse the conceit) for yours too. I feel in the very best of humours with all the world which is owing entirely a reaction after arriving a few moments ago in myown room and finding it in utter confusion. The books piled round in chairs, the contents of the closet in the middle of the floor, the broken neck of a bottle, previously full of madeira, in the closet, several of my pictures lying on the floor; and I think even the gentle Mittie will think this sufficient to aggravate one. My first thought was the sweetness of revenge and I turned to the door, then it suddenly struck me that my revenge would really fall upon mother a very innocent party, besides I had heard a rumour of house-cleaning; so I determined to try how long it would require to repair what evidently must have taken long to undo. In a quarter of an hour the mischief was all repaired and my ^{good} humour is a consequence of violent exercise and the picture of horror which I know the woman will present to morrow when she discovers what a night has brought forth.

There was a stampede last night from Airfield proposed, and our own immediate family are the first who have acted upon it. Yesterday morning I had heard all agree that we would stay our usual time; in the day Mary went into town and (how could she help herself?) talked a great deal. In the course of this conversation she learned that chills and fever grew worse and were confirmed by staying in the same atmosphere and often became bilious fever; in the

Chapter III

meanwhile at the place one of the servants had apparently an attack of the latter. In the evening a general discussion ensued which terminated in immediate arrangements being made for a remove, the first fruits of which is this letter. I will not write quite so often until you return to Roswell as I know that you will hardly like to receive so many letters together, as the irregularity of the mail will oblige you to; I am sorry that I did not know this sooner as I would have acted upon it.

All are improving bodily and mentally, mother is down stairs and I have just persuaded her to take a trip to West Point when she recovers a little more. I was telling her how I enjoyed the quiet here and that I thought I was intended for a quiet man when she very naively enquired if I thought that was Mittie's bent too? She gave as a reason for refusing going to Europe the pleasure she anticipated with you next winter.

Mr James Bulloch arrived in the Black Warrior and took dinner with me twice which allowed all the time that we could expect for quite a long talk. He spoke of writing you a "sober" letter but I particularly requested that he would not, and I think he gave up the plan. Before leaving he received a telegraph that Lizzie was worse and this hurried his departure a little. He seemed to hope and indeed imagine that it was nothing serious; he has received no letters from Annie although I told him of her good intentions. His arrangements seem perfect on board ship, indeed in every particular he seems suited now. The last trip he has not been quite well but as it is nothing that confines him from duty he does not regard it as anything and is determined to cure himself entirely during this three weeks on shore.

During one week over two hundred people died here from the heat, in one hotel some twelve or fifteen servants. It seems to me that the masters are about as accountable

August

as some of Mrs Stowe's [Harriet Beecher Stowe] favorites. "I am going down to read now to mother" but it will not interfere with my finishing the letter afterwards. If you ever give such a reason ~~again~~ and then do not send the letter again for two days I will give a worse lecture than for beginning at the wrong end of a book, although I do not promise entire freedom on that head either. -

Mother has a severe head ache and was just retiring so, after reading an Esay of Lamb, not to give it too premeditated a look, I have returned to my room to finish my letter to you prior to indulging in the luxury of a croton water bath.

When leaving the country was first proposed all felt in very low spirits as father seemed rather disguted with country places, but he seems now disposed to hire for next year with the privilege of buying and in the meanwhile proposesy keeping this one which allows the retention of all the horses dogs chickens ducks turkeys pigeons etc ready for the other.

I don't know why I should write more unless to assure you of what you already ᵏⁿᵒʷ that I regret exceedingly your inability to write as often at present as you intended, and to request you to remember that ⁿᵉⁱᵗʰᵉʳ the length nor number of your letters will ever tire me; indeed the latter deficiency I hope you will make up for as soon as you return ᵗᵒ ᴿᵒˢʷᵉˡˡ. Do not be shocked at the number you have received from me and remember that I presumed they would reach you on different days always.

If it is clear next saturday I anticipate driving out to Yonkers to spend sunday as I had promised to at the Morris. Although they know I am engaged not an allusion was made to it and no teazing done. In every particular I was treated just as though we had parted but a few weeks instead

Chapter III

of eighteen months. I look forward to introducing you to them one of these days.

How many plans I have laid out for the combined future of little Mittie and myself!! It seems so natural in all my projects now to include another that I will scarce feel the change when it will become necessary to do so. -

Excuse the gilt edge on this sheet but it is a remnant of Paris and I had intended it merely to prevent a view of the letter by the curious. I find it so pleasant to write upon however that I expect I will try it again.

And now dearest "Good Night." Oh could I only feel your arm round my neck and receive one kiss! I would run up many a flight of stairs for it. Would you think if I claimed a good many more than one that I was asking for too many?

Your Own
Theodore Roosevelt

After being relieved of his assignment as captain of the SS *Georgia*, James Dunwoody Bulloch accepted assignment as the captain of the United States Mail Steamship *Black Warrior*. Its typical run was from New York to Havana to Mobile and back.

In referring to an incident that occurred in New York, Thee referred to "Mrs. Stowe's favorites." Thee referenced the slave masters in *Uncle Tom's Cabin; or, Life Among the Lowly*. This widely-read book, published in 1852 by Harriet Beecher Stowe (1811-1896) a Connecticut-born teacher at the Hartford Female Seminary and an active abolitionist, featured the character of Uncle Tom. In this sentimental and somewhat overly dramatic novel, Tom, a long-suffering black slave, is the center of a tale about the treatment of slaves in America's southern states. Many historians cite *Uncle Tom's*

Cabin as one of the fuels of the abolitionist cause which rose dramatically in the 1850s. More than 300,000 copies of the book sold in its first year of publication.[40]

Stowe's direct experience with slavery was limited to one brief trip below the Mason-Dixon Line into slave-holding Kentucky. Her book also popularized several stereotypes about black slaves, including the affectionate, dark-skinned "mammy"; the "pickaninny" stereotype of black children; and the "Uncle Tom" or dutiful, long-suffering servant, faithful to his white master or mistress. Many of these stereotypes continued in popular culture for decades.

Thee may have been reading an essay by Charles Lamb (1775–1834) to his mother. Lamb, an English writer and essayist, became well known for his *Essays of Elia* and for the children's book *Tales from Shakespeare*, which he produced with his sister, Mary Lamb (1764–1847).[41]

Thee wrote of indulging in a "croton water bath." Due to a limited supply of fresh water, Manhattan Island began construction of dams and aqueducts in 1837 to divert water from the Croton River in upstate New York. A receiving reservoir of rusticated retaining walls was located between 79th and 86th streets and Sixth and Seventh Avenues (now the site of Great Lawn and Turtle Pond in Central Park). From here water flowed to the Croton Reservoir, built to resemble ancient Egyptian architecture. Water began to flow from the aqueduct on 22 June 1842 and by 1844, 6175 homes were connected to the system. The Croton Reservoir provided clean drinking water and clean bath water to wealthy homes in Manhattan.[42]

Chapter III

Croton River Dam, 1843 Engraving

Croton Reservoir in Manhattan, erected in 1842

Sulphur Springs
Aug 20th

My dearest Thee
    I had just been reading aloud to Mother and became so very sleepy that I thought I would write you to wake me up, when I heard a knock at the door and your last letter was handed me together with one from Anna. I was immediately

wide awake, and commenced reading intently - I received one too on last sunday so this is to be the answer to them both following out my original proposition, namely two letters from you for every one from me, however dear Thee-a-te when I go back home I shall keep my last promise to you and write twice a week, here I really cannot. I have received all of your letters commencing with the one from Charleston if I am not mistaken I told you I had gotten that one. Anna says in her note that the box with the ear rings had come, and goes off in a perfect excitement of description about the cuff buttons, and clasp button. I must hurry home to see them, she also says. "I am perfectly crazy to see into dear Thee's letter it looks so interesting" so she at all events is not fearful of applying to you that epithet. So sensitive Thee cease your scruples. We leave on Tuesday for Roswell and will have been here three weeks with the exception of one day - We are perfectly delighted to get home again, 'tho I have enjoyed myself very much and found it much gayer than I had expected to, There was a party made up from Gains Ville to go to the falls. Talulah [Tallulah] and Tacoa [Toccoa] in Habersham county you may remember I told you I was very anxious to go - The party however was not one in which I cared to go 'tho I would have disregarded almost every thing to see the falls, still I could not stand being in company with rowdy young men, and crackerish girls without a married lady to matronize us. 'Twas such a disappointment to me, one young man who had been very attentive to me, said he would not go as "Miss Bulloch" was not to be of the party - Since then his attentions have been redoubled 'twould amuse you to see us together - he is very pleasant and gentlemanly - but rather unrefined, his dress would put to shame Tittlebat Titmouse - There has been one of Mr Pratts school boys here who reported about that I was engaged, at last but that there had been a young man

Chapter III

from the North visiting us and it was believed I was engaged to him - To my surprise yesterday Mr Branum (the attentive youth) asked to see cousin Charlie privately - asked him to tell him candidly whether I was engaged or not, he did not wish to be satisfied from mere idle curiosity - but if I was not he would come to Roswell to see me. Cousin Charlie told him that such was the report but that he did not feel it ~~write~~ right even if I were engaged to tell anything of the kind to perfect strangers - The affair stands just in this critical position - if I hear any more of it I will tell you, what could have made him fall in love with me I cannot imagine, I never could have, with him, not as present Thee-a-te could I?

Your poor Mother! I fear she never will again trust herself on horse-back. how surprised she must have been to find herself suddenly in the road. I hope you have not had to drive discontented little boys to ferrys six miles off- and back again with the same discontented little boy, that too on a rainy disagreeable night, hereafter dear Thee tho I wish to encourage your kind feelings - let me beg of you for my sake to find out where any little boy is going to pass the night positively before he is brought to take tea with you.

I am going on this page to give you a small list of commands which I wish you to obey - But I will not call them commands only my wishes with regard to your "deportment" -

1st That in future you will not stay in town to read my letters - and take tea or dry toast and tea - but will enjoy your "social meal" as in the olden times, before a thought of Mittie lessened your appetite for chicken and something substantial.

2nd That you follow out my theory, and enjoy yourself as much as you did before we met.

3rd   That you take care of your dress, and never even think about wearing a green coat to church 'tis perfect treason, it is of more importance to the family than you imagine - but seriously dearest Thee a te, please for my sake dont think of me in that kind of way and never go out, just think when you had not been at home a week you had staid in town two nights! - I wish you would think about this and follow my advice, be assured tis much the better plan- I love you all I am capable of loving "<u>except Mother,</u>" yet I enjoy myself as much as I ever did - only more because I can think of you with so much pleasure. I only feel impatient to see you some times, but then I am so confident of your entire love for me that I am happy - I think it is our duty to make ourselves as pleasant to those around as possible. Thee ate please, p-l-e-a-s-e-- for my sake be as you always were - Sister in a letter received from her lately says that Mr West & herself will pay a visit to Airfield after they leave New Port which she is enjoying very much - Mother says I must give her love to you. I think she will be better when we get back home, when she can have proper food for an invalid - I will write you as soon as I get home When Henry comes for us on Tuesday I expect another letter from you. I think I too am "<u>insatiable</u>" -

    Give my best of loves to your Mother and all of them - I am glad Lizzie Ellis liked my note, Thee read this in a blaze of light, or else you will loose your eye sight-
           yours aff.
           Mittie Bulloch
           good bye my sweet Thee a te-

    By the 1850s, north Georgia's attractions such as Tallulah's gorge and waterfalls and Toccoa's waterfalls were well known to locals and visitors as outing destinations. While the journey would have been difficult, many made the trip, on

Chapter III

horseback or by carriage, to see these natural features located in the north Georgia mountains near the North Carolina border. It was not uncommon for the younger folks to climb down the steep walls of the gorge. Tallulah is now located in Rabun County and is about 36 miles from White Sulphur Springs. Toccoa falls was located near the road from the Springs to Tallulah.[43]

The character Tittlebat Titmouse comes from Samuel Warren's *Ten Thousand A-Year*. This British legal satire concerned the rise and fall of Tittlebat Titmouse, a London dandy. The novel was quite long for its day, but became widely popular.[44]

In the 1850s, men's clothing took on a bolder look with frock coats having wider lapels and looser cuts both in the body and the sleeve than the previous decade. American Frock coats were almost always black, however, charcoal gray and dark brown were acceptable colors along with midnight blue. Thee may have purchased his green frock coat while on his European tour as fashion on the continent favored more colors. Metal buttons were very stylish. In the early part of the decade, men continued to wear extravagant, heavily starched, asymmetrically tied cravats. Most men favored the side part hairstyle with an extreme front wave. All businessmen wore vests daily over fine white dress shirts. Pocket watch chains, of heavy gold, continued to be the norm.[45]

The next letter to Thee arrived from Anna rather than Mittie, who was still at Sulphur Springs. Anna brings Thee up to date on family news, especially about the whereabouts of her brother Daniel Elliott, still traveling in Europe with Robert Hutchison. She also asked about her brother "Jimmie" whom Thee had more contact as James Dunwoody Bulloch's ship operated out of New York City. James had transferred to the United States Ship *Black Warrior* in late July of that year.[46]

Roswell August 22nd

My dear Thee

Your letter came to me this morning and at the same time a long one to Mother from brother Dan He is still uncertain with regard to return to this country as he may continue to spend some time in England and Scotland. It is more probable that he will come home about the end of September. Mr Hutchison had informed him of your engagement, brother says it is almost impossible for him to realize it at all – He says that when he left he regarded Mittie as so completely a child and that she expressed herself so positively a sceptic upon the subject of love that nothing could have surprised him more. Mother and Mittie will arrive on Wednesday – you can not think how anxiously I am expecting them. Mittie in her last letter to me said that neither Mother or herself had experienced the full benefit of the change and water because their diet was so totally at variance with anything that could be expected of invalids – I think that when they get back home they will find that the water has been better than they now think. Mother says Mittie has been induced to take a great deal of exercise and you know how good this is for her. Roswell has improved vastly since the earlier part of the summer – we have very pleasant reading parties almost every day, and Mrs Habersham and some of the pleasantest school boys walk out with us whenever we do not ride. I should have mentioned before the safe arrival of the letterbox with our earrings and the other little articles – Thank you for the trouble you must have taken. The earrings are altered exactly as we wished. I did not venture to send Mitties to her as I know how irregular the mail arrangements are. The buttons you selected for Mr King can not fail to please

Chapter III

Mittie – Thee I think you are very thoughtful – She asked me in her last letter if I liked the buttons, and seemed so pleased at your remembrance of that one little wish – You remember how oppressed she seemed with the idea that she must give him something – It was inconceivable to me what a disappointment to the whole family the discovery about Airfield must be – I always thought it must be so exactly the place to make you all comfortable – I do not like to think of your dear Mother being sick she looked so very delicate when we saw her - so give my love to her - Cousin Mammie says I must remember her to you. I am afraid she will have left for Charleston before you visit us in the fall – Do you not think it a little strange that a young gentleman of your cheerful disposition should leave the city and visit a little upcountry village at that inclement season under the most auspicious circumstances you know Georgia is not a pleasant state to travel in – As it is merely a whim, suppose you visit a more interesting portion of our state than Roswell. It is only two days now before I will see Mother and Mittie – it is so dreadful to be separated from Mittie – I think I will not let her ever go away again! Irvine was quite amused with the piece of paper you sent him which contained so exactly his own sentiments – Have you seen brother Jimmie! I have not heard from Lizzie since Mother went to the springs – just before she left she had a pleasant letter from him – "This letter was not exacted" at all, I am only afraid you will be surprised at this very prompt reply to yours. I felt you would like to know if the box arrived safely – Much love to Mrs Weir Roosevelt remembrances to all – I really would like to know why you think Thee, that I have been "so kind" to you – In the first place if it was not really the case it was not any thing at all. And you know too you really merit all the love and confidence your friends feel in you – If this reaches you when you are occupied just put it away – Good bye Yours truly

Anna Bulloch

Anna's reading parties probably included Mary Ann Stiles Habersham as she was of an age with Anna and Mittie, being 18 or 19 at the time. The buttons for Mr. King were no doubt selected for Tom King. Anna in particular sent regards to Mrs. Weir Roosevelt, as Mary West Roosevelt was the sister to Hilborne West, husband of Susan Elliott West.

Roswell Aug 26th

Dear Thee

We reached home on wednesday of this week, quite worn out from travelling a day and afternoon, notwithstanding all this however I went out to tea the very afternoon I arrived, 'tho I had gotten up that morning at four oclock! was that not a feat for me? We were not able to stop all night at the place we had expected to, on the road between here and the Springs on account of typhoid fever being at the house - 'tho we had made all of our calculations to do so, and left the Springs just allowing time to get there by dusk - knowing how perfectly impassable the up country Georgia roads are by night - particularly with no moon, We had therefore to drive six miles farther (coming within one of being up-set). To you it may seem a short distance, accomplishing as you have, thirty miles from six to twelve oclock besides paying a visit, but it took us an hour and a half. Could you see the place we actually staid all night, you would scarce believe your eye-sight, a common cracker house - they had no candles in the house, so we had tea by torch light, a warm, summer evening - dogs went about the house as freely as the family, you may imagine my fright when I was eating, nominally to find one under the table playing (so

Chapter III

they said, but I thought biting) with my feet, at this juncture the maid of all work had to put the torch on the floor (she being the only candle stick) - to rescue me from the dog - a scuffle ensued - the dog and herself were not heard of more, whether she was killed I know not, one thing was certain we could get no one to wait on us, The bed we slept upon, beggars descriptions. I realized the Irishmans theory for the first time, "if one feather was hard to sleep on, what must a feather bed be." We forgot all these dreadful misfortunes 'tho when we arrived safely at home on the next day - found Anna looking the picture of health, she had been taking so much exercise - riding and walking with the school boys - even her lips had color. After waiting a propper length of time, Anna rushed up stairs and I after her to see the cuff-buttons and other things, I was very much pleased, Thee-ate with your taste, I wrote a note and sent them to Tom yesterday. (Anna seems perfectly disgusted with me, cannot imagine my having a fancy for pleasing Tom in the slightest degree) he seemed perfectly charmed. said their beauty and neatness had captivated him at once and they seem to be treasured as a memento of a sincere friendship - he spent last evening with us and made him self quite agreeable. We heard from Brother yesterday he was then in London with Mr Hutchison, had just made a most delightful trip through Switzerland and France with some American friends. he said to hear of my engagement made him feel old and useless, could not possibly realize such a thing. He will be at home by the last of September unless Mr Hutchison persuades him to travel with him in Scotland. Airfield vacated! and in account of chill and fever - if the place had been in the southern part of Florida I might have given credit to such a story - but on Staten Island, a healthy Northern climate, we do not hear of such a thing even in Savannah this summer, When are you all, in New York at your respective houses.

August

I should think 'twould just be the most disagreeable season of all others to be in the city. How could William run away - choosing the most trying time of all others your Mother sick and Airfield proving false to its fair promises - & I hope Mrs Roosevelt is a great deal better do give my love to her. I am glad she made you remember my bent was not to be <u>too quiet</u> Thee-ate. I told you as early in November as possible something dreadful might happen but dearest Thee I am going to say some thing that I wish you would be perfectly good about - oh I would so infinitely prefer December, some where <u>positively</u> between the fourteenth and twentieth -Think about it dearest, and think too that it is my wish, I know you so well you will begin to imagine tis because I love you less - but Theeate, when I trust my life happiness ^{to you} ten days later, makes no difference atall in my love for you. If you really love me you will tell me that it will suit you just as well, I trust you with perfect <u>confidence</u>, I could have remained silent about it and let the time come with you proposed - but darling dont you know you told me to ~~true~~ tell you every thing I thought, I have done so, and when I assure you that it will add <u>materially</u> to my <u>happiness</u> and <u>comfort</u>. I know you will not think tis because I love you less - by October I will be able to tell you even the day <u>positively</u>. Write me exactly what you think, and be careful what you write, think how far away from you I am, and if anything you should say might wound me, you would not be here, to explain a different meaning. After this we will not mention the subject, for dearest Thee I am perfectly foolish when I begin to think over it all, and about leaving home, and have to think "well I will be with Thee ate and if it was not for this, darling, I never would be comforted, I am so thank ful 'tis you and <u>no one</u> else. I have received three letters from you lately, one the very day I left the Springs and found two awaiting me. You have been very good about writing

95

Chapter III

- believe, they are always interesting to Mittie who loves you dearly. I would have liked to have been with you the day you wished for me, for Thee ate some times you are more entertaining than at others, 'tho always lovable and loving. I should like to have a "quiet talk. (Thee's favorite expression) with you now. I had almost forgotten to congratulate you in having at last been able to have "Eggplant" cooked to suit your fancy. We miss you so much at lunch - sand-witches and lemonade dont seem the same thing as of yore.

I anticipate making the acquaintance of the Morris' Would we not have had a delightful drive together out to their place? Anna sends much love, and thanks for the three numbers of Punch. I will write again the first of next week - you will hear from me the twice a week that I promised. good bye. yours with love.

I hope poor Lizzie Ellis will have a slight season of rest, she must be having an awful time, but I don't think Robs being away shooting made it a bit worse.
If you can decipher this letter, 'tis more than I can do upon reading it over, but I have not time to write over, as we are to have company to tea. How is Mrs James I Roosevelt?

                Your own
                Mittie

Mittie's use of the term *cracker* occurs several times in her letters. *Cracker* was a term used in the nineteenth century to describe a poor, uneducated, white person. The use of *cracker* was somewhat contemptuous and illustrated Mittie's recognition of her social status and in this case, that of the boy they hired to reset the bowling pins. No doubt the boy had never seen the inside of a bowling alley and had no idea how to reset the pins. It is very likely he would have taken on just about any chore in order to earn the small change the party offered for his services.

Mittie sent Thee Anna's thanks for three copies of *Punch*. This magazine, once subtitled *The London Charivari* as it was based on the satirical French paper *Le Charivari*, began publication in July of 1841 and introduced what we now know as cartoons. Known for its humor, satire, and cartoons, the editors insisted that it be less bitter than other British publications and hold to a higher literary standard. Volumes XXIV and XXV were published in 1853.[47]

New York Aug 28th 53

Dearest Mittie

Over a week had passed without my receiving one letter from you; this was however easily accounted for, when one did arrive, by your evident devotion to your theory of enjoyment.

I do not expect, like yourself, to be able to enjoy myself "<u>more</u>" because we are seperated, but I will try to follow out your "wishes" as far as possible.

It is sunday, and were it not for the subduing influence of the day I would request you to look over those portions of my first letters that you skipped and answer a question contained in one of them, the answer to which might have had an effect upon my occupations for today. - Whose life was it that your mother requested me to read? -

We had quite an amusing though slightly disagreeable scene yesterday. You may remember that I mentioned the neck of one of my bottles being all that remained of what had once contained something stronger than water. The disappearance I naturally applied to those who had access to my room, it now however looks as tho the cook deserved the credit.

Chapter III

Yesterday mother was rather unwell, although her general health has recovered itself, and she lay down before dinner time. The dinner hour passed, four o'clock came and with it one of the servants to say that Clara (the cook) was high, had let the fire go out, would not cook dinner nor allow anyone else to. This difficulty was atlast overcome and sometime afterwards mother wished some dry toast and tea as her meal; this the cook positively refused to give and father (for the first time in his life I believe) was obliged to go down in the kitchen, determined if necessary to toast it himself. Clara told him he had been a father and a mother to her ^{at last}, that Cornelius (who has just arrived) had come to a "heavenly home" and, after a little more conversation of the same nature, in a few moments sent up the toast and tea. My dinner was delayed till half past seven instead of seven, but as all the vegetables had been forgotten for their dinner they were cooked for mine, and I was rather overwhelmed.

Since our arrival in town the weather has been perfectly delightful and to day reminds me exactly of a sunday morning in the spring when I employed myself just as I am doing now. Then I had <u>that</u> delightful month to look forward to; now, a little farther off, a whole lifetime of pleasure. How I wish that November followed after August and not October, it seems so far off.- Do take great care of yourself remembering that another's happiness is dependent upon you too, and if you should ever have anymore palpitations or be sick remember to tell me myown little Mittie.

Afternoon. I have just returned from church (the Dutch Reformed) after having enjoyed a really good sermon, upon the different amount of interest shown in worldly and heavenly affairs. The church was full and I walked home with Miss De Witt; on the way up she mentioned that there was to be a magnificent concert with a newly imported band from Europe, tomorrow night. Remembering your wishes I suggested that we should go together which proposal she agreed to with evident pleasure, saying that her mother and brother were in the country and she was having a miserably quiet time in town. It seems rather ludicrous and I think must have puzzled her amazingly as I have never before paid her any attentions at all. She probably thinks (as indeed in this case she has reason to) that my engagement has improved me. Unless stopped by some relation before hand she will probably receive what will generally be considered a well merited lecture from her mother for going with me alone when that respected lady returns.

Fortunately there are few New Yorkers in town or I don't think I would have exposed her to the temptation.
6 PM. Evening. Father who has been convincing himself for the last three days that he was not sick lay down for two hours this morning, something he scarce ever does, and this afternoon had what appeared very much like a chill followed by fever, he made an immense number of rhymnes and seemed a little light-headed, mother has just persuaded him to retire [again] for the night provided she will go with him, which as it is broad daylight seems asking a good deal.

We are accustomed to it and do not mind it [Incomplete- last page missing]

Miss Dewitt was the daughter of Dr. Thomas Dewitt of the Collegiate Reformed Protestant Dutch Church of the City of New York. In 1853, the church was located at Lafayette Place. The Roosevelt family regularly attended this church.

Roswell August 30th

My dear Thee

To days mail brought your last letter together with one from Brother Jimmie, short and pleasant, (not however

Chapter III

on account of its brevity) quite the reverse of what he threatened namely long and sober - also one from Mr West. Imagine how enviously Anna looked at me, as she had to hand every letter separately to me, and expecting the next always to be hers only to be disappointed. The next request was that I should read a little bit of every one to her, which I endeavored to do, consequently if I should answer any of Mr West's or brother Jimmies questions, attributive it entirely to the confused mass which three letters completely irrelevant produced upon me. Thank you Thee-a-te for your letter and believe I always love you quite as much as right, and as much ^{as} I am capable of loving, 'tho not so much as you love me (Conceited Mittie!) It is the most deliciously cool afternoon, quite a fall feeling in the air, and the trees have some what the appearance as tho they were giving up the idea of mid-summer - just such an afternoon as I think walking in the Fifth Avenue would be delightful particularly if you were with an agreeable person, Thee ate I think I would like to walk with you, provided you were in an entertaining humor, I wonder if you were here, if you would gallantly say - that <u>you</u> would like the walk with <u>me</u>, independently of my humor. I had almost forgotten to tell you of the finale of my love affair at the Springs - it became currently reported that I was engaged (strong supposition) and Mother one day very innocently confided in an old lady that such was the fact, the simple minded old lady told the young gentleman, effect, I was treated with greatest indifference as tho I had done some-thing dreadful when all the time you 'Thee were entirely to blame. I could not help it then, Think only dearest how wanting in taste, if he wanted to show that he did not care for me the proper course would have been to continue his attentions, where as the other plan adopted made every body suspect I had refused him. The day he we left the Springs, he did also without ever saying good-bye, so excessively green when I had never been any thing but lady-like to him. Thee please excuse me but just as I have finished, it suddenly occured to me, that I had given the above account in my last letter, if so skip to here - This morning after breakfast Anna and I walked up to see Mrs Habersham and Mrs Dr Bulloch (that much abused lady) they returned with us and we had a long game at the alley, hired on the way a little cracker boy to put up the pins for us. After officiating the whole morning he knew nothing of the arrangements. When we left, always with a stupid look brought the balls up <u>in his arms</u>. This evening all Roswell spends with us. We meet on a grand consultation. Tableaux are on the carpet - and tonight we arrange which are to take which character and other necessary arrangements, before Wednesday evening which is appointed as Tableau night, we will have some really pretty ones, you know Mrs Habersham will make a fine picture, but know that is no compliment to her as almost the uglier a person is the better they look in tableau. We have all become on a surprising state of intimacy. rides on horseback and walks home become quite the order of the day. So you see we take a great deal of exercise, and all of us going together makes it so much pleasanter. Tomorrow afternoon there is to be a <u>large</u> walking party on the creek, and the evening after we are going on a graping [grapeing] frolic. Mr Thomas and the Flats and boats will come in requisition. Our number of Harpers came to day. We have read aloud "Bleak House"- so very thrillingly interesting- and ending so unsatisfactorily, oh! then I had the whole work I h should <u>immediately</u> read the end. Please send "Agathas Husband." I know I shall like it. Irvine [Bulloch] has been at home all day he had a severe spell of sickness as the hour for school approached, which however wore away amazingly as that hour became more distant and by the middle of the day became well enough to shoot at marks with a pistol, a

Chapter III

performance which has been kept up unceasing - making Anna and I jump at every report - he begs me to thank you for the paper, containing advice with regard to a wife - he agrees with it perfectly he says. Mother sends her love, she is far from well. Anna sends hers too.

I expect you laugh at my two little notes every time, but a great sheet of paper seems so interminable, when you commence, 'tho this is as long in reality. Give my love to your Mother. I wish she were only out here with us in the country - no chills and fever, now it is delightful. But even the latter part of October begins to be disagreeable - at least to me, you know I like a <u>warm climate</u>, but I love New York, and some of its inhabitants - I write again the last of the week.

Your more
affectionate
Mittie Bulloch

poor Lew West; please remember us to him. I hope he is better.

Born Dinah Maria Mulock in Stoke-on-Trent, England, Dinah became a poet and novelist. Her third novel *Agatha's Husband* was published in 1853. A well-educated minister's daughter, Dinah moved to London about 1846 where she found encouragement about her writing. Her first novel *The Ogilvies* was printed in three volumes and obtained great success. In 1864, she married George Lillie Craik a partner with Alexander Macmillan in the publishing house of Macmillan & Company.[48]

Chapter IV
September

As the wedding date drew nearer, Mittie and Thee's correspondence continued at a rapid pace considering that each letter took between seven and fifteen days to reach its destination. They often wrote to each other on the same day. As the following correspondence noted, Mittie sometimes received multiple missives from Thee in the same post.

New York Sept 3rd 53

Dearest Mittie
    The confusion which might have ensued upon your receiving three letters, in answering them, brought up a very amusing picture before my mind. Hilborne [West] astonished at your apearances of unvarying love, as much as you "were capable of"; and "brother Jimmie" reminded of sand-wiches in which he took a very slight interest. My letter did not contain anything incongruous the part you thought a repetition not proving so; the conduct of your quondam lover showed as you say such a desperate want of tact as I could not conceive possible even for a cracker; it must have amused you, (who I think rather pride yourself upon having a great deal of it), exceedingly.
    The day after writing you last I felt quite well (having acted according to the Doctor's advice) and in the evening "sister" was so kind as to come down partly as she said to see me individually. I did not feel very lively but considered myself well and enjoyed her visit together with one from

Chapter IV

cousin James (lame) very much Mrs West looks to me a good deal better.

Mrs & Mr James J Roosevelt were here at the same time; had she ever alluded to my engagement with you I would have informed her of your enquiry with regard to her health. As it was I talked to her about the English Lords and Ladies who she is proud of having entertained and she proved very benign.

Yesterday I woke up and passed the morning pretty well, in the afternoon I took a glass of water and found to my astonishment that I had in a measure lost control over my hands, which you know I do not possess the best of control over in writing at any time. I of course knew what it was and jumped into an omnibus and went home. Before reaching home what I should never call a chill, a shake perhaps, had all departed and I felt as though some malicious individual had placed two coals of fire behind my eyes. This together with an insatiable thirst and very great restlessness under a large amount of covering lasted about three hours. As it will probably take tomorrow which is my sick day (something unknown to me for nine or ten years) before it is broken up, I was afraid I could not write to you then and so have written this saturday afternoon, being made to come home early from the store by the threat of father, that he would not leave till I did. He seems to have recovered entirely and as it has only taken each member of the family three or four days to break it up, I will be perfectly well before you hear from me again, always provided quinine which I indulge in every hour or two has its usual effect. The family are coming down here to tea tonight (want of a waitor prevents their appearance at dinner) and I [am] hoping most anxiously that I will be allowed to indulge in the ice-cream. My feelings on that hot day in Roswell were comparatively cool.

Mittie what a good arrangement of days we made for writing, one of your letters always comes on saturday to me, the other in the middle of the week; the first I allude particularly to, it is so pleasant just to reread it over quietly and feel that no one will interrupt me while I am answering it on sunday. It is a day which I can devote a part of it at least to myown thoughts, and to own the truth I find this very difficult during the rush of business of the rest of the week; you know I scarce regard this as applicable to you, as there seems to be a kind of dreamy shadow of you hovering round and softening my whole existence, it interweaves itself without interfering with my other pursuits. And now Mittie unless I am very much shattered tomorrow, I will finish this then.

Sept 4th. The day proves an exceedingly warm one, the first since our arrival in town; which under the prospect of drinking hot lemonade and lying under blankets by no means agreeable; this I am to undergo soon after dinner. You can ^{not} imagine ^{how} absurd and impossible to realize it seems for me to be sick, they have been talking of all of us going to Newport, which I of course would do at present merely through compulsion as my business needs me here. I am doubtful if they will make up their minds to go. Poor Weir is the most melancholy looking subject as he has had combined with it a severe attack of his dispepsia. Last night when father proposed that he should give up smoking he said it was the "<u>only pleasure</u>" he had in life. Upon being reminded of a wife and family he made no exceptions.
I am glad to see that Dickens has more influence over you than I in as far as finishing before reading Bleak House is concerned. I don't think you deserve any pity.

Don't let your intimacy with Mrs Bulloch [Mary Eliza Adams Lewis] cause a rupture between Anna and yourself, for fear you will be innoculated with her views matrimonial. With love to Anna and your mother, who I sincerely hope is better
I remain

>Yours Devotedly
>Theodore Roosevelt

Cousin James Nicholas Roosevelt (1836-1856) was most likely Theodore's visitor. James, the son of Judge James John Roosevelt, never married and died at 20 years of age. Theodore's distant cousin James Roosevelt (1828-1900) of the Hyde Park Roosevelts, could have been Thee's visitor; however, the families were not close friends during this period.

Thee and his family discussed going to Newport, Rhode Island. The wealthy of New York, Philadelphia, and Boston had recently begun summering in this small seaside village with its cosmopolitan resort atmosphere. Earlier in the 1830s, wealthy southern planters seeking to escape the heat had begun to build summer cottages in the town. Other visitors stayed in local boarding houses that catered to the wealthy. The more wealthy Yankee visitors began building "cottages" for their own use. This period proved to be the beginning of the gilded age for Newport.[49]

While Thee apparently did not note the date when he wrote the following letter, research, based on the 1853 calendar and his mention of his recent illness, indicates it was the 7th of September.

September

New York Sept Wed 1853

My own Dearest Mittie

    I had intended adding a postscript to my last letter, but found myself on the morning when it was carried off by father too weak to do so.

    I have always regarded fever and ague [a fever, usually associated with malaria) marked by paroxysms of chills, fever, and sweating that recur at regular intervals] heretofore as rather a practical joke but judge from one nights experience that this is taking too easy a view of it. Imagined myself in the deserts and the Arabs leagued together to prevent my having any water and when sufficiently myself to reach the water finding that it merely added a fresh pang to my head which was already splitting. I tried to walk from one part of the room to the other but found it was too much for me and had to give it up, this lasted till five in the morning, the longest night. I ever passed. I could not help thinking of your enquiry if I was "strong" how unequal I would have been ^{then} to answering it in the affirmative.

    Last night I was successfull in breaking it by being pinioned down so that no air should come in, rather a warm situation with the thermometer about 86° or 88°. My expression of face as a mosquito lighted and insisted upon staying under these circumstances is beautifully represented by "Mr Jones" while table turning in the Porch which I will send you if possible today. Newport was fixed upon decidedly and if it clears up we will start tomorrow; as everything has gone wrong however so far for this season, it is hardly to be expected that this plan should prove an exception.

    I evidently never ought to have left Roswell where we were all so happy to join my fortune with those against whom the fates seem at present leagued. Fortunately there never was a tide that had not turning and by the time you

Chapter IV

reach here I look forward to the brightest possible prospect in every way.

Mary and Weir have made about twenty plans the last of which was to go to the Lewis' and then to Philadelphia, all have either fallen through of themselves or been vetoed by the Doctor. Do apologize to Annie for me if my letter proved incomprehensible or unreadable I can give no other excuse than slight indisposition, but I find that it is of a kind which distracts yones mind without his being aware of it.

Rob has just been in, inquired if I was writing a love letter, borrowed a couple of books and seems altogether in the happiest of moods. I am going to ride in the carriage to the store half expecting a letter from you. I am perfectly well now and only want something of the kind to brighten me up and as this will make the last part of my letter I hope a little more agreeable to receive. I will leave it until my return.

Afternoon. No letter from you and it will have to be forwarded. The mail arrangements are however good and one day will be all the difference in receiving my letters, probably none in yours. By the bye there was one irregularity of the mail at the Springs, where you were which I wanted you to account for, how my letters seemed to come to you so often when you would could not send yours to me. The ancient fact so often exemplified at school of "whatever goes up must come down" seems not to operate at the South. If it had anything to do with shame at acknowledging who they were for, I would prefer the enquiry remaining unnoticed.

We will stay in the house with George Morris' sisters at Newport and they are about the only people I will probably know at all intimately; if he was there of course I would see a great deal more of them, but he unfortunately leaves in a day or two. I just received a letter from him apprizing me of a sudden change in his plans produced by the prospect of shooting on the western praries. I know he would stay if I should ask him but do not feel sufficiently good company to repay the sacrifice, besides I am going "for my health."

And now Mittie as it is proved I can be sick, although four days is not very long, it shows the still greater necessity of taking every care of yourself and with this request once more repeated (selfishly for the first time) I will close remaining your ever
affectionate
Theodore Roosevelt

Night. The trunks are all packed and now as it looks really as if we would go how much I would like to have dear little Mittie as one of a party which will probably, although starting under difficulties, prove a very pleasant one
Your own
Thee

Punch published the cartoon of Mr. Jones to which Thee refers.[50] The magazine satirized "table turning," a popular parlor game of the period writing:

> "TURNING THE TABLES. Somebody wrote an excellent farce called Turning the Tables, but it is not so great a farce as one that is now having a run in private circles, where the entertainment of turning the tables is being got up in a very novel manner. The performers are linked together by a finger of one hand, while they place the thumb of the other on the table, which they surround; and it is asserted that, after they have continued in this position for about half an hour, the mahogany will begin to spin round with fearful velocity. That a table will go round, occasionally, in the eyes of those who are sitting at it we can readily believe; but we suspect that the circulation of the table is rather

Chapter IV

intimately connected with the circulation of the bottle. We have not much faith in the experiment of putting the thumb to the mahogany, but we believe that, if the fingers, with a full glass between them, are raised very often to the lips, the phenomenon may be at last realised. We have seen cases in which a rotatory movement has been imparted to objects of a more fixed nature than furniture; and, indeed, it is not an uncommon thing for a lamp-post, a pump, or even a pubic building, to commence a series of rapid whirls under the influence of what — without reference to the rappers — may be called the "spirits." We suspect that, if the cause of the revolution of the tables were to be closely investigated, it would be found to result from that species of electricity, of which — although glass is said to be a non-conductor — the glass and the bottle are the principal agents. Perhaps Scotch philosophy may be able to throw some light on this subject, for now that Scotland is proved to be the drunkest of the three kingdoms, we may safely leave such subjects as that of turning the tables in the hands of our staggering neighbours."[51]

UNCOMFORTABLE POSITION OF MR. JONES DURING A TABLE-TURNING EXPERIMENT.

Roswell September 8th

I hope you too have not been attacked by chill and fever, my dear Thee, I suppose you had been seized with the symptoms, from what you said in your last, alas! even the beef-steak proved ineffectual aided by "medicine". I have dreamed about you lately several times, and I suppose should feel quite superstitious about some of the strange things you said and did, in some of the dreams. 'Twould greatly distress Anna, as she has become of late a perfect "Melanie". By this time I hope you are quite well again, ready to escort Miss DeWitt about. I wonder you are not some with your old flame Mary Lee. We have been reading aloud lately "Beatrice" and have been charmed with it, from the manner in which you spoke of it, I did not think it worth the while to read, but since I have read it I have presumed you have not, or you would not have spoken thus, however it may just suit my fancy, you know tastes differ so very much.

We leave tomorrow on a Pic-Nic to the Stone Mountain, we will be absent two days. intend tenting out at the foot of the mountain, our party consists of nineteen, so I expect we shall have quite a merry time, Mother seems to be afraid of cold, but we always have large fires upon such occasions, and have plenty of blankets and shawls. Carrie Shackelford and John Franklin [Dunwoody] are to be of the party. The last time we went upon such an excursion the young men of the party got drunk (failing of high life at the South) and kept us awake all night by their dancing and singing. I hope we will have better fortune this time, as a young theological student is to be of the party. Our hope is in Tom King and himself. Before breakfast a few mornings ago a servant brought to my room a waiter full of splendid bunches of grapes and blue figs from Tom King. December then will be the time, and I think it will be best to inform your friends, as it can make no possible difference to them,

Chapter IV

as I had never positively decided the precise time everything depending entirely upon circumstances, dear Theeate I wish you could tell me whether there is a probability of your Mother and Father coming out. Mother seems anxious for them to do so, but I am very much afraid they will find both the season of the year, and the inconvenience of getting here (I allude to the stoppage in Atalanta) rather too much for them, of course we will be happy to see them, Mother I know will be disappointed if they do not come and Uncle John and Aunt Jane are very anxious to become acquainted with them, the latter I suppose wishes to hear from your Mother a direct and succinct account of the "Dutch Reformed" church together, with the private and public life of both the former and present life Pastors of the church. Your poor Mother has quite a trial before her, we have all been sacrificed to the altar of Aunt Jane's hobbys.

Anna has just been up to me to see if I could possibly know what was the matter with her, as she sees various colored spots dancing on whatever object she looks. I strongly suspect drink in the shape of a private tap, but this charge she indignantly denys, and seems perfectly oblivious that there are such things. So I have mildly suggested the possibility of her having knocked her head without being aware of it, at this she left the room in complete disgust, asserting that she did not believe I knew anything. Altogether I am in bad reports with the family. Maum Charlotte called me into the pantry to taste something which is being fabricated for the Pic-Nic, and pass my judgment as to whether it was flavored right, I very gravely tasted, (and I am sure did what I thought was right, for I knew not what else to say) then said Maumma I don't think it's sweet enough, received in return a withering look of contempt, accompanied with the remark that it was a perfect sugar-barrel then, and that I had better go up stairs. All send love. Must leave the rest of this sheet to ward off prying. I suppose sister has left this with love to your Mother.

>I am yours truly
>Mittie Bulloch

If I survive the Pic-Nic, will write again next week.

Mittie's reference to Anna becoming the perfect *Melanie* has not been identified. Perhaps the reference was made to a character in one of the many books they both read. It is interesting that the character Melanie from Margaret Mitchell's *Gone with the Wind*, published in 1936, came to exemplify the Southern belle.

The book Mittie read aloud each evening was *Beatrice: a Tale founded on Facts* written by Barbara Hofland in 1829. Hofland, the daughter of a Sheffield, England, manufacturer named Wreaks, was raised by a maiden aunt before marrying her first husband, T. Bradshawe Hoole, a merchant. After her husband's untimely death, Hofland published a volume of poems which attracted over 2,000 subscribers. Using her proceeds, she opened a boarding-school for young women at Harrowgate. She later married painter Thomas Hofland and settled in London. Here she began publishing novels.[52] *The Literary Gazette; and Journal of Belles Lettres, Arts, Sciences, &c. for the Year 1829* wrote this about her novel *Beatrice*:

> Beatrice is, we think, one of her most successful productions: the story, though romantic enough to be extremely interesting, is quite rational enough to be also very instructive; for few mental lessons are more instructive than difficulties supported and overcome by principle and exertion.[53]

Chapter IV

For a trip to Stone Mountain from Roswell, the group of young people needed to cover about 26 miles cross country. By horseback and carriage, the trip would take the better part of a day. George Hull Camp told a similar story of an outing to Stone Mountain taken in July of 1845 by the young people of Roswell.[54] Stone Mountain is a quartz monzonite dome monadnock located directly east of the current city of Atlanta. It measures five miles in circumference at its base and rises 825 feet above the surrounding area.[55]

In the early 19th century, Stone Mountain became a natural recreation area. Young men commonly took their sweethearts on horseback from Decatur to the mountain. Entrepreneur Aaron Cloud built a 165 foot (50 meter) wooden observation tower at the summit of the mountain in 1838; however, it was destroyed by a storm and replaced by a much smaller tower in 1851.[56] Most visitors traveled to the mountain by rail and road, and then walked up the one mile mountaintop trail to the top, where Cloud also had established a restaurant and club.[57]

A granite quarry started operation at the site in the 1830s and by 1847 the quarry could be reached by a railroad spur. Unfortunately, these early quarrying operations destroyed several spectacular geological features on Stone Mountain, such as the Devil's Crossroads, which was located on the mountain top. An interesting coincidence of history brings two generations of the Bulloch family together via this mountain's quarry. Mittie's future son, President Theodore Roosevelt would organize the building of the Panama Canal using Stone Mountain granite for some of the construction.

Near the end of her letter, Mittie makes a comment about the young men all getting drunk on an outing, how it was "failing of high life at the South." Mittie's view of alcohol consumption reflected that of her father, church, and community. Many of the founding families of the Colony of Roswell had early on signed an abstinence pledge that forbade the use of all alcoholic beverages. Mittie's father James Stephens Bulloch had joined the temperance cause as early as 1829.[58] In Roswell, with the formation of the Washington Total Abstinence Society, the members pledged:

> We whose names are hereunto annexed, desirous to forming a Society for our mutual benefit, and to guard against a pernicious practice which is injurious to our health, standing and families, do pledge ourselves as gentlemen, not to drink any Spirituous or Malt Liquors, Wine, or Cider.[59]

James kept the minutes of the society's meetings that began with hymns, prayers and thoughts on temperance. The society's members included white residents of the new "colony" as it was called and several black slaves. The minutes reveal a number of "backsliders" who would confess to their sins related to alcohol and then retake the pledge of abstinence. In December of 1842, the Society modified the original pledge, excluding wine and cider.[60]

Newport Sept 11th 53

Dearest Mittie

If this letter was commenced as you deserve it would be with a very severe lecture for neglecting writing to me when you could, after leaving half a dozen of my letters unanswered previously. It was not certainly doing as I had done towards you, but as you so entirely know my desires I will try not to refer to them again.

Incidents have been multiplying rapidly since I last wrote - we fairly started for Newport atlast and after being on the way two hours met the boat from there which had

Chapter IV

been seriously damaged and would not be able to make the evening trip. We were obliged to return to carry the evening passengers notwithstanding all our representations as to the outrageousness of this conduct. We expect to sue the companys for damages and have published a condemnatory article in the papers, but what was this satisfaction compared to Mary's coming home to rooms painted during her absence and ourown house all in disorder. I went in the evening boat with my horse, the others followed next morning in the Rail R cars which opportunity Mary took to have a chill.

I found plenty of ~~friends~~ acquaintances up here among whom the Morris rank first. I have ridden or driven out with them generally in the afternoon, and spend a portion of my mornings in their parlor.

From this you may judge that my recovery has been a rapid one, which indeed is the case with all the family who are looking the perfection of health. I begin now to hope that the tide has turned and the bright future is opening. My horse behaves as only _he_ can.
Miss [Beliden] is here, but although I do not blame her for an affectation that from long practice has become nature, she seems a little faded and does not take as well as in days gone by. She plays beautifully and Miss Morris by the bye sings in the same way. I saw a little piece of whit practiced at the supper table last night that allowed one to conjure up very brilliantly Savannah society. A young man had been indulging freely in champagne and would, half as a joke, occasionally fall against the young lady next to him. She was from the South would laughing request him to move away and evidently regarded it as intensely witty, decidedly encouraging it.

We had the full Germania band all the evening, to which some young men with pale faces and thin extremities danced, generally moving the young ladies' right arm as though "hoeing corn". The better portion of the community here decidedly look down upon it and amuse themselves by criticising and laughing at the dancers.

My window looks upon all that is most interesting at Newport. I have merely to look up from my letter to be reminded of the ancient Norseman by the tower in which "the skeleton in armour" ~~which~~ according to Longfellow was found ~~there~~. A little below is the town romantic looking from here but becoming very contracted and city looking on entering it. Next are the bay and battlements and far off as Weir says on the top of the trees is seen a faint glimpse of the ocean.

The beaches are perfection for riding never either mud or dust and since our arrival the weather has been superb for enjoying it. You would regard everything here as perfectly delightful, indeed it is only ~~that drop~~ your company which is wanting to make me think it so; but that drop makes a very large vacancy; particularly when I do not hear from you.

The scene which you depicted with your mother was perfectly frightful.
Little Mittie will find herself in Oliver Wendell Holmes' position as far as restraining her wit is concerned. Do give my love to your mother and Annie and believe me your devoted

      Theodore Roosevelt

P.S. Mittie without desiring to be "blue", I was reading one of Lamb's letters to a friend in China, in which he explained the difficulty of giving news a year old. This your letter reminded me of as of the request to deliver a message to "sister" is concerned. She is almost as near to you as to me, indeed you will probably be the first to see her again.

      Your Own
       Thee.

Chapter IV

In his letter, Thee referred to Henry Wadsworth Longfellow's *The Skeleton in Armour*. Then toward the end of his letter, Thee mentioned two additional authors. First, Oliver Wendell Holmes, Sr. (1809-1894) who although educated as a physician, was also a poet, professor, lecturer, and author. He lived in Boston and held membership in the Fireside Poets, a group of 19th century American poets in New England that included the aforementioned Henry Wadsworth Longfellow, William Cullen Bryant, John Greenleaf Whittier, and James Russell Lowell. Holmes began writing poetry while quite young and his most famous work *Old Ironsides* was published in 1830 and became influential in the eventual preservation of the *USS Constitution*. It is not clear to which of his works Thee was referring; however, Holmes was well read during the period.[61]

The second was the previously mentioned Charles Lamb, the English writer and essayist who was well known for his essays and letters. Lamb became obsessed with the mysterious empire of China later in his life and wrote many letters concerning that nation. (See endnote 41.)

Roswell September 14th
I have been so sorry for you dear Thee, reading your doleful account of your attack of chill and fever. However yesterday when I was at Uncle Johns [Dunwoody], some one asked after you I laughingly gave your information of your misfortune, Cousin Mammie thought me quite heartless to do so, and that really I was the wildest girl she had ever known, and would have been much better pleased if with tears and sobs I had announced the fact. but the thing struck me ludicrously - consequently, all my would be tears were turned to smiles. I do sincerely hope dear Thee you have entirely recovered,

September

I am hoping a great deal from the change to New Port, and the company of the Misses Morris - my next letter I hope will contain the news of my invalid Thee being quite restored, if not I shall advise a change South for a few weeks - you know you need not come to see me unless you particularly desired to do so, we use no <u>compulsion</u> whatever. I can assure you 'tis the most delightful way of living, so entirely independant. Thee you would have been horrified to have caught a glimpse of me, on Friday and saturday of last week. Our Pic-Nic party started most bouyantly on Friday morning. but when we had nearly gotten to the Stone Mountain we had quite a shower, which gradually set in to be a regularly pouring rain, however it cleared up sufficiently for us to conclude to have the Tent pitched, which was done, and a large fire made up before the door, we in a delighted state 'tho anxiously watching the clouds, which became more threatning looking rapidly - presently a perfect torrent of rain poured relentlessly down, we just sheltered by a cloth tent, Night had set in, dark as pitch, the thunder rolling, and the lightning flashing vividly showing our disconcerted faces. we had one candle burning - but I for fun got one of the boys to extinguish it, thought it would be such a good joke, only for a moment, when to my consternation found all the matches had gotten wet, and we had no hopes of light - till one of the negroes could go to the Hotel, which was about a half mile distant. We had a perfectly ludicrous wet funny time, when the storm continued we found ourselves getting so soaked that we must immediately rush to the Hotel, a party of fifteen, and three umbrellas! we arrived safely - all of us took quite a stiff "Brandy Smash". fortunately had dry clothes, in a few moments, we were all ready and danced in the Ball room, (so called, looked more like a deserted barn) till one oclock! When we woke up the next morning, 'twas still <u>pouring</u>, however we braved it, went down to the Tent,

Chapter IV

had damp biscuits, floating ham and chicken, and tea and rain for break fast, After this delightful meal we concluded that Home was much better on a rainy day, and consequently acted upon the principle, and reached Roswell about five in the afternoon, after not having ascended the mountain, not even seen the top for the constant rain, Mother was perfectly frantic when we rushed home, had any quantity of hot water and tea, and wanted us to immediately to go to bed, - Our Wet Pic-Nic is regarded with horror, and the old people all say. "I told you twould be so but you would go" - this of course is not so, but *as it* pleased them to say so and does not hurt us so we allow it. How many of you are at New Port? only the chill and fever ones, or all? I direct this letter to New York. I suppose you will get it, you did not say any thing about sending it to New Port. Thee your pen which was bad at first has become awful next letter I write I am just going to use a little piece of stick, which will answer quite as well.

Last night we all took a moonlight ride. Tell me all how you pass the time at New Port. I do not mean to answer any questions about the mails - so you need not trouble yourself. I made a mistake, the life Mother advised you to read was that of John Newton, however I do not think 'twould seriously injure you to read both. Sarah sends this jasmine to you, how much more romantic she is than I am, you know who I mean, the little girl about the house, she came to me and said, "please Miss Mittie, send this to Mr Roosevelt, and tell him it came off of our vine". It is meant quite as an attention, I hope you will appreciate it as such, Do give my love to your Mother. I hope she is quite well. Anna sends love,

Your affectionate
Mittie Bulloch-

We are going to have quite a gay week in Roswell. Miss Hand [Julia] & Miss Bayard [Florida] have arrived - we are there fore to undergoe parties, similar to those, during your visit. Excuse. Whether congratulations or pity is required.

We can get no stamps in Roswell, so have to use these huge governmental envelopes. it makes me so ashamed.

In this letter, Mittie referred to a recommendation that Martha had made to Thee concerning reading material. While some confusion apparently occurred, Mittie now set the record straight by telling Thee that he was to read the life of John Newton. That Martha would recommend highly that Thee read about this evangelical Christian and abolitionist provides a glimpse into Martha's character. While she was known as a deeply religious woman, her recommendation indicates Martha may have also have held serious concerns over the practice of slavery. Other historic documents indicate that Martha had taught several of her slaves to read and write, despite Georgia laws prohibiting such measures.

Born in London to a shipmaster's family, John Newton (1725-1807) began his career as a young sailor on one of his father's ships before being impressed into the Royal Navy. After a desertion attempt, he was flogged, reduced in rank, and transferred to a slaving ship. He soon found himself in Africa as a captive of slave trader Amos Clowe and his wife Princess Peye where he was abused. During the voyage home in 1748, after being rescued by a sea captain friend of his father, Newton had a spiritual conversion to evangelical Christianity during a severe storm off the coast of Donegal Ireland. Newton credited the saving of the ship and all hands to his prayers.[62]

Chapter IV

In 1806, Newton published anonymously his autobiography entitled *An Authentic Narrative of Some Remarkable And Interesting Particulars in the Life of _____ Communicated, in a Series of Letters, to the Reverend T. Haweis, rector of Aldwincle, Northamptonshire.* His un-attributed autobiography, written in an easy style, became widely read after his death.[63]

Newport Sept 14th 53

Myown Dearest Mittie

All here are gradually departing and the place is acquiring that doubly desolate look which unoccupied rooms and immense houses always give. I rather prefer it to the full season as now I can enjoy myself entirely in myown way. There are still enough here to make it a society if one is disposed to enter [it] and still one can be alone if he pleases taking away thus the principal objection I have to "Watering Places." It is so disagreeable I think always to know that someone is looking at you ready and anxious to find something to take to pieces. I rode yesterday afternoon with Miss Thorn, thus for the first time in my life being followed by a groom in livery.

She is beautiful rides beautifully and her horse had gaits very similar to my own so that as far as the asistants went everything was delightful but unfortunately she is a young lady who (to judge from her want of conversation) does a great deal of thinking. Horses seemed to be the topic in which she took most interest, and as she evidently enjoyed the ride and did her utmost, I was agreeably disappointed. She rides a trotting horse. Her father has five and as many servants here; he is regarded by everyone as an exceedingly disagreeable man in his family and from the way in which she suggested she would be willing to run with me when he was not near I don't think the world belies him.

September

The Morris go away tomorrow and with them depart all whom I know well at all at Newport, indeed almost everything that I should call decidedly ladylike. The rest seem to be rather disposed to be "fast" and you know ^{how} utterly I despise a woman who forgets her true character so entirely. One young woman of this description Weir has made the acquaintance of, but she kept him three quarters of an hour at supper the other night and then performed ^{the} witticism of telling her mother she "lied" before him; ~~and~~ I think it cooled off his desire to cultivate her materially.

I have been taking father a drive in my wagon this morning, and fortunately nothing broke. I always feel half afraid of venturing with him, as I know one accident would prevent him ever trusting his life, to what he considers a very unsafe conveyance at any time, again.

All are perfectly well as I consider it as necessary to put in that announcement as I look for it anxiously from you. The gong is sounding out I will be obliged to conclude after dinner. <u>Au revoir</u>.
After dinner. Dinner is the one meal of the day which does not quite equal expectations engendered from the size of the house and its pretentions. But your own description of utter want during your little watering place existence this summer so far outstrips myown, that it is not worth mentioning. Indeed my discontent is merely a proof that the more we have the more we long for. I sometimes think what a relief to all this turmoil "love in a cottage" would be but then I recall little Mitties serious objections to that style of life unless driven to it by necessity and remember that after all it would be necessary for both of us to be happy in order to make either of us so.

Give my love to your mother and Annie. I could unfortunately not remember you as requested to Cornel, he

Chapter IV

is reported to have gone to Philadelphia to visit Miss Anna Cochran, and old acquaintance, [-re], of his.

Yours Devotedly
Theodore Roosevelt

Newport Sept 18th 1853

Myown Dearest Little Mittie

You have had a decidedly evil influence upon my thoughts this morning, diverting them notwithstanding all efforts on my part from the sermon to which I ought to have been listening to far distant scenes. You know how very much "tenting out" shocks our northern views and to own the truth not receiving any letter at the usual time has made me a little (I scarce know what term to use the sensation being a new one) anxious.

I am sorry to be unable to answer your question about mother's coming to Roswell positively but I will comfort you with the probability that owing to the lateness of the season there is very little chance of it even should mother's health permit it. She still has a faint hope however.

Cornel is in Philadelphia according to Rob who went on with him visiting Miss Cochran three times daily. He has cried Wolfe so often that the family await the finalty of this in perfect tranquility.

We leave here tomorrow all very well contented to return home once more. I feel this most as every moment away from New York now is time really misspent unless for my health as so many things there require my attention.

The Misses Morris left last night, their mothers sudden indisposition having prevented an earlier departure. They are different from the general style of young ladies, but have certain views with regard to etiquette that render them very hard to become acquainted with. I would like to think otherwise (although not at all what I should call friends of mine) but I am perfectly certain you and they will never like each other. Their cousins on the other hand I know you will like.

Mary Lee for whom you so affectionately enquire I am not in the habit of visiting more than about half a dozen times a year. My intimacy consists in having spent six weeks in the house together some six or seven years ago, and being treated when sick with the utmost kindness and care by the mother.

There are two Thornes left here yet but I never thought it paid to be devoted for prospective dinners and because the people were rich and I have confined my attentions to several rides on horseback which is really agreeable as our horses go well together and she is just as well satisfied when I don't talk. We came down to the beech just after a storm the other afternoon and the waves were dashing against the rocks magnificently.

She turned her back to shield her from the wind and said "how cold it is." For once I regretted very much having a lady companion.

Why you should wrong me in your dreams Mittie I cannot imagine unless it comes from a guilty conscience in not being quite so candid as usual when writing. "I had never positively decided the precise time." Little Mittie must not forget her promise of entire candour with me, she will see the effect of the want of it most beautifully exemplefied in Agatha's Husband.[64]

We had quite an interesting little scene the other day, you will scarce beleive anything so revolting as occuring in real life. In the first place a young man named Morgan eloped with a Mr Sellden's daughter. She acts exceedingly improperly after they are reconciled to her parents and

Chapter IV

travelling in Europe, until Morgan one evening throws her out of the window she merely being saved from death by catching with some part of her dress on the railing round the window. This gives old Selden a fit from the effects of which he lies at the point of death in Paris. The Morgans come to Newport to live where she continues to conduct herself very improperly. Atlast he gives her several blows in the face with a cane, after which she puts herself under the protection of a Mr Winthrop who consults a Mr Hone an old man of over seventy. Some days afterwards Mr Hone is about to leave Newport when Morgan rushes at him with a cowhide and thrashes him awfully. Mrs Morgan in the meanwhile her face still showing the marks of the beating comes to a dance at our hotel. No comments are necessary.

And now dearest I will bid you good bye remaining ever

Yours Devotedly
Theodore Roosevelt

We return to New York to morrow.

New York Sept. 21st 53

Dearest Mittie

Dan [Elliott] arrived here to day and had I not promised to spend tomorrow evening with him I would have written this then after the receipt of the letter which I expect on that day. He seems to be in uncommonly good spirits, talks as though entirely heart whole and altogether appears to have overcome those feelings of the love-sick youth for which we have given him credit.

He said he intended going to Philadelphia but waited over to day to take a drive with me, he however accepted an

September

invitation with me for tomorrow and Weir the day after ⁽ᵗᵒ ᵈⁱⁿⁿᵉʳ⁾ so that I suppose he will stay several days, indeed he seems to have determined to see the Chrystal Palace and "Lyons" of the city generally before his departure. He talks a great deal of Europe but says there is no country like our own. He talks of the climate debilitating him but that thermometer in which I place much confidence, the appetite, does not show any signs of this.

All the family spent the evening with us, it quite looked like the return of old times.

Your doubts with regard to my having read Beatrice are I am happy to say unfounded, my objection to it was the same which I urge against "Uncle Tom's Cabin," that the book is not adapted to doing any good while it creates great ill feeling among the catholics. You know no one could despise more than I a sect which does not allow private judgement but obliges one to take the interpretation which another chooses to give to what they are perfectly able to understand.

But I will not argue upon a subject upon which we both take the same view.

Sarah's jasmine was duly appreciated although the source might have been one that would have gratified me more, please return my thanks.

I was very sorry that your Pic Nic should have proved so unfortunate although my prejudice against such a thing made this rather a relief to what I had feared. I would have been in favor of sending you to bed as your mother proposed.

Rob is at present the subject of numerous family jokes for having bought a sewing machine as he says to prevent Lizzie from sewing all day, otherwise her occupation. As it is to replace Lizzie it has been suggested that he will carry it with him on any expeditions instead of the original. We have all agreed to send in to his house all clothing that requires

Chapter IV

attention, but to own the truth if it operates as anticipated I think the family will be soon converted entirely in its favor.

My pen I have nothing to say in favor of except that I never write as other people and think should you try every side but the ᵘˢᵘᵃˡ point you would probably find one to suit better. Should I not forget it you may expect to receive some postage stamps in this letter so that you may not feel "so ashamed" when writing to me again. Give my love to Anna (who ought to write to me) and your mother, and should you remember it to Tom King my remembrances.
I will if possible send a little book you once asked me for belonging to the episcopal service by Dan, but as I had not expected him it may not be ready.

All have arrived here safe from Newport and without any serious inconveniences although a boat holding two hundred more than it was arranged to accommodate did not prove a very agreeable means of conveyance. Indeed the most serious objection to Newport is the means of access which I must own I do not feel disposed to brave again. Fortunately there seems to be no necessity at present as we all seem perfectly well at present.

And now my own dearest Mittie as it is half past one I must close, almost regretting the discontinuence of the chills and fever if the doctors would only give as pleasant a prescription as yourself, another visit to the south
Your Own
Theodore Roosevelt

In 1844, English inventor John Fisher combined all the inventive sewing machine elements of the previous half century to create the first modern sewing machine. Isaac Merritt Singer and Elias Howe followed his lead and produced similar machines within the next few years. Singer, an engineer, included several innovations, especially the falling

September

shuttle, vertical needle with basic tensioning system, and the presser foot to hold the cloth in place. Howe however held the American patents and sued Singer in court. After winning, Howe agreed to let Singer continue manufacturing machines for a fee of $1.15 per machine. Singer was the first to allow purchasers to pay over time for their new sewing machine.[65] By 1853, the new invention was readily available, but at a hefty cost for most households. Rob may have purchased a Singer, patent model 1851, commonly called the *Jenny Lind* after the famous Swedish singer.

Singer Sewing Company Advertisement, 1851

Chapter IV

Roswell Sept 22nd

My dear Thee

Anna and I have just driven over from Marietta, where we have been spending a few days with Carrie Shackelford. Mother had a letter for me from you, which had made its appearance during our absence, and as she had not read it, therefore could tell me nothing about you all, I concluded to find out for myself. I have received two letters from you from New Port.

I mention this because I see you like your different letters separately noticed, this is in answer to your two last. I felt confident New Port or change some where would do you all good, and am glad to find my anticipations realized. Notwithstanding all your difficulties in commencing your trip you have all arrived safely.

Having your horse must add so much to your pleasure, in fact I suppose you will never be able to leave him again, after his having been so very delicate and you far from him. I plainly see that I am destined to be jealous of that horse, in some future day.

We had quite a pleasant time in Marietta one of our old school mates at Barhamville was also paying Carrie a visit, this was delightful remembering and talking over all of our old school life. We had not met since we told each other good bye at school. My hands are so cold and I am so sleepy from driving in the wind (we have had a very cool spell) that I will wait till morning to finish.

23rd We had a party last evening fortunately every body seemed roused from their usual state of lethargy, and willing to make an affort. We danced till half past twelve, the Redowa with Ralph King - but mostly quadrilles, we have had some additions to our Roswell society lately, which makes it more agreeable infinitely. The Dunwoodies from the far South (I do not think you have ever seen any of them) are here visiting. today we are to have a family reunion. 'tis so cool I am in absolute dread being obliged to dress for dinner. Theeate pity me I will gradually get accustomed to the cold. Cousin Jack (you remember him I suppose) with some other gentleman are coming over to Roswell to day, with their dogs and guns to have a regular shooting time, the season is to be wound up with a grand supper party given by Anna and myself. I am afraid it will be quite rowdyish. Was the southern young lady who let the gentleman fall against her at supper a Miss Rosa of Savannah? I wish to know particularly I will write soon again.

am your truly aff.
Mittie B.

My love to your Mother-
    Anna sends hers.

    The redowa dance originated as a Czech folk dance and appeared in Prague salons around 1829. This round whirling dance was the forerunner to the waltz and soon appeared in Paris and then London around 1846. It remained popular for only a few years before being replaced by the waltz which was faster. Both the redowa and the waltz allowed couples to dance close to each other while holding hands. Just imagine, Mittie and her friends dancing the redowa across the King's dining room in their pounds and pounds of petticoats.

Roswell Sep 27th

    Anna has gone off "Graping" [picking grapes] with the boys, dear Thee, and as I cannot go (Mother will not let me) and feel like being with you, I have concluded to commence a letter, being able to finish seems rather doubtful, Irvine is in the <u>Entry</u> <u>carpentering</u>, consequently making any amount of noise and doing no good. I think little boys are

Chapter IV

some times awful bores. He has suddenly stopped, joy joy! Mother has proposed his following the Graping party. He has absolutely consented - has gone - such stillness. I do not think I can write now, because having become accustomed in a measure to the thundering noise, I miss it. Capricious Mittie. How will you please me ever?

Cousin John Franklin [Dunwoody] has been spending sometime with us. he came over in order to shoot Partridges and Doves. We have had delightful little dishes of poor inoffensive little birds but it pleased us and did not hurt them, then at all events. He left today, we miss him very much, not as much however as we once missed another gentleman. It is unpleasant being in the House with no gentleman, tho we will not have to endure long - as Brother Dan will be with us shortly. He must be in New York now. I do hope he will not just miss you, at one time I was fearful of your being at New Port when he passed through on his way South. We expect a beau in Roswell next week. one too, who while Sister was at New Port, was decidedly the "observed of all observers:" I should not feel excited about him as my future is made. he is very handsome, that will be very much valued in Tableaux - which are to come off again, next week. You see what a mania we have for them, and there is rather a dearth of handsome men in Roswell, with the exception of Henry Stiles. in one tableau I am the Virginian to his Virginnius. Tom King has gotten up quite a flirtation with Mrs Habersham, he has been her constant attendant devotedly for all the summer, when we were arrangeing the different scenes it was proposed that she (Mrs H) should be the Miranda to Toms Ferdinand, but she refused most positively. upon being asked her reason she replied that she had never acted that scene with any one but Mr Habersham, before their marriage, and would not like to act with any one else, as to her their was such an association, so I suppose she must love her husband, something which Anna and yourself doubted so very much.

Sep. 28. I received your letter from New York this morning, the family are in quite a state of excitement about Brothers arrival which we had not heard of before - and we are all in a state of expectancy as to his appearance in Roswell, which I do not think will be till the middle of October. We have been perfectly engrossed with the last number of "Bleak House, such a conclusion; some of the last scenes are perfectly inimitable. Richards death - Anna who attempted to read it aloud became strongly affected in articulation towards the close, and Mother and I became slightly blind. I have not been very well lately, have had a very bad cold, I cannot speak out of a whisper in fact, but my colds always <u>do</u> me that way, they seem more alarming than they in reality are, my throat is so very easily affected, that I lose my voice immediately as a cold attaches itself to me. Mother is going to dose me up extensively to night - and I hope to be quite myself in a day or two. Nothing for you to be uneasy about Thee. now mind, you are not to feel at all badly about it, for 'tis nothing. Anna sends her love and says she will write you soon. I am so much obliged to you for the stamps, 'twas so very thoughtful Thee, I appreciate I assure you, for none are to be gotten here, for love or money. If Robs sewing machine should prove successful, I will try introducing it into our family. 'twill be regarded as a heaven send.

    Mother who is in the room with me begs that I will give her love - mine to <u>your</u> Mother if you please - Where is Miss Lochnar?

Your very affectionate
Mittie Bulloch.

I have given the clasp button to Willie Smith. I did not think it pretty enough for Alfred Gordon.

Chapter IV

Mittie's mention of *Tableaux* being acted out referred to the practice of suitably costumed actors carefully posing without moving for the reading of a narrative. A term borrowed from the French language, *tableau vivant* literally means living picture. *Tableau vivant* as an amateur venture in the drawing room became extremely popular during the mid-nineteenth century. The tableau where Mittie plays "the Virginian to his Virginnius" came from a Roman story, of the year 504 B.C. In this historical tale, beautiful young Virginia, the daughter of Lucius Virginius, dies at the hand of her father to save her from a life of slavery and defilement by one of Rome's ruling Decemvirs named Appius Claudius. Several paintings of the event had been completed and presented as engravings during the previous years. These include three entitled *The Death of Virginia* beginning with Gabriel Francois Doyen's between 1756 and 1758; Francesco de Mura's circa 1760; and Guillaume-Guillon Lethure's circa 1800. The tableau with Miranda and Ferdinand is from Shakespeare's *The Tempest*.

The Death of Virginia by Guillaume-Guillon Lethière

September

New York Sept. 28th 53

Dear Mittie

I received a juvenile epistle from you to day and have come up from the store early in order to answer it and still keep an engagement with Dan. He has spent most of his time since his arrival here with me and is quite at home at all the respective houses. We have been to see the Chrystal Palace together and both of us found it much superior to our anticipations. The building is so immense that one has an opportunity of seeing each article well. The statuary and paintings attracted most of our attention although the machinery is also very interesting and we found a representation of Gulliver waking up while surrounded by the Lillipuetians which amused us exceedingly. I am so sorry that they intend closing it in December. I have been with Dan over to Mr Hodgson's in order to see a Miss Terrell or rather to allow him an opportunity of seeing her while I divert the attention of the family with whom she is staying, whom however much they may merit respect, I cannot bring my conscience to saying I admire. There is a Miss Tellfair who mother insists on it does not carry out her appearance in her actions but Mrs Hodgson she is perfectly quiet about, rather a bad sign.

From the tone of feeling pervading this letter you will already doubtless have surmised that I had not had my tea but I must add as farther extenuation that the life of John Newton seems to be regarded as not adapted to the age and is not be found in the New York book stores. So that I have not the advantage of his example.

After tea. It was not Miss Rosa who I alluded to as not acting according to northern impressions of propreiety. I saw that young lady however; she staid at the other house, merely favoring us when there was dancing; to which she

135

Chapter IV

seemed so devoted that I knew I would merely be in the way and was not introduced as I thought of being, remembering having heard you speak of her.

There was a comparaison made between Miss Morris and herself which from its perfect absurdity impressed her more upon my mind. Dan has been to see the Misses Morris and will tell you how beautiful they are, he will also probably abuse them for not talking which I don't think they merit, he does not seem to appreciate them as fully as Miss Terrell. I have not been to see them since their return and do not expect to see them, except perhaps a casual visit, until I go south when if I find myself down there before I am desired remembering that you wanted one not to appear until as late as possible, I may pay them or rather their brother George a visit. The mother has several times requested that I would bring you also as I returned, but I know you would not enjoy it and so "much regretted."

Hilborne West telegraphed Dan that he was coming to day and he is presumed to be at Weir's now but Dan is at present devotedly a lady's man and does not expect to see him until tomorrow, preferring the visit I spoke of. I hope he will include you in his general devotion to the sex and not resume what, by your accounts, was his ancient tone at Roswell. His spirits are, when I see him, much better and he talks resolutely of finding <u>some</u> occupation.

Do give my love to Anna and send me up your united (they are always so united!) views with regard to "Agatha's husband." I am reading now "The Roman Traitor" but fear, owing to its being bound, it will have to wait to be read [by you] until you come north.

With my love to your mother I remain

Yours Ever

Theodore Roosevelt

All the family are well. Robs' sewing machine excels his utmost hopes and served to amuse us (Dan included) during a visit to - it the other evening.

T.R.

Henry William Herbert (1807-1858), a classical scholar, wrote numerous fiction volumes and many histories. *The Roman Traitor*, published in 1846, was actually entitled *The Roman traitor, a true tale of the Republic : a historical romance*. The second, T*he Roman traitor: or, The days of Cicero, Cato and Cataline. A true tale of the republic* was released in 1853. Thee could have been referring to either volume. Herbert also wrote sports articles under the pen name Frank Forester for one of the early sporting magazines, the *Spirit of the Times*.[66]

Chapter V
October

Not all of the Bulloch and Roosevelt family members saved their letters from 1853. In particular, Anna seems to have saved few written to her at this time. So October's letters began with a note to Mittie included in a letter from Thee to Anna. Anna's portion of the letter remains undiscovered.

                                      New York Oct 2 53

For Mittie's eye <u>alone</u>

    Myown Dearest Mittie

    I cannot close this letter to Annie without a few words of love for one whom I long so continually to be with, once more.

    Do write your love for me as in days gone by. If you are tired of writing twice a week don't write so often, but do, when you write express (if you feel it) all the love you used to feel for me.

    I was reading over again your first letter after my return from Roswell, and its tone seems so very different from that of your last. You promised me too what it was not necessary to promise but (promised) I so much wish you had <u>thought</u> of sending me. It is not the chain I would have prized so much in itself, but it would have proved that out of sight was not out of mind. Don't send it now, unless already sent it will have lost that charm, its greatest one, of being a gift prompted by the feelings of the giver.

    Then there is one change but you think it a very slight one and I will not allude to it.

Chapter V

And still this does not make me doubt your love but merely makes me long so very very much to have again an opportunity of talking with you, and trying once more to persuade you to show such love as one ought to feel for one another and as I am I certain I entertain for you.

Little Mittie will call this a "rhapsody" I suppose, but I assure her it does not deserve the name, being merely an expression of feelings which I restrained until, having received but one note for the last two weeks, I thought she might have forgotten that love only prompted the request that she would write often, and that she would like to be absolved from a promise which of course the moment it became burdensome I would sooner should not be kept.

If you could have regular times to write to me I would know when to expect the letters and would not feel so frequently disappointed. But do remember if it is a pleasure for you to write how intense a one it is for me to receive news from you and write as often as you can <u>with pleasure</u>.

And now myown dearest Mittie after my note has covered so much paper pride and love have had a severe battle together, the first desiring to burn an expression of sentiments which I had half determined to keep to myself.

Do love me dearest as I love you most devotedly.

     Your Own
      Theodore Roosevelt

Thee mentions a chain which he desired and wished had been given. Based on references from later letters, it appeared that Thee desired a chain made from Mittie's hair, a common courtship custom of the time. Thee's outpouring of love and "sentiment" to Mittie and his desire for more frequent letters from her were answered in Mittie's reply. It is however very likely that Mittie had not received Thee's letter when she put pen to paper on 3 October.

Roswell, Oct 3rd

    I did not get your usual letter today my dearest Theodore (ahem) and concluded of course that as I wished to hear from you so much, that you might like to get one extra letter from me, I am a great deal better, is my first peice of intelligence, because I think you may have felt slightly uneasy about me - Mother has kept me a close prisoner. in fact I have only been allowed to promenade the piazza, since I last wrote. I have heard of you, instead of from you through a letter from Brother Dan. he says he cannot tell us when we may expect him, as he is "sparking" around the Misses Morris and Miss Tyrrel [Terrel]. this is his own expression. What a funny fellow he is - has he told of the finale with Miss Lewis yet?

    Anna encloses a letter to you for brother Jimmie 'tho he sent us his direction we have misplaced it. I suppose this is the letter she was to have written, soon after you left. Thee only think two months have passed since the morning we told you goodbye on the piazza, I can scarcely remember how I have spent the time; just thinking about it has made it fly. yet it seemed as if I had spent nearly all my life at those horrid Sulphur Springs.

    Anna and I are expecting Mary Cooper Stiles on a visit, and you cannot imagine how excited Tom King is, you know he admires almost any young lady he happens to be with, not caring much for identity in his different loves. You would be so amused to see how Anna encourages this passion in him, makes it convenient for him to be with her when we are all out together, such interested motives, Mary wishes Anna and I to return to Cass with her, but I do not know if we will or not. Have you ever had to finish a letter with a little negro boy just by you wanting to take it, and every member of your family entreating you to close, or else their letters which have just been finished in an agony of

Chapter V

haste will be also late? if you have not, you know not with what tribulation this dreadful little note has been written—good bye.

Mittie Bulloch

I am trying your pen up side down to day. scarcely any improvement, but variety is pleasing.

New York Oct 3rd 1853

Dearest Mittie

Dan will spend tomorrow evening again with me (we went to Wallack's together to night) so that I have to make the most of the few tranquil moments after his departure.

I was very sorry to hear of your cold although I convinced myself that it was not serious because I would not allow myself, even in thought, to doubt that you would not deceive me. I am going to make you a present, so that you may not catch cold again, in December of a set of furs unless you object. Perhaps this is not proper ^(to tell you) but I would much sooner if you do not like it know it now, otherwise don't say anything about it. Mother is having manufactured a sett of silver, but I will not shock you further.

I regret also not being at the tableaux and will try to send you a correct engraving of Virginia's position which will explain part of my reason; the rest, as I suppose you have not read the cause of her fate or would not have acted it, I will not enlighten you upon.

Dan has got the prayer book in his trunk. It is in a package and, if you do not care about making it public what it contains, you need not, as he does not know and it is sealed. I merely did this thinking you might fear that some of them would laugh at you, although I know some would not. It is a present that gives me great pleasure to give, always remembering your promise never to think of it as compared with the bible.

Do remember another promise you made Dearest Mittie to take care of yourself doubly for my sake, and above all things to tell me just how you are; you cannot tell how much it relieves me to feel that I can place full confidence in what you tell me about your health.

Hilborne left for Philadelphia to day, and Captain Bulloch arrived in his vessel, he is in quarantine however and I have not seen him yet. Dan's being here and George Morris just out of town make three people all of whom I want to pay some attention so that my time is well occupied. There does not seem to exist the feeling here that you had about not arriving before the wedding, and I hardly know how I will keep myself at George Morris' within a day of you; so unless you write me that I positively must not (politely speaking your "wishes" you know), if I find myself at the south a few days sooner than expected I will spend them at Roswell; and you know I must arrive too soon so as to allow for the chance of accidents. In other words dearest every day makes me want to see you more.

One o'clock is approaching and I must say good night

Oct 5. Captain Bulloch has just left me. We went to Mrs Plummers together and engaged rooms for his wife and Miss Caskey who are coming here to see him. They come under the impression he is sick although he has really entirely recovered from an attack of yellow fever which he had at Mobile. His having had it is very fortunate as it takes away any probability of his ever being troubled with it again. He abuses you both, Annie particularly as a correspondents; unfortunately I could not with conscience take her part.

Chapter V

He, Dan and several other friends take supper with me tomorrow night. If you enjoy "doves" how much you would enjoy the woodcock and champagne. Cornel was slightly ferocious at first as he had proposed giving a supper to Bob Macky and other youths of a similar stamp who mother will not allow to enter the house, with good reason, if she can help it, his desire was consequently frowned upon. All she asks is within the bounds of respectability, but she had a little experience of the other class last winter.

I have invited Joe Mc Allister who brought Miss Clay to stay with us to day although I did not quite approve of a remark of his, "It seems but yesterday that I kised Mittie as a child." Now this is something I desire entirely to monopolize and don't like to hear anyone able to recall; of course I kept my views to myself.

I have sent the promised engraving in this week's pouch which contains, by the bye very little I am afraid to amuse you; the engraving is beautiful for itself, without its moral.

Lizzie Bulloch has been steadily improving during the last month, which the Doctor says he considers much more favorable than a rapid improvement would be. I hope to see her soon and judge for myself.

Dan is rather down-hearted, he says he will write home in a day or two, an observation I have heard him make before.

Mrs Habersham's proof of love for her husband was more than counteracted by the announcement that she was carrying on a "flirtation" which atleast gave him good and sufficient reason for not returning an affection that she could disemble so easily out of his presence. You will probably have a laugh with me over his success, more especially as I suggested that I thought she was one of <u>that kind</u>, when he was hoping but doubtful.

And now dearest I have no subject left but love which little Mittie knows I cannot express when speaking to her fully, so I cannot hope to write it and will only say my <u>dearest</u> one, good night

Theodore Roosevelt

Four New York City theaters played an important part in American theater history. The first three, including the one attended by Thee and Daniel Elliott, served as the successive homes of the stock company managed by actors James W. Wallack and his son Lester Wallack. The first Wallack's Theater opened on 1 November 1852 at 485 Broadway in a building most recently holding Brougham's Lyceum. The Wallacks were actors, entrepreneurs, and theatrical stock company managers. The building had been built to specifications for its previous owner John Brougham as a theater. As the company developed, it quickly realized a reputation as the best theater company in the country.[67]

Performances at Brougham's Lyceum were principally burlesques and farces. The venture was not successful and after two seasons, James W. Wallack leased the house and renamed it *Wallack's Lyceum*. After extensive renovation, Wallack opened his new theater on September 8, 1852, with *The Way to Get Married* and *The Boarding School*. Admissions were fifty and twenty-five cents.[68]

In February of 1854, *Putnam's Monthly* reported:

> There are two theatres in New York, and but two which are devoted exclusively to the performance of the regular drama; these are Burton's in Chambers Street, and Wallack's in Broadway....Wallack's Lyceum, in Broadway, is an exceedingly elegant little house, the

Chapter V

style of the interior decoration is in excellent taste, and the effect of a full house is light, cheerful, exhilarating, and brilliant....Great attention is always paid to the production of pieces at this brilliant little house, and the costumes and scenery form an important part of the attraction. English comedy and domestic dramas form the chief attractions at Wallack's, and the house is generally full. The utmost order and decorum are maintained...and everything offensive to the most delicate taste carefully excluded from the stage.[69]

Yellow fever, historically known as yellow jack or yellow plague, is an acute, often deadly, viral disease which brings on symptoms such as fever, chills, loss of appetite, nausea, headaches, and muscle pain, particularly in the back. Symptoms typically improve within five days; however, some people within a day of improving experience a recurrence of the fever with severe abdominal pain, and liver damage begins causing the skin to yellow. This viral disease is spread by the bite of the female mosquito. Those who survive the infection possess a lifelong immunity with no permanent organ damage. Yellow fever epidemics occurred frequently in American cities, especially in the South.

New Orleans, plagued with major epidemics during the nineteenth century, most notably in 1833 and 1853, was one of the stops on Captain Bulloch's route. The 1853 epidemic began in May and by the autumn of that year had sickened thousands and killed at least 7,849 people. It is estimated that the true death toll numbered between 8,000 and 10,000, approximately 10% of the population. Officials quarantined all ships coming into US ports with yellow fever victims on board, usually for 30 days. At that time, it was not known how yellow fever was transmitted.[70]

October

Roswell Oct 5th

My dear Thee

It is after tea, and we are all in the parlour, writing different people. of course we will be interrupted by visitors as we wish particularly not to be disturbed. I took a long ride on horseback with Irvine, we forded the creek and altogether we had quite a pleasant time, except I had to converse about all kinds of dogs, pigeons, marbles, and other school boy topics. You see I am quite well again to be able to be riding about as usual, and last evening I acted in Tableau, To Morrow evening we are going to attend a party. All this looks quite revived again, does it not?

You must be having a charming time, conversing with the youthful and artless Mrs Hodgson, and her lovely sister who I suppose has not yet entered company. why Thee she would be quite a "spec" for you. Miss Tyrrel used to be an old flame of Brother's - he said just a little school girl friend, but was always quite tender about her, however, I will never again believe any thing about Brothers love affairs till I hear that the p Parson has said amen. By the way alluding to such a thing as a wedding makes me think of ours to be. You remember when you were here, I said I would have no Bridesmaids at all - well then I did not think it would be necessary - but since we have been thinking over things in general and have come to the conclusion that some of my five dozen intimate friends must be asked to officiate. If I had had a strictly private wedding, for instance married in the morning and leaving immediately, nothing of the kind would have been expected but as it is I must submit to having four attendants. The great difficulty I know of course will be the groomsmen, well I have been thinking that Corneal would come out, then Brother Dan you might ask, and I would like to have you ask Tom King (besides the compliment to him his being in the place makes it so

Chapter V

convenient) this makes three. Mr Morris if you think so would complete the number. I know the season of the year is exceedingly unpleasant, but perhaps with pleasant girls the young men might be able to get through with a few days. Dearest Thee I do not mean to dictate to you who you should ask, but thinking it over we concluded those gentlemen would be pleasant, and suit the girls. Do not speak about it, or take any measures in regards inviting the gentleman, till you hear from me again, after that letter which I will write next week. I want you to proceed in the usual form - I am not perfectly certain if Mary Cooper Stiles will be one or not, but if she is I would like to have you bring Mr Morris. otherwise I do not think he would be interested, and consequently we would be bored all around.

Please write me what you think of these arrangements, I have asked the girls already because you did not seem to think it would be very difficult to secure gentleman. I hope I have not acted too hurriedly. Would it not be ridiculous to have a line of Bridesmaids with no escorts?

We have just had visitors. I knew they would not let this evening pass, as we were anxious to write. Two of the school boys intensely dressed, and tight gloves. They are gentlemanly boys and have only staid a very short time, for the sake of entertainment we commenced telling Ghost stories - and Anna and I have gotten quite excited, our door and windows will be doubly attended to, we would not go up stairs by our selves on any account. Enclosed I send a little note to Mrs James Roosevelt, which will you please deliver for me. You know when we saw her in Philadelphia she asked me to write, which I have not done till now, for no reason that I know of was it put off from time to time. Thee you have no idea what good policy it is to keep up the appearance of a cold. Mother has such delightful nice little hot drinks every night just as I am going to bed. It seems so queer for

October

Brother to be so quietly domesticated in your family - from his letters he seems to be so comfortable that he has no idea of coming to Georgia. as to "<u>Some occupation</u>" I am afraid the seat of that occupation is picturesquely situated in the moon. I have not yet read Agathas Husband, but Anna has, and says she will [in]form you with her opinion, when she writes. I presume she likes it judging from her oblivious manner to every thing else. I heard Mother the other day say after having repeatedly questioned her, to which she gave no reply. "Well I do wish you were not so much interested in other peoples husbands." Please give my best love to your Mother, I hope <u>now</u> that they will be able to come out.
      Yours most affectionately,
      Mittie Bulloch
You may kiss me like a gentleman when we meet perhaps.

      Roswell Oct 10th
My <u>dearest</u> Thee,
  I received to day your little note enclosed in the letter to Anna and I cannot tell you how badly I felt, to think you should distress yourself about the reality of my love for you. I did promise to write twice a week, but you may remember I said only a <u>note</u> the last part of the week - well I did keep that up for sometime till I thought once a week would do, besides Theeate, somebody else's letters fail sometimes, for instance, last week I received one from you on monday and none again, till the note in Annas letter. How is that the promised two letters in a week? what I have just stated is only the repitition of the week before. Hereafter I shall always write on every monday (unless something not thought of should happen) and sometimes again on saturday, if the spirit moves me. Would you not rather have this free will offering? If you really desire me to I could write positively

149

Chapter V

twice a week if it would add materially to your comfort, any for two weeks before you come south, the two weeks before we are married (does not that sound bold and decided?) I am going to give you quite a little dose of my letters in the shape of two missives a week.

Now for the other charge, breach of promise. I feel mortified when I think about that chain, but I had concluded to wait till I went North in order to have it done to suit my fancy, this I thought would do as well, because I do not wish to have you wear it with similar vests, 'twould not show at all my hair being so dark. My dearest Theeate - I am afraid you will not love Mittie with all her faults (what you promised once in the piazza voluntarily) - I own in somethings I have behaved rather badly - I only can say that in almost every thing <u>you</u> have acted just to please me - and I can not follow out my usual tactics, namely carrying the war into the enemys country. Never mind one nice talk will make all up. I expect we will find time for such an one, 'tho since I have determined to have so much larger wedding than I had expected to, <u>we</u> will have to be devoted to the company. I am rather anxiously expecting your letter, to hear what the prospect of groomsmen are is. I think the day will be some where either in the first or second week of Dec. I will tell you positively in my next letter or the one after - I wrote you a long letter last week with one enclosed to Mrs James Roosevelt. I will write again this week, you must not feel anxious about me, for see I am able to write on the very day I have had a palpitation. I mention this because Anna says she is going to tell you about my having been sick as she promised (which I am very sorry she did, as it will do no good) I love you Thee indeed I do because I do not always write a rhapsody is no proof against the first, believe me you would sicken were my letters to like the first I wrote, which I regard as decidedly weak minded - It is so late I can scarcely see to write, I hear Mother singing down stairs all alone. I must go and be with her. Thee I <u>love</u> you or I would not write you.

Entirely yours
Mittie -

New York Oct 10th

<u>Evening</u>
Dearest Mittie

Even running the risk of utterly shocking the post master I must add a few lines to my morning's letter.

I mentioned to mother the probable change of programme and while she agreed with me in as far as enjoying most a quiet ^{wedding} she severely reprimanded me for presuming to interfere at all. Now I thought and still think you would have preferred a candid expression of opinion and merely write to request you to do as you think best entirely, merely requesting you not on our account to increase the number of guests. I would mention too what I did not like to allude to this morning the precarious state of Mrs. James Bulloch's health. So many things may occur which would interfere with a large, while nothing but a change in ourselves, and that dearest is impossible, could derange our plans for a quiet wedding.

As to the four groomsmen I don't object to them in the slightest degree (it would be quite unnecessary as you have invited the bridesmaids) as I do not anticipate any difficulty in obtaining them. Of course Dan would be one, Cornel probably another, George Morris who is handsome (though you will not call him bright) certainly ^{third}, then I would first ask two or three here to whom I ought to pay the compliment and if, as they probably will not come, Tom King is not objected to by Anna, he will be the next choice.

Chapter V

But first of all things do send me word the exact day, as I of course cannot invite anyone until I know it, and <u>do</u> Mittie make it an early one in December if it must be as late as December.

Mother and father expect to come unless the former is worse. I was suspected of having some reason for not wanting them to come, but was able in consequence of your letter to day to ask them for the first time with my whole heart.

I am glad you have changed your views in desiring their presence; although I must acknowledge that the utter change in your views with regard to other spectators is utterly incomprehensible. Do explain it.

Dan was very much shocked at the change in Mrs Bulloch; she has gone to the Havana, probably to pass the winter there, he fears never to return.

Dan talks glowingly of matrimony but does not seem any nearer it than when he first arrived. He stoutly denies any foundation for the rumour about Miss Lewis and even denies having called or had the desire to as he passed through Boston.

I hope now dearest that I have convinced you that more thought on the subject has determined me to be "good" with regard to your arrangements and not object to them, but do try to recall some of those conversations on the sofa, when we both agreed how much better it would be to leave Roswell soon after the marriage, and do not alter your views very much on the subject.

You know my dearest little Mittie always insisted upon it she was not at all changeable.

With my love to Anna and your mother I remain as ever

Yours
Theodore Roosevelt

Thee passed the word to Mittie and her family about the state of Brother Jimmie's wife Lizzie. James' ship departed New York on 9 October en route to New Orleans via Havana. Lizzie accompanied her husband on the trip.

Anna weighed in with her thoughts on this date while responding to a personal letter from Thee. That letter and a portion of this letter are missing. Anna explained to Thee how things worked in Roswell and exposed her one of her mother's personality quirks.

Roswell Oct 10th 1853

Dear Thee

I was so glad to get your letter by the mail today. It was very kind as you are generally so particular about having your letters replied to. The inhabitants of Roswell are quite willing to have you and Mr West discuss them. They have no fear of two persons who over look every failing. Now before I write another word I must keep my promise to you. Mittie has not been perfectly well lately. For some time she has had a pretty severe cold. I did not write about that because we thought it would soon pass away and because as numbers of others had colds so we thought very little of it. To day she had a slight palpitation. Nothing at all like the one when you were here. Mother thinks the cold was the exciting cause. Now the reason I enlarge so much more fully upon this than Mittie wishes, is because I want you to trust entirely in me Thee, of course if I feel bound to mention at once, so slight an attack I would not leave you in ignorance if she were really sick. I tried to persuade her that I would be so interesting she need not write by this mail, but she could not agree with me at all, so my letter will take hers to you. Carefully I hope, as I know it will be so much more welcome. The only reason I can not give you our <u>united</u> views of upon Agatha's husband is that Mittie has not read it. I was delighted with

Chapter V

it I really think Agatha's husband is a parallel case with the unfortunate individual who married the four Miss Hilsons. I will only come in as far as arranging and discussing and all that goes. Mittie and I really hope our "Indian chief" will come out. He will "not be at all in the way." I was sorry to trouble you with my letter to Brother Jimmie, but I did not remember his address perfectly, and I was so anxious for him to get it, so this must be my apology. We have not heard anything at all recently from Lizzie. Mittie is quite brighter to night, does not seem at all as if she had been sick this morning. the weather is <u>so</u> delightful now that we are taking very regular exercise, this will soon restore her entirely, since her cold she has been more or less confined to the house in the afternoon, but now we will commence again to walk in the mornings and ride in the afternoons.

[one or more missing pages]

the only one I have ever coveted! I am a dreadful reprobate. Mittie and I regret exceedingly that brother Dan has been flirting so, with Miss Mary Telfair. We are not at all shocked at her brother in law's coolness. Of course he protects the young thing. You can not think how much better Mittie is than she was when you were here, so much so, that Mittie and I have changed all of our plans about the wedding. What do you think of having quite an old fashioned county wedding? You know what Roswell is, do not bring any one who could not remember themselves to it, but we would be <u>so</u> <u>delighted</u> to see, first of all your Mother and Father, and in truth any of the family whose powers of endurance are great. Now Thee from what I have written about "our plans"! don't think your

[one or more missing pages]

in everything we do or say, as Sarah always is. I never hint to mother about any thing I mean to do, a <u>moment</u> before the right time, for if I do my strength is <u>all</u> <u>wasted</u> in useless

October

efforts to keep her from sweeping everything before her. If I in an <u>evil hour</u>, ask her please when it is time, to tell Henry to have the horses ready for us to ride, that I will just go up stairs to read a little until time to go, I am lost – She will send Sarah out immediately, to tell "Henry Miss Anna wants both of the horses <u>now</u> <u>right</u> <u>off</u> to stop what ever he is doing and get them, he runs how <u>slow</u> <u>motion</u> he is." Just imagine the shock to the constitution, sitting in a dark room reading quietly not even remembering anything about horses to hear them lead around to the door, and at the same moment have your <u>room</u> door hurriedly opened by Sarah, saying "Misses says come down Miss Anna, the horses ready and Uncle Henry aint got time to hold them. I don't know why I write this for you have been over taken by the same much love to your Mother from us both. Please remember us to all

      Yours truly,
      Anna Bulloch

Mittie insists upon my adding what we have both forgotten to tell you that Mother will determine <u>the</u> day just as soon as possible, you will then hear immediately.

      Roswell, Oct 12th

My dear Thee,

  I received to day your last letter together with the Punch and the beautiful engraving of Virgenius, for all of which I am duly obliged. I am so sorry I did not get the engraving before as the position in that is so much finer than the one I had to assume, however the Tableau was pronounced beautiful (I do not mean to be vain as Henry Stiles was the most conspicuous figure) by all who saw it. No one here thought it at all wrong to act, and I suppose

155

Chapter V

every one who had studied Roman History understands the scene. I am sorry you should be so very particular. I am afraid you will make quite a prude of poor "little Mittie." Indeed dear Thee I am under the impression you had been rather bored by Brother Dan and things in general when you wrote the last letter, your enmity against poor Mrs Habersham (who, I think the most exemplary of women) to say nothing of your cuts at the innocent Bob Mackey and the good natured Joe McAlister. He did know us when we were extremely diminutive and I have often played with his beard, since I have been grown (such a long time!) I have been very little in his company in fact not at all until last winter in Savannah, then we were not quite so <u>familiar</u> as in the days of my childhood. My dear Thee I kiss a great many different people and always expect to, I cannot allow you monopoly there why just think what the world would would be with out my kisses, I could not think of depriving my friends of the <u>pleasure</u>.

    I hope your supper party passed off pleasantly. I should think it would have been delightful. How extremely embarrassed poor Cornel must have been to have had his company so looked down upon. I am quite well again my dearest Thee. I am telling you the truth I am not going out at all this week in the evening so as not to renew my cold. this is quite a trial to me as tomorrow evening Horace Pratt (one of the Ministers sons) who had just come to Roswell with his Bride is going to have a Bridal Reception – and every one is going to attend. Thee I cannot think of such a thing as your appearing in Roswell until the <u>day before the wedding</u>. it may be a southern idea, but remember it is a <u>southern young lady</u>. should you come I shall immediately drive over to Marietta and pay Miss Green a visit. Thee I have asked <u>six Bridesmaids</u>, and am in a perfect fear of nervousness for fear you will not be able to find Groomsmen. Mother has asked Lew West to come out at the time, how would he do for one? I know of course that he would not be at all exciting but still he looks like a man – and I cannot have any of the young ladies disappointed. this would make five. So you will only have to find one – please unless every body else positively refuses do not bring Mr Robert Campbell. I do not mean any disrespect at all but I did not fancy him. Do tell whom you ask what a very stupid place Roswell is – and do not let them expect anything in the slightest degree pleasant. You, I know will think you are doing penance all the time, but dearest Thee as the thing is obliged to be. I want you to be in your most agreeable of humors, and help me in the greatest possible manner. I made the wedding large because I was obliged to have it so. Be sure and write very particularly as I wish to know positively who to expect, all the gentleman will stay at Uncle Johns [Dunwoody]. Anna has just come in from riding on horse back, and has thrown herself in a complete state of exhaustion on the sofa. she says Jim (you may remember his horrid gates) instead of having a pace has a <u>hard jump</u>. I never have seen her so completely overcome her pulse is almost gone – she sleeps. I am much obliged to you for the prayer book and will remember my promise, particularly as I think the Bible the book of all others. We do not expect Brother, or a letter from him as everything is perfectly uncertain connected with him. I always intend writing Brother Jimmie but never know when a letter will meet him, as soon as I should hear he had arrived the letter I write would arrive after he had sailed again. I think I will give up the idea entirely. Anna says she sent a letter to him to your care, in the very mail that a letter which you spoke of having received from me was sent. I hope he has gotten it ere this. *Do you think you will be glad to see me? I will be to see you more than any one else except Mother. I am going to be quite grave and dignified before my Bridesmaids

Chapter V

so to show them how to do <u>the thing</u>, particularly as I am much younger than any of them. My love to Mrs Roosevelt. I am beginning to be afraid of her again.

Lovingly
Mittie

New York Oct 12th 53

My Dearest Mittie

    I had determined to devote the early part of this evening to you but fortune ordained that duty and a little pleasure mixed should interfere with unmitigated pleasure. Miss Clay is staying with us and being deaf found no-body to talk with after tea so, after discussing Dr Quincy's writings with her in a stentorian tone of voice, I suggested that if she felt a disposition as I was going up stairs I would be happy to have her company. She said she had a delightful impression of a previous glance at $^{my\ room}$ it and was very desirous to repeat the visit. Of course I tried and presume as it is nearly ten that I must have succeeded in amusing her. She is very intelligent and consequently of course very easy to entertain and one of the few [...tern] people against whom noone ever says a word.

    Julia Lochnar (not correctly spelt) has sent us word that, "if convenient" she will pay us a visit which mother agrees to of course; and all I will insist upon is her departure at the earliest possible date. I intend bribing mother to tell her that she must not stay long by the promise of some extra politeness on this condition. Do you ^{not} pity me? Chrystal Palace an indefinite number of times, interspersed with a general desire to be gratified of seeing everything that is going on in New York. Would I could ^{hope} that the time would not exceed my maximum of two weeks that this was to last, but she will think a month short. It is [then] especially hard when ^{since} my love for you has rendered it so disgusting as to be impossible for me to take those little liberties which used to be my greatest resource in amusing her. There is only one little waist that my arm has a longing to encircle, one pair of lips ^{that} to kiss would be indeed happiness, one from with whom it would be such a very great pleasure to be seated on the sofa, or she on the little stool. If Julia had any mind it would be so very different, we then might talk together.

Make Dan give up some preparation which I found very useful for chapped hands last winter. A little is rubbed from one hand over the other after washing, the lips at the same time. The vial is <u>very</u> small and I want you to preserve it for fear that it may be needed at the time of the wedding, then I want you to look your handsomest. I put "Mittie" on it in pencil, and tried to impress it on Dan's mind.

Miss Eliza Clay says that if you are like your mother I have been fortunate. I tried to discover the points of resemblance but must own I was slightly nonplussed.

I am very much amused to hear the views and interest taken in me by each. Miss Ann Wallace says she intends making you a wedding present of a book on cookery, something I very much fear will give you a distaste to literature.

Each of my acquaintances has a different picture of my choice in his mind's eye. The only authentic picture is drawn by an acquaintance who met me going down in the omnibus with Miss De Witt who he presumed to be you. I have never seen her since that night.

Mittie the more I think of coming South, the more I feel the necessity of coming directly to Roswell, it will need three or four days before the marriage to make us feel fully at home together, and I really don't think it worth while to stand upon any miserably cold etiquette upon the subject.

Chapter V

Do tell me how you intend to act. If I reach Roswell it will be impossible to prevent me from seeing you just on the old footing, and I know you would not in your heart desire it.

Our house is in a state of general starvation; after enduring a miserable cook for a month we changed for one atleast fat enough to be good. After cooking us one dinner execrably she determined herself unable to do the work and left without any notice. The work that she objected to was walking from the kitchen to her room in the garret. She insisted upon a bed down stairs. Now we have noone and quite a small supply of company. Fortunately the loss is merely felt in the variety as another servant can do the common cooking.

With my love to Anna and your mother I remain
       Yours Only
       Theodore Roosevelt

Tell Anna that I sent her letter to Captain Bulloch's direction, it arrived before his departure.
Letter written just before leaving to New Port to day with Mr George Morris

Mittie's growing list of potential bridesmaids included her friend Carrie Shackleford. Carrie's letter mentioned several personal friends of Mittie's and was written from Welham which may be the name of a community or a plantation. It appears to have been within riding distance from Roswell. Carrie called James Dunwoody Bulloch, "Cousin Jimmie" denoting the family tie as her mother was a Dunwoody.

      Welham Oct. 15, 1853

My dear Mittie,
  It is with the utmost reluctance that I address you at this time, for while all my inclinations and wishes lead me to comply with your request, still I am obliged to decline,

October

and to deny myself the happiness of being one of your Bridesmaids. Your marriage is to be so late in the season, dear Mittie that it is quite out of my power to remain to it, <u>duty</u> strongly calls me elsewhere, and I can not disobey its voice. My thoughts will be constantly with you Mittie and, believe me, my <u>best wishes</u> for your happiness.

You must know how very sorry I am that I can not be with you. For from child hood have we idly talked of this week when of course it was but ideal, and with me the impressions of child hood have but deepened and strengthened.

I very much fear I will not be able to see you before I leave as I may go down in a fortnight. Clara Green and I had intended riding over when the carriage went for Grandma and Aunt Mary and spending the day, but when the time came Clara was sick, and we have had no opportunity since. Do you and Anna still intend visiting Miss Stiles, if you go before I leave, do stop at least a day here or at any rate notify me of the day you will be over, so I may see you at the cars. I can't bear the idea of not seeing you again. Ask Anna what has become of her contemplated gallop (?) over here on horseback.

Aunt Evans leaves to-morrow for Savannah. The rest will go before long, no exact time fixed however.

Uncle Jack is far from well, he is troubled with chill and fever, Aunt Jane is very feeble still.

I suppose you have received Sarah G.'s letter. I trust your friendship may continue, and no misunderstanding again interfere with your kind feelings for each other. I did not see her letter, but she merely told me that she had written to you. I sincerely hope that all unpleasantness will now be over. I hope your Mother's health is better Mittie dear, between you and Anna let me hear of your arrangements now & then before the "<u>grande finale</u>". How was Cousin Jimmie's wife when you last heard?- I am the only person in

Chapter V

the house, but I will send the ^{love} of all the family, as I know they would desire it. Give my love to your Mother, Anna. Good-bye my darling

your affectionate friend Carrie

New York Oct 15th 53

My own Little Mittie

cannot imagine how much pleasure a little missive which I received in one from Anna yesterday gave me. It brought the writer up so vividly before my mind's eye that I fairly after reading it almost felt as though I had paid Roswell a flying visit. There was something so ludicrously matter-of-fact in a young lady not giving her lover a piece of her hair for fear that it would not suit his winter vests. I would have regarded this as a sarcasm on my object in wanting it which you seem to think was entirely for use did I not remember other speeches of a similar nature made in earnest by the author of this one. The effort to carry the war into the enemy's country was a decided failure as you really knew that when my letters failed it was merely a consequence of my having received none to answer.

I felt so "so ashamed" but I really cannot fix the tribe to which the "indian chief" invited by Anna belongs and must request further information immediately lest he may be out on some hunting expedition. I suggested to Robert Campbell the possibility of my needing his services in a sociable conversation last evening, but he could not well act. On the other hand he may come South to the wedding to which I promised him an invitation if there was to be any number there. If you have not already written "the day" do write it immediately when you receive ^{this} and request your mother to fix one as near the one we appointed together as she can, as I see from your letter you have thrown this all onto her shoulders. Remember how long it takes for letters to go between here and Roswell. If you answer this immediately I will not receive it answer until 1st Nov. Then to write to Tom King if no one offers from here would make the 15th Nov before I could hear from him. Don't forget to tell me if I am to be shut out from seeing you ^{before the wedding} as my plans depend on that; if I once reach Roswell I will see you just as I used to, even if Henry positively affirms that you are out and Maam Charlotte tries to disuade me so as to preserve your dresses for service after marriage. Do wear a dress that can be "tumbled" indefinitely without ruffling the temper of the owner when we meet. I must send you down a list of those I want invited and that will depend somewhat upon the kind of wedding, so you see what a call there is for all your decision of character.

Afternoon. Dan said he was going and is presumed to be now in Philadelphia. Miss Norris and Sara Emlen are staying at Jim's and spent last evening with us, and now Mittie I must tell you a scene dearest which while it is painful I feel that you ought to know under the circumstances. Captain Moore a friend of Lew West sent by him some Idols of China to, as Lew understood, Cornel. He then told Mary and Cornel also in the presence of others that they were for Mary. Mary while the Philadelphians and our own family were present asked him where they were. Cornel denied that they were hers and excited himself until he used the rather strong language of "swindler" and "cheat" to her and inferred more. Of course all the family were up in arms and this morning he received some decided views from father on his conduct. He brought up the Idols to Mary's but I have not had an opportunity of speaking to her since and hearing the termination. I get along very well with him now, weeks pass in which we don't exchange a word and as Jim's Lizzie says that is such a relief

Chapter V

in comparaison to being called "Liar" and "Thief". Now you know Mittie why I tremble to bring him as a representative of our family to the South, although he always behaves so much better among strangers. Don't fear his ever being rude to you dearest, he would never be so more than once. As we never any of us bear malice I suppose no more will ever be said about the affair last night; and a scene of the kind occurs very seldom; but I thought it was my duty to show you that there were small troubles to be met with as well as I hope a very great many pleasures in your future lot in life. I wish so much you were here this evening to hear Dr. De Witt preach on the Waldenses, I am reduced to going with Lizzie's aunt, I knew Sarah would not appreciate it.

Evening. Dr Dewitt did himself and his subject full justice, he gave a glowing account of all the past persecutions and present position of this people of which we know comparatively little.

Lizzie says she will answer your letter when her company goes, She seemed very much pleased with it.

I will commence a new piece of paper with an old request do above all things take care of your health and never think of leaving me in ignorance of any sickness to save my uneasiness. You don't know how much you have added to it by the desire to conceal even that little palpitation.

How very much I long to have you under my eye, so as to try at all events to take better care of you. I won't talk about it but you can't imagine how I regretted the change from November

Thank Annie from me for keeping to her promise and believe me
Ever Yours
Theodore Roosevelt

I don't feel as though I have half finished what I want to say.

Dr. DeWitt preached on the Waldensians or Waldenses. They are a Christian movement and religious cultural group organized in Lyon, France, which soon spread to the Cottian Alps in the late 1170s. The Waldensians originated with the Poor Men of Lyons, a group organized by Peter Waldo, a wealthy merchant who gave away his property around 1173 while preaching apostolic poverty. The group's teachings, which also included the denial of purgatory, conflicted with the Roman Catholic Church. By 1215, they were declared heretical and subjected to intense persecution. In the 16th century, their leaders embraced the Protestant Reformation and joined with other Protestant entities.[71]

Waldensians arrived on American shores during colonial times, especially in New Jersey and Delaware. In 1853, a group of approximately seventy Waldensians, including men, women, and children left their homes in the Piedmont Valleys and migrated to Salt Lake City, Utah, after being converted to Mormonism by Lorenzo Snow. Active congregations remain in the United States, and the American Waldensians Society maintains their history and doctrine.[72]

After Thee's last letter, Mittie and Anna take it upon themselves to "explain" to Thee how society acts in the South and, in particular, Roswell. Anna wrote first to explain why the wedding was now more grand than previously decided upon. While her letter remained polite, Mittie's letter revealed to Thee a bit of her personality.

Roswell October 17

My dear Thee
I just want to write a few lines because I am afraid my last letter may have misled you about the wedding – well first Mother is better than when you were here so that

Chapter V

she will enjoy everything very much. Mittie is going away entirely from the quiet stiff little village of Roswell, as all of the people here are really kindly attached to her she could not do anything to hurt or offend them now there is no way in which she could more positively do this than in not letting them see her married. So from this very first it was understood that they all should see the ceremony, we have not invited, (or rather will not) invite any strangers at all. Mittie felt that she would be so conspicuous to be the only person to be looked at that she asked me, Julia Hand, Miss Stiles, and one other friend Miss Atwood to stand with her. She thought that four would be a pretty number and would give you no trouble to find gentlemen. As I will wait with Tom King, you can induce Corneil to come as Miss Stiles and Miss Atwood are both reasonably pleasant. You said when you were here that you did not know how to keep Mr Morris from coming. So perhaps you can depend upon him, and then brother Dan. He can not fail to be pleased with Mary Cooper. I take Tom King because the other girls shall have a nice time and be with pleasant gentlemen. These young ladies would have been at the wedding under any circumstances. They do not increase the number of guests at all. Mittie only makes use of them to take away from the prayer-meeting effect of the whole affair. Now Thee please excuse this interference on my part it was entirely at Mitties suggestion, she did not feel equal to a plain statement of the case. Do always give my love to your Mother and my kindest regards to all who have remembered me. Mother begs to be remembered.

 Goodbye please forget that I have written this
        Yours truly
        Anna Bulloch

October

I expect Thee will be vexed with me after reading this letter.

Roswell Oct 17th

Dear Thee

    I received two letters by to days mail. the first written in the heat of your displeasure, the other slightly an improvement on the first in as much as there is an air of resignation. it may be assumed, but still gentlemanly, and with some slight regard for the rules of etiquette and civilized life generally. Before I say another word, let me request you to thank your Mother for me for her well merited reprimand. Thee let me tell you it is a thing unheard of for a gentleman to interfere with any of the arrangements made by the lady and her family - he is generally "<u>done up</u>" in the style decided upon by them unless principal is involved or circumstances occur which would be regarded of course by any well bred <u>lady</u>. Thee I grant it may be different entirely, your Northern customs, but will I ever be able to impress upon you the <u>fact</u> that it is a Southern young lady, and in a Southern village that the wedding is to occur, consequently I must observe the rules and customs prevalent in that village. I cannot imagine you for one moment supposing I would like the step decided upon unless I had thought well of what I was doing. My Mothers health would of course been the first consideration, being in the same house with her. I knew what that was, and it was by her suggestion entirely that I decided upon having the <u>four</u> attendants, as far as I am concerned I would infinitely prefer being married in the morning and leaving on the same day, but to this Mother was very much opposed, consequently I was obliged to have all the Roswelltes [Mittie's term for residents of Roswell], then again your Mother and Father coming out, 'twould have been rather rude to them to leave on the very day they arrived. So much is expected of me upon such an occasion then the number of invited guests would have been <u>large</u>,

Chapter V

but this was never dreamed of from the first on account entirely of Lizzie Bulloch's precarious state of health, which you remind me of. Mother has considered this from the first. Indeed my dear Thee I understood you once that George Morris you would probably bring. Corneil of course would come. Brother be here, and Tom King on the spot. If you brought any guests it would bore me exceedingly. The groomsmen you are of course required to bring but I always thought the other invitations went from the Brides Parents, of course all friends of yours we would be most happy to invite, but you said we would have a Reception in New York which would take away from the necessity of written invitations from here - I am not going to invite any but my relations from a distance as it is such a private wedding – In my last letter I said <u>six</u> groomsmen, but I have concluded to have only <u>four</u>. I can not tell you how much I regret all this as you have been so bored believe me I acted from the best of motives and it really was <u>required</u> from me. I do think gentlemen are so hard to get along with well however as the thing stands the four girls have been asked and the only thing is to secure four gentlemen for them. Otherwise I will not know how to explain this non appearance. I cannot imagine the necessity of bringing Mr Campbell - you might say you had been requested to ask Tom King. I hope you understand, I wish I could talk with you about it, I <u>know</u> I could make you understand perfectly. We can not fix upon a <u>day</u> yet, but as the young ladies have been <u>asked</u> and have <u>accepted</u>. I think the gentlemen can be asked also, the time either the first or second week in December the day to be told them as soon as fixed. Mother of course intends writing your Mother and inviting cordially both herself and Mr R together with all members of the family who may be able to attend. I still think it will be a very unnecessary trip for your

Mother to take as nothing pays for the excessive fatigue of the journey.

I am ready to leave Roswell any time after the ceremony you think best. My answer to the charge of being thought changeable is that "circumstances alter cases."

I hope you will feel more comfortable after receiving this. dearest Thee I so much regret your being worried.
Yours very truly,
Mittie Bulloch
After tea. Anna has gone on a moon light ride. I being left quietly to myself have been reading over this letter, which Anna says is not at all as she would write to her <u>Lover</u>, and she thinks it sounds cross. well Thee I do not mean any such thing only you wrote, "your change is incomprehensible, do explain it" and this letter is the only way I can explain. I own the first note I was so provoked with you that I tore it in atoms. But since, I have thought perhaps I was not explicit enough and it might have seemed queer the change, tho you might have known I would have acted properly.
yours with love, Mittie Bulloch

During the early-to-mid-nineteenth century, meals followed a particular pattern in affluent Southern households. Served early in the day and often as a buffet, breakfast consisted of a rather substantial meal. By the middle of the century, women often took a light luncheon at about 1 p.m. or at times a heavy mid-day dinner was served to the entire family. A light tea might be served around 4 p.m. if guests called, otherwise, a more substantial or high tea would be served at 6 or 7 p.m. Sometimes, particularly in the summer, a light supper prepared the family for the evening's rest. So Anna probably went riding about 8 or 9 p.m.

Chapter V

New York Oct 18th 53

Dear Mittie

Your letter has made me more low-spirited than I have been before for months. I had indulged in so many dreams about, and looked forward with so much genuine pleasure to, what I was now to "do penance" at. Of course as soon as the day is fixed I will do my utmost to obtain the six groomsmen, although success at present seems rather doubtful. It is so far to go that I would not ask it of anyone but a particular friend or indeed accept an obligation such as I should consider this from any other, and you know my list of intimates is very small. But I feel that my spirits have not quite recovered their tone yet, and I will lay this by until I regain my control over them. I lay down on my sofa for a whole hour brooding over the absurdity of anticipating pleasure. The present plans of course render me still more anxious to take my departure from Roswell as immediately as possible after the ceremony. We will see so little comparatively speaking of each other here, that I had looked forward to that one week's unalloyed pleasure as an epoch in my life from that reason if no other, but - I will give up writing for the present.

19th. I had a very amusing visit at Lizzie's [Roosevelt] discussing the choices of groomsmen, and their various characters should any I ask go. I took dinner there and we then adjourned to the Chrystal Palace, I taking charge of Sarah Emlen. The evening passed off very pleasantly, Sarah although generally very quiet regards me as so old an acquaintance, and connection besides, that she throws off all reserve. Poor Sarah! but I will have to keep the explanation of why I consider her unfortunate until we meet. I paid a visit to Mary Lee the other night and discovered to my astonishment, something she never told me before, that she prefers <u>engaged</u> to unengaged young men. She demanded an accurate description of you but soon showed that Miss De

Witt has given her as graphic an account as I could. I wish you would ^{write} out a little description of yourself for me to repeat to my many enquiring friends. Julia Lachenour has come now, not being expected the latter part of the season. I found ^{her} here, stopping as I went up to Jim's this evening; as I had promised Sarah to go with her I could not offer to take Julia. You can imagine the pleasure with which I would have done it otherwise!!

  Mother has retired early, the moon is shining in at the window and the feeling of being utterly alone makes my thoughts revert to those pleasant times when we would either at this hour have walked the piazza together, or inhabited the parlour while Anna was in regions unknown and merely discovered at bed-time. How much I long to see that bright face which is to dispell all thought of loneliness from my heart for ever.

  I have been reading Kirwan's travels, he wrote the best letters against the Catholic church I have ever read and of course ^{as} noone could pass through Europe without seeing its deceptions he alludes to it very freely. At the same time there is a good deal of humour about him, and some of his accounts are very amusing. By the bye a catholic priest got a bible away from a child in our city the other day and burnt it in the street. I like this much more than I would to have them sailing under false colours. There is no fear of their having many converts if they will only show their real principles.

  I had a good opportunity this evening of seeing all the jewelry and silver these being according to my companions taste, and there certainly are beautiful specimens of all kinds.

  There is a statue too of a girl threading a needle which has such an intent look, and is altogether almost as natural as life. But I suppose you have read accounts of most of the articles, besides I hope we will be able to catch a glimpse of it together before it closes.

I wish you could only have your first impression of New York weather now; during the last two or three weeks it has been perfect.

Your fear of mother Mittie I know will take unto itself wings so immediately upon finding how entirely she is prepared to love you that I do not consider it worth combatting and so will bid you good night remaining
Ever Yours

Theodore Roosevelt

The slowness in the exchange of letters left Thee agonizing over groomsmen in New York. He also continued to "go out" with several young ladies of his acquaintance to such places as the Crystal Palace. Per his reference, Thee was most likely reading *Letters to the Rt. Rev. John Hughes, Roman Catholic Bishop of New York* by Kirwan, a pseudonym for Nicholas Murray (1802–1861), Moderator of the General Assembly of the Presbyterian Church in the United States of America. Murray, an Irish native, emigrated to the United States and apprenticed as a printer with Harper Brothers. Years later, he was ordained a minister. He wrote extensively of his travels and on archaeology and his anti-Catholicism views. His letters were first published in 1848.[73]

New York Oct 23 53

Dearest Mittie

It is a delightfully warm sunday, one of those days which we prize doubly at this season of the year as the approach of winter renders them more rare. It is just the time which, with very few exceptions, since you left here in May I have set apart for you; and it has thus insensibly become almost sacred. This feeling makes the hour pass doubly slowly when I have none of your letters to answer as is the case at present, so I will merely commence this and keep it open in case there should be anything needing an answer in your letter which I suppose has been delayed on the road and will be here tomorrow. The slowness of the mail is doubly aggravating now when we have so many arrangements to make and plans to decide upon. If it were possible I would go down just to spend one day with you and settle everything; as it is the principal cause of our trouble in the shape of groomsmen seems improving. Fred Elliott unless the day proves different from the one which I expect will act. Henry Roosevelt who lives in Charleston I will ask and he will probably act too unless too late in the month, as he always spends the latter part of that month in New York. These with the three first enumerated and _{one friend you do not know} will leave Tom King to be called upon in case there should be any difficulty with one of them at the last moment. If they accept I will not have cause to be ashamed for one of those who with good reason will be looked upon as samples of my friends; but <u>do</u> tell me the day that I may ask them.

Evening. I have just inveigled Dan into a conversation with Julia and left them alone in the dining room. I have requested him not to object to your plans with regard to the wedding which he seemed disposed to do; and should he, remember dearest that so long as we consult on our own happiness nothing else is necessary, and I am determined to be happy whatever plans you have arranged for the wedding; after it I will claim a vote. You ought to have sent me an extract from that letter to "sister" written in the scriptural style, so that I might have been able to share his amusement which seems to have been very great over it. He intends starting not later than the 9th November and hopes to have the company of

Chapter V

Hilborne and Mrs West in the steamer. What would I not give to go down with them?

I hear mother come in from Mr Kermit's and as Dan's tête a tête will be interrupted. I must go down again, and try not to look as if I was thinking of you – good night. 24th. Your letter, which had been delayed as I supposed, arrived to day and so far from feeling "vexed" at it, tell Annie that she could not have composed one for her "lover" which I would have preferred receiving, so that her objection was unfounded. If she judged so ^{harshly} of yours I am sorry she had an opportunity of judging of mine from Maiden Lane; if the one written ~~from the one~~ from the house merits the comparaison of "gentlemanly" what must it have been?

I am very sorry that I should have so entirely misunderstood you; of course there can be no possible objections to the four groomsmen and if it is to be a small wedding Tom King would be much more in place than a youth dragged down from here. I had unfortunately acted too hastily upon the impression that there were to be six and asked Fred Elliott who had provisionally accepted. As it would have "bored" you to have him, I went to see him as soon as I had received your letter and without retracting the invitation myself persuaded him to reconsider his determination, and now I will ask Tom King and George Morris in a few days, both of whom I have no doubt will serve. The then two young men already bespoken.

Mother requests information with regard to the colour of the dress to be worn by your mother on the occasion, that is she wants to know if it will be black, otherwise she will not appear in that colour herself. She was telling me her plans to night for trying to make ^{you spend} so very happy a winter here; you don't know what pretty things I said about the happiness of your disposition. I promised to do my utmost to help her, and Mittie dearest I do feel confident we will

October

all be so happy here together. Mother spoke of how near the time was approaching but it seems to me an age to wait before I will see you. She is going first to Miss Clays with that lady, and to fix the time of their departure ^(for her place) ~~as they will go there first~~ she is anxious to know "the time" as soon as you can conveniently determine it, when she will be expected at Roswell.

In looking over this letter I am afraid there is a slight air of resegnation about the first part which in my present state of feeling seems very absurd; as I now feel how impossible it will be for me to do otherwise than enjoy myself.

Tell Annie I will write to her in a few days, and have a message to deliver from mother with regard to the singularity of her not being first bridesmaid with Cornel as first groomsman. I refused at first point blanck to deliver it, fearing lest it should be against the etiquette of "civilized life generally" but she insisted and, as I could not give my objection, conquered. She thinks it might cause remark. And now Mittie with my love to ^(your) mother and Annie I remain

Your Ever Loving
Theodore Roosevelt

<u>over</u>

Your mother will be so glad to hear it that I must add that Dan sang for me some hymns, among which were several that you used to sing. He was in good voice and you can't imagine how delightfully it recalled you all.

Chapter V

Roswell Oct 24th

My dear Theodore

Anna and I have just returned from walking with Mary Cooper, the day being so cold we have taken any quantity of exercise if I remember rightly this will rather please you, as you always wanted me to walk on those warm summer mornings, when I never felt like doing so. I received your last letter to day and was very glad to see that "Richard is himself again". I think you have gotten reconciled to the idea of having attendants. The wedding however is not large enough to warrant your asking Robt Campbell if he is asked there are several stiff girls I will be obliged to invite, Anna and I being so much occupied at the time, it will […] entirely upon you to entertain them, they will only be here however if Mr Campbell comes. I shall have a divorce immediately after the ceremony if he is one of the groomsmen. You may arrive <u>two</u> days before the <u>grande finale</u>, but if one minute before the consequences will be fatal to you. seriously Thee you must not be in Roswell sooner than two days before. Mother will write some time this week to Mrs Roosevelt telling the all important day which you seem to really want to know. I cannot imagine your taking so much interest about such a trifle. Not one of my dresses shall be tumbled. Maum Charlotte says you must not injure them as you did last summer. indeed Thee, I am going to bring you up better and teach you how to take care of lady's dresses. I cannot <u>afford</u> to have you "rumple me" as you did in the summer. No more tearing my morning dresses - no more childs play, you forget that I am eighteen! Ask Tom if you can, remember he is in the place. I was sorry to hear about Corneal and Mary, and am delighted that I was not there. You need not fear bringing him here I am confident he will behave well. I hope he will come, Dont you think Thee you might get along with him perfectly and yet speak to him oftener? why it seems perfectly dreadful to be in the same house and not speak to a person more than once during two weeks. Imagine Anna and myself upon such terms. I dont mean to be intimate with him but seems to me you all think too little of Corneal.

Anna and I had a party for the Bride last week and I never remember passing so pleasant an evening - in the first place there are a great many people up here now. visiting the various families, we commenced by playing games, hearing that the Bride was opposed to dancing - but she would not play games - so I determined we should dance, and we did until two oclock - we were afraid the Bride had had a most stupid time, as she would neither talk, play, nor dance, but as we have since heard she had enjoyed herself very much I have met her out several times since, and she still preserves the same silence apparently she is under a vow not to speak, and entirely much more fitted for a deaf and dumb assylum than Bridal entertainments. We have had quite a little excitement in Roswell, one of Mrs Habershams letters to her husband was opened and vilely presented and numerous additions of a very singular character made as soon as he received it he sent it immediately back for her to make inquiries at this Post office, while he was to do the same in Savannah. 'Twas proved conclusively that it did not occur there, (so they say). consequently suspicions rested here. Mr Camp and Adams have been greatly distressed and have written on to Washington about it. They prove that no such thing was perpetrated at this office. We all feel so sorry about it for every body liked Mrs Habersham exceedingly - she has identified herself so much with the place and been so generally lady like. Tom in the meantime seems to think he has flirted with her when poor green thing he has only been made use of.

Chapter V

We are going to have an Egg-nogg frolic tomorrow evening, I am going to have it quite stiff decidedly as the southern young gentleman would like it. Thee did you ever notice in the Harper, the September number a fashion plate called the Bride? It is thought to be very much like me almost every body in the place has noticed the likeness - Mother had cut it out and placed it in her bible, she says it is as good as 'tho it had been taken for me. You must be sure and look at it and tell me if you think it like. Do give my love to your Mother be sure and do so Mother and Anna send theirs to you. Irvine just enquired who I was writing and begged me to remember him, He is not on very good terms with me at present, reason, I had his favorite little dog brought in the house, and we dressed it in a complete suit of clothes. jacket, cap - in this way he was sent to meet his master coming home from school, Irvine was very indignant. good night ever the same.

Mittie Bulloch

Do tell me when to write Brother Jimmie so that a letter may reach him when he is next in Port?

Your pen, which in its best day never suited fell on the floor, and stuck up straight. Only imagine the state of the nib.

Roswell October 31st 1853

Dear Theodore

I really was quite glad to get your letter to day and relieved to think you had received my cross letter, I must tell you immediately by your last two letters are quite improvements on their predecessors - still you all have a few directions to give, we will endeavor to fulfill them, what

October

Harper's New Monthly Magazine's Bridal Fashion

Chapter V

possible difference could it make whether Anna waited with Corneal or not? They might both be first Bridesmaid and Groomsmen and yet not wait together, as it is often done, however as it is we are quite pleased at the arrangement for Anna would infinitely prefer waiting with Corneal to Tom King, she only suggested the latter as we wished to procure pleasant gentlemen for the other girls and she could reconcile herself to fate (or she says). Please say to your Mother that my Mother will appear in black as she has been in mourning for the last six years and is still. At first I was charmed at the idea of Fred Elliott being out here, you know what a fancy I conceived for him at first sight but think considering the size of the wedding it is much more advisable to have the other four attendants - for really I do not think it pays to inveigle a person out to Roswell in December, Mr Morris being a Southerner may have some idea of what the northern part of Georgia is in that month, and Corneal as your Brother may survive the first shock. Your Mother and Father will only come out to spy the nakedness of the land. I know they will be intensely disappointed and disgusted, the only thing that reconciles me to the idea of their coming is that Mother and themselves will be acquainted. With regard to Brother objecting to any of my arrangements, tis a matter entirely of minor importance as he would not have been consulted, had it either been small or large, we never in the family think of such a thing as taking <u>his</u> advice, he may be perfectly able to give it but still our habit is not to receive it in the smallest particular. Sister writes that <u>she</u> does not think she will be out for a month to come yet and that Brother will come with them. I wish he would make haste and come for we are crazy to see him – you know 'tis a long time since we have parted. How does he like Julia 'tis to be hoped slightly more than the Roosevelts generally or else I fear with his

October

impetuous disposition he has been quite rude I should have liked very much to have heard there conversation.
How is Mr Kermit? (I am trying to look quite grave for your sake) he certainly has not been in the state all summer, tho he was last spring or he could not survive.
Thee to ease my conscience, I have had another palpitation. I dont think so violent as the last, at least I am not so nervous as formerly, it may be because I am becoming accustomed to the horrid things but tis my firm and candid oppinion that I have some disease of the heart, I don't mean to distress you but really I think it my duty to tell you. I may be wrong. Anna hopes so. she thinks it some serious affection. You know I wished my Cousin Mr Dunwody to perform the marriage ceremony - as he had accepted and seemed quite flattered by my thinking of him, but to day we heard of the death of his wife. So I suppose he will not officiate. You saw Mrs Dunwody when you were here, she only passed through the place we told you she had been such a beauty previously.
I would like to see you very much - indeed I wish you could come down for a day there are so many things I could tell you which I cannot write. I am sorry I said what I did about my heart if you were here I would laugh and tell you the same thing. You know 'tis just a way I have and may not mean any thing.*Tom King had a dancing party the other evening which was delightful. Eva his sister has just come home from school and it was given to her, we had double sets of quadrilles in both rooms - and after supper the fancy dances. You cannot imagine how gay we have been, there have been so many visitors in the place. Mr King who is said nominally to object to dancing (In reality does not care either one way or the other) was quietly put to bed by the judicious Mother of the family. Notwithstanding this precaution Mr Pratt (the Pastor) is quite offended with

Chapter V

everybody in general, and it is reported that we are to have a sermon on the next sabbath, stating his views. I am regarded as a perfect reprobate by them all - good night I am always yours (unless something else should "turn up")
affectionately
Mittie Bulloch

Give my love to your Mother and any others who may ask after me

Chapter VI
November

Although Mittie and Thee resolved the issue of the number of bridesmaids and groomsmen, other matters related to the wedding remained to be settled. Additionally, Thee's travel arrangements and those of his family filled the letters of late October and spilled over into November.

In this letter, Thee called James Roosevelt's wife Lizzie Emlen to differentiate her from "Lizzie" Ellis who was married to Robert Roosevelt. With two women named "Lizzie" in the family, confusion must have often occurred.

New York Nov 6th 53

Dear Mittie

First I must appropriate a little of this letter to eradicating from your mind if possible the impression that those palpitations are at all dangerous.

I have asked two or three doctors about them in a general way, and find that all your symptoms are such as a change to our more bracing climate and a little more age will probably entirely overcome. It is a very common complaint, Fanny Morris had one when I was out at her place the other day.

Continual suspense has reduced me to that happy frame of mind when killing time seems the only object in life. I have devoted the last week to nominally paying

Chapter VI

attention to Mr Taylor & Morris' party. I have been out with them every night and after leaving the ladies a supper invariably followed. A little more practice and I look forward to meeting the southern youngmen on a footing of quality; unfortunately Mr Taylor's departure in the early part of next week will take away my excuse, and my family would be at a loss without it to account for so sudden a change. His sister proves quite an addition to my acquaintance, she seems unaffected, natural, and to have a disposition very much like Julian her brother had. Her smile reminds me of him sometimes very painfully. I was very much struck with the difference between her and those whom I had visited the Chrystal Palace with previously, when it chanced that I had charge of her the other evening. It is forcibly exemplified too with the Misses Morris. One of them was positively tired of the Palace after having been there an hour. At the Opera too Miss Taylor seemed to enjoy everything with so much zest. It was her first Opera and proved fortunately a very good one, Masinello. It is a love plot founded on absurdities of course through out, but the music of course is everything. The spirit with which she entered into everything reminded me of you, but not half so forcibly as hearing Miss Willis sing again last night for the first time since that eventful evening did. Lizzie Emlen says after her being so much in the way that night, she positively dislikes to hear her sing now.

The continuance of such delightful weather makes me regret still more that you should not have followed out your original intention and so obtained so pleasant a first impression of the climate. I wrote to Tom King a week ago, and don't know anyone here who might ought to be invited out of our own family except Mr & Mrs J J Roosevelt and Mr James H Roosevelt, to both of whom I would like you merely to write a formal note. (Of course they will not come.) If your mother writes the invitations and encloses them to me I will see them delivered here. I have prepared George Morris for a strictly private wedding and so do not look forward to having him feel very much disappointed but still if there is a choice of bridesmaids do remember that his position is the least enviable of any and that a pleasant companion would render it so much more pleasant for him.

My opinion of Miss Willis had dwindled away into even less than it was before since she has formed quite an affection for Julia. It is a little unkind I know but I cannot help judging of a person by their associates and to own the truth rather despise a woman who cannot see want of refinement in one of her own sex. It is to me convincing proof that she is wanting in it herself. I have scarce ever visited Mary Lee since she formed an attachment to Margaret Mason, although in this case my conscience smote me, as she commenced it because Margaret was staying at our house. I think this is one reason why I like Lizzie Emlen so much she never forms a sudden friendship, but when formed it is generally a lasting and dependable one. And I never saw a friend of hers wanting in qualities which command respect.

I gave one of those "Night Watches" to Mr Taylor last night for his mother. Neither of us alluded to the past (indeed we have not done so since he has been in town) but the tears immediately rose to his eyes and I could see how very difficult it was for him to overcome his feelings, there was but one hope which I knew had always comforted him, dependence upon a higher power; and it is this which sustains his mother, who was four months after hearing of Julian's death confined to her room. He was her favorite son and the fifth grown up child she has lost.[74]

Yours with love
Theodore Roosevelt

Chapter VI

Remember me to Anna & your mother. Captain Bulloch is in town and I will forward a letter to him if he should have left before it arrives.

Masaniello, originally named *La muette de Portici* (*The Dumb Girl of Portici*, or *The Mute Girl of Portici*) is a French opera by Daniel Auber with a libretto by Germain Delavigne. The opera is loosely based on the historical uprising of Masaniello against Spanish rule in Naples in 1647 and centers around a love story. Generally regarded as the earliest French grand opera, its English translation first opened in New York City in 1831. The 5 November 1853 opening at Niblo's Gardens, attended by Thee and Miss Taylor, was widely heralded in the New York papers. The *Home Journal* wrote about the opening night:

> The rain fell steadily and fast. The streets were as forbidding as the fireside was agreeable. Yet on that evening Niblo's was crowded literally to the ceiling, and the adjacent streets were one prodigiouse turmoil of omnibuses and carriages—so irrepressible is the desire of New Yorkers to be at the birth of a novelty.[75]

Niblo's Garden, a New York theater, located on Broadway opened in the 1820s under various names before becoming the property of coffeehouse proprietor and caterer William Niblo. The first theater burned on 18 September 1846 and reopened in 1849. It seated approximately 3,200 and featured the best equipped stage in New York. Seats sold for $2 each in 1850. The theater complex featured an exhibit room for panoramas and a refreshment hall.[76]

Thee mentions giving one of those "Night Watches" to Mr. Taylor as a gift for his mother. During a *Grand Tour of Europe*, nineteenth-century tourists often returned with

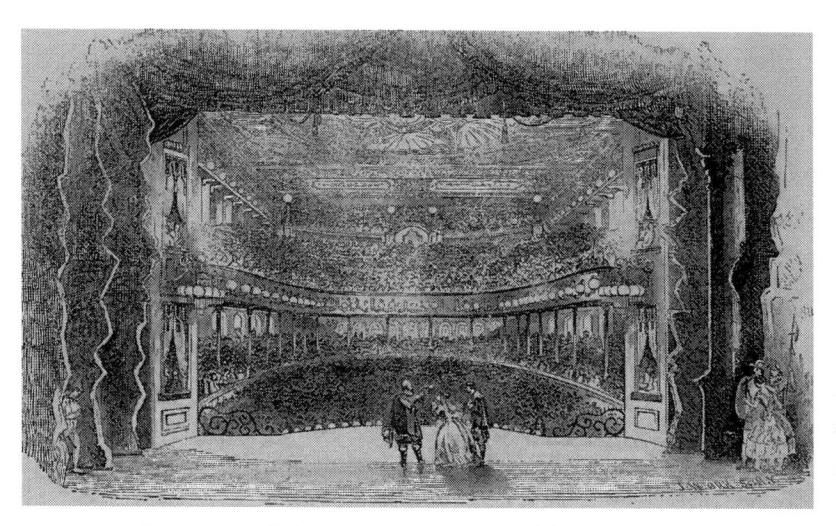

Interior of Opera House at Niblo's Garden

copies of famous masterpieces as gifts for family and friends. No doubt, Thee wrote of giving a copy of the painting known as the *Night Watch*. Properly titled by its long since forgotten name *The Company of Captain Frans Banning Cocq and Lieutenant Willem van Ruytenburch preparing to march out*, this 18th century masterpiece was housed in the Trippenhuis, which at that time housed the Dutch Academy of Sciences. The *Night Watch* is one of the most famous Dutch Golden Age paintings and now hangs in the Rijksmuseum, Amsterdam, the Netherlands, as the best known painting in its collection.

Roswell, Nov 13th

My dearest Thee,

Today, not more than five minutes since I received your last letter one I had been looking for all last week. Theeate you must not <u>do me so</u>. I will begin to think you are getting tired of me already - however the letter was interesting to me, in fact I feel quite a little spasm of love for you to day - you know I am quite fitful about my love spells, at least you used to accuse me of being so.

Chapter VI

Yesterday after we had given them up entirely. Miss Rees and Brother arrived. Anna and I were quietly seated in the parlour reading our Bibles (do you ever?) when the servants came rushing in to announce their arrival. You may imagine what a state of excitement we have been in ever since. Last night until very late, we were all only affectionate and inquiring, but this morning immediately after breakfast we made a vigorous attack on the trunks and boxes. Brother has brought for each of us a beautiful Florentine mosaic, perfectly lovely - Then from Cairo he brought me an opera cloak which has been a great cause of amusement to Anna and myself he says that it was considered beautiful by all who saw it. We think it perfectly frightful, and much more appropriate as a present for an indian squaw! of course I have not expressed myself in quite such strong language as he seems to think it such an extremely handsome affair. I will show it to you when you come and see what you think of it. We have been trying to get out of him a description of his wedding present to me, but cannot succeed, we hope in a day or two to make him give up by dint of persuasions. The next letter I write will probably be after I have been flushed with victory - He seems to have been very much pleased with his stay in New York, and delighted with you all including Julia, but says that you told him she could talk of nothing but dress. Now my dear Thee after warning me not to by any means let Brother know his private opinion of Julia, himself tells him - inconsistent Thee!
My Prayer Book is beautiful and exactly what I wished in every respect & for this all thanks - and the little bottle for chapped hands has been delivered in a state of perfect presentation much to my surprise knowing Brother of old. Every one admires my Prayer Book dearest but I will remember my promise about it.

November

I will be sure to remember the people you wish invited, we are going to see about invitations shortly as the time is drawing near. I will try to secure a pleasant Bridesmaid for George Morris but Tom King being a groomsman and having both a sister and first cousin of his for Bridesmaids he of course can wait with neither of them Anna waiting with Corneal leaves only Miss Stiles for Tom, and Anna and Mary Cooper are the only really pleasant girls. He need not tho be all the time with the young lady he attends with, I think that so stiff particularly as we will be so very an informal party. We are expecting Sister and Mr West out shortly and soon after them, you all will come, I expect to have you to form bad habits. however I will exert a better influence over you. I am not at all <u>fast</u>.

I have been very unwell lately, but am quite well again and expect to be robust by the <u>20</u>th - another palpitation, I am not taking near so low a view of them now, as I did formerly - Now I think them entirely nervous.

Dear Thee how are you going to behave when we meet, if I see you first before them all mind seriously please don't kiss me or anything of the kind I would not let Brother see you do so for worlds. I am in earnest I would regard my affection as misplaced if you should take any libertys - please read this carefully and act like a perfect gentleman. I do want to see you my dear dear Thee, quite as much as anyone except Mother.

Brother has given Anna and myself at least a weeks work repairing his broken kids [gloves]. I think Brothers are so troublesome when they take a sudden fancy to become the gloss of fashion. Will you not have wide sleeves to your coats? I think them extremely <u>graceful</u>. They are calling me to dinner so I must say good bye as this afternoon, some relatives are coming who have to be shown my trousseau. (Mittie's french!). Anna sends her love of course.

Chapter VI

Your own\
"Little Mittie"

Give my love always to your Mother. I wish I could be with you for a little while. Again yours

Mittie

"Brother Dan," Daniel Elliott, finally arrived home after his extended *Grand Tour of Europe* which included a trip to Egypt. Mittie's descriptions of Daniel's character exist as the only family record of it in any historic document from this early period.[77] However, two creative stories written by Brother Dan for Mittie provide the reader with an idea of his sense of humor and artistic talents (Appendix A and B). Thee's introduction to Daniel of his cousin Julia Augusta Lachenour proved to be yet another passing fancy for Daniel.

The "Miss Rees" who arrived with Daniel could have been Elizabeth "Lizzie" Rees, age 35, but was most likely her younger sister Matilda, age 31. Although residents of McIntosh County, the family owned property in Roswell. Their mother, Mary Dew Rice Rees, a widow, died in 1853. Daniel and Mittie would have been familiar with both daughters from Darien, Savannah, and Roswell society.

New York Nov 20th 1853

My own dearest Mittie

If you only knew how very much pleasure your last letter gave me I don't think you would allow your "love spells" to be quite so "fitful". You know I always told you I could not help allowing your mood to govern my own love a little, and that I cannot express myself cannot feel quite so ardently when you do not seem fully to reciprocate it; not answering three or four of my letters seemed so different from the way in which I would have acted towards you. Little

November

Mittie would not be afraid of my getting "tired" of her if she only knew with how much pleasure I was looking forward to seeing her again, never more to be separated.

Four months - how long it does seem; and still another long month to wait. I feel very rebellious even now but have determined not to talk any more about the appointed day. Dan must have been quoting his own thoughts and attaching my name to them, when he spoke of Julia's inability to talk of anything but dress. I was very guarded in the expression of my feelings about her when with him, although of course I could not - tell him I loved her very desperately.

Dan's bridal present was discovered up here, but as you are of course "victorious" by this time it is unnecessary to tell you. It is too late now, but I am so sorry I did not ask you before to mention something you are in want of. Jim's Lizzie was saying yesterday in the case of previous weddings she had not felt so much interest but this time she really wanted to find something you would like, which as she never says anything she does not mean was really a compliment; although her search will probably be unsuccessful. They were all here last night including Miss Lewis and Miss Willis, the evening passed off very pleasantly.

I was sorely tempted to desert the family mansion this morning by the promise of a particularly good dinner which (don't let it break your heart Mittie) I am sorry to say that on Sundays we do not always indulge in at home. It originated in the superstition that it was beneficial to servants, but the time which they thus have for themselves proves rather a disadvantage than an advantage to their morals and mother has about given up her ancient views upon the subject.

The invitation came from one of our clergymen's sons and his wife (Dr Knox's) they also congratulated me, which comes rather late. One of Dr Dewitt's daughters is to

Chapter VI

be married at about the same time with ourselves, it is the one you saw at Mary's.

Just as I left the Knoxs, (it was after church where I had met them), I unexpectedly lighted upon a little terrier dog which looking particularly lively and bright attracted my attention. The owner proved to be Nelly formerly Lathrop with her husband. I walked with her to her destination and while taking off my hat to bid adieu the Miss Morris' passed. Thus I was enabled to kill numerous birds without any difficulty, and you certainly ought to give me a great deal of praise for the way in which I carry out your "wishes."

Mary was asking me last night about Mr Hutchison's compliment to you as she said she had received a letter from Annie in which an allusion was made to it which she, as she could not understand it, was very naturally puzzled with. I repeated it for her benefit, and very much to her amusement; she could not find the resemblance.

A lady made some very pretty observations to Miss Clay in a letter about you I think her name was Nesbitt [Martha], she told her of the engagement as a piece of news.

Miss Clay spent several days last week with us and she and mother have made their plans to start a week from tomorrow, taking the tripp down of course very slowly.
With my love to Anna & your mother I remain Yours "with quite as much love as I feel for anyone except mother"
     Theodore Roosevelt

Does not that look cold to you? It did to me.

     Roswell, Nov. 21st 1853
My dear Thee
 I am up stairs with every window open, the weather is as warm as summer, in fact has been so far this last week,

November

but we do enjoy it so much for riding on horseback. I wish it would be just such a spell when you are all out here, but of course it will be extremely unpleasant. I received your letter to day and Mother hers from Mrs Roosevelt with which she seemed very much pleased. Mothers message I must give at once as it is important. She has made a mistake in the wedding day and wishes me to correct it immediately, it is to be <u>Thursday the twenty-second of December</u>. If your Mother has left for Byran, she begs that you will let her know immediately as it may make some difference in her plans.

Thee this is important, so please do not forget it. We have held a family consultation and have concluded that it will not be advisable for you to be on the field till Wednesday the 21st. Mr Morris and Corneal will of course come at time also, and find us in all readiness to see you. Thursday December 22nd will be the wedding day - positively no change.

These are all entirely Mothers arrangements and "I tell you the tale as 'twas told to me." We expect Sister and Mr West on tomorrow week, you cannot imagine with what pleasure. Mother particularly invited Lew West to the wedding, but he cannot come, tho of course we wished to pay the compliment. I am rather glad he will not come. Imagine a stiff person one of our party which will only be tolerable provided every body is lively and perfectly easy.

On Saturday Brother had a Dinner company in honor of his return which would really have been pleasant had there been a few intelligent people present. After dinner it was really amusing to see them all seated Turkish fashion (that is the gentlemen) in the piazza smoking Brothers different meerschaum pipes of which their name is legion, and taking coffee from small Turkish cups. You will find no difference at home except that Bess has been sold and Anna and I have another maid in her place. We were obliged

Chapter VI

to sell in order to prevent her being separated from her husband. Anna and I had a dreadful time after she left till she could be replaced, but we "harsh unfeeling Southerners" have to become accustomed to such things. Everything else is as stationary as ever. Tom King has returned from the South. I have met him but once since, then he said nothing about having received a letter from you, but I presume that of course he has. I think I told you about the gas having suddenly gone out at a party in Philadelphia, there it was quite a relief as it took away slightly from the ennui of the evening; it has been a mystery to me how we ever managed to survive those evenings spent at Parties in Philadelphia. You must enjoy having Miss Lilly Lewis with you, she sent out to Anna by Brother a daguerreotype of her pet dog. The renewal of an old joke tiresome even in Phila__. The violet is not this time from Sarah, I must close as it is time to get ready for a ride with Anna and Irvine.

Ever the same
Mittie Bulloch

Meerschaum, German for *foam of the sea*, is also known as sepiolite, a soft white mineral, often used to make smoking pipes. Meerschaum, opaque and off-white, grey, or cream in color, is soft when first extracted. However, it hardens on exposure to solar heat or when dried in a warm room. The first recorded use of meerschaum for pipe manufacture occurred about 1723; however, these pipes quickly became recognized for their flavorful smoke.

New York Nov 26th 1853

My own Dearest Mittie

Although it is very late I find myself indulging in that painful feeling of "hope deferred" which has rendered me so restless as utterly to preclude the possibility of sleep should I retire; how very delightful a talk with you would be. That abominable post office, to delay a so long expected letter; it is all in vain that I try to reason myself into the thought that it will be but two days more, I always conjure up all sorts of "odd and uncomfortable looking" images in my mind. Mother's departure on monday too seemed to render me still more anxious, and tonight when she asked me if I had heard from you, she seemed to regret the negative answer; which of course I gave as though letters were such a common occurance that it was merely <u>today</u> I had not heard. Mrs. James J. Roosevelt was standing by.

On Thanksgiving day we had a sermon that I would have liked so much for you to have heard. It was particularly preached - at ladies, telling them their duties toward their husbands; the clergyman spoke with so much feeling that I should have suspected him of being married to one devoted to "women's rights." It was intended as an incentive to religion in the family circle and showing how much members of such a circle had to be thankful for. Dearest little Mittie must use all her influence to make me remember to whom I owe all this, and not allow me to indulge in mood, which sometimes I cannot help now, but really believe that her society will dispell; as they seem caused by her abscence.

Before I forget it, do answer this to the care of Roosevelt Hyde & Clarke Charleston, instead of New York as I will spend some days either there or at the Morris' near the city. It will be so much pleasanter to be able to hear from you without such a very great delay, besides it saves the chance of accidents. George & myself will have to arrive on saturday before the wedding. I do not regret this for myself but do a little for Uncle John. Please dont object as it can't be helped.

Nov 27th.   You can't imagine what a relief it is to have such a letter as your last to look back to, it was so

Chapter VI

affectionate. Sometimes when I try to analyze the feeling it seems so impossible to say why I love you so much and long so much to have it fully returned; but the fact is always the same.

There is a young lady you may have heard me speak of with whom I acted the part of lover in private theatricals once - Carey Stuyvesant. She paid Lizzie a visit the other day and heard for the first time of my engagement; the next evening I met her at a party. When I came into the room not one of my acquaintances there knew of it, but she had not been there five minutes before I heard her tell it in a loud voice to everyone that she came in the neighborhood of. She then felt a sympathetic drawing towards me, being in the same position herself, and became unexpectedly confidential. I had always disliked her and had every reason to believe it mutual as I was introduced by an ancient lover who I think she gave me credit for persuading away from her. She said she believed she loved him at the time but now of course had found out to the contrary. I was very much amused as her views of love and mine differed so materially, but even she said she had not danced nor cared to since her engagement, generally. I would not have written this sentence did I not know that it was too late for my thoughts to interfere with your pleasure which I would not have for the world. After we are married I hope - but you know already what I have in vain tried to school myself into not desiring. I must leave for church. —

I had intended leaving this to finish until tomorrow morning after the receipt of your last letter but will add a postscript if it arrives in time. Last night was our farewell saturday night to mother who leaves tomorrow morning and rather a larger gathering than usual. The spirits of the party were a little damped by the arrival of Mrs James J R. in rather a bad humour, but she did not stay very late. I will

bring over the invitation to her in person when it comes, (I hope tomorrow), as I want to see how she will take it. She has never alluded to my engagement although uncle James has frequently. She came over to have a talk with mother about the cause of her anger, but I will relate this to you when we meet and also one or two other little pieces of our experience with fashionable women which may amuse while it will disgust you. With love to Annie and your mother I remain
     Yours devotedly
      Theodore Roosevelt

Little Mittie shall have the coat sleeves altered to suit if not sufficiently large already.
     Yours ever
     Thee

 Thee requested that Mittie direct his mail to Roosevelt Hyde & Clarke, a hardware, cutlery, and guns company in Charleston, South Carolina, so that it would reach him during his layover with the Morris family in Charleston. Henry Roosevelt was the leading partner in the Charleston firm and Thee's first cousin.

     Roswell, Nov 28th, 1853
 Well dear Thee I have only just a little time to commence my letter, as I have promised to go with Irvine to the Alley, in reality it is now the time I should be there but I never exactly keep my appointments so I intend to encroach a little. The two Punch's and your last letter have been received. we had quite a dose of Punch, as the same mail which brought mine, Brother received the same two from Mr Hutchison. I have just returned. Mother called for me at the Alley and we took a walk together. I think

Chapter VI

I am stronger than I was a few weeks ago. I am taking a preparation of Iron called "soluble citrate of Iron." Dr King thinks I have not enough Iron in my blood, and really since I have been taking the Iron regularly I have felt much better, and have quite a color, before I was very pale, Brother has been out ever since breakfast shooting with Dr King - he has been supplying me with Partridges for some time as they all have all taken up an idea they (the birds are good for me) – are good diet for me. Anna left to day for Etowah Cliffs the Stiles' place - she is going to spend a week with Mary Cooper. I could hardly spare her, but did not like to disappoint Mary, and Mother said she could not think of sparing me when I had so very short a time to be with her - I should have liked to have gone very much had I not been on the eve of leaving my own dear home. Mary will soon be down now - she is coming some little time before the wedding. I have mortally offended one of my friends by not having her for one of my Bridesmaids. had I had six she would have been one, but only having four, there were others who I had to ask first. I think it is a very great pity - one cannot please themselves and not cause offence to friends, but a young lady at such times is generally a perfect martyr, Do think during the wedding times - my Brother is going to play on the flute for our dancing. this is the only music we can engage, but he plays in such perfect time that it will be delightful -

We met both of the Miss Dewitt's at Mrs Weir Roosevelt's - so I do not know which of them is to be married – is it the one with the dark eyes?

I am delighted to hear of your different encounters with the ladies but cannot understand whether you walked home with Nellie Lathrop or the fascinating Terrier. I would like to hope not the latter, if it should prove however to be the case I should feel so ashamed.

November

Your Mother I suppose left with Miss Clay today. I hope you received the letter telling the change from the twentieth to the twenty second of December as the Wedding day - If not I hope you wrote immediately telling her of the fact as it may make some difference in their plans. Mrs Dr Nesbitt the lady who I suppose was the one you mentioned as having written to Miss Clay about me, I know very well - she is Dick Taylors sister, I think I told you about Dick Taylor, did I not? - he was married a few weeks ago. Mother is very anxious for my old Mamma (Maum Charlotte) to go on North with me, in fact has concluded that it is necessary for me to have an attendant. She says she would feel anxious unless she should accompany me, but we have not come to a positive decision till we can talk the matter over with sister and see whether it would be practicable.

She certainly would be a great comfort, and I am very anxious to have her, she is so accustomed to me and is so good. What do you think Thee? Mother has her heart set upon it, says she would feel very badly if I should go with out her, she would of course only remain the winter, as her children are here. I will not mind leaving home half so much if she is with me, I do hope she will be able to go with me. Anna and I succeeded in making Brother [Daniel Elliott] tell us his Bridal present for me, we all think Brother so much improved by his having been abroad - he was always affectionate, but his temper is so much better. We have had quite a touching scene in the yard. one of Irvines dogs was taken sick and finally died. This was a most awful tragedy to poor Irvine, it made us feel Badly to see him. Irvine is now my constant companion while Anna is away - walking and riding, at such times quite agreeable. It is his vacation at present and you have no idea how he bores us in the mornings and times we wish to be quiet. I frequently hear Mother say to him "I do wish your school would begin again"

Chapter VI

- such standing truths and so very personal you would think they would have some effect, but alas a schoolboys sense of delicacy is not over refined. Please give my love to Lizzie Ellis and tell her I anticipate seeing her very much. Mother also her love. I must go to tea - goodbye my own dear dear Thee.

Always the same
Mittie Bulloch

On the same day, Thee sent Mittie a postcard containing one last message.

Nov 28th 53

Dearest Mittie

I have just received your letter enclosing a little token of affection that it is useless to tell you I will prize for the thought that actuated the giver and as recalling myown dearest one to my mind.

Mother has just gone but I will write about the change to her and also request you to answer this here and not to Charleston, which letter remember I will <u>expect</u> and be very much disappointed if I do not receive.

Tom will act

Yours Only
Theodore Roosevelt

Chapter VII
December

The month of the wedding finally arrived. Susan and Hilborne West arrived from Philadelphia on 26 November, one week before Mittie penned one last letter to Thee.

Roswell Dec 3rd

My dearest Thee

    I have just left Brother [Daniel] and Mr West smoking away in the parlour for the purpose of commencing my letter to you, I do not generally write you on sundays, but I was at Home all this morning - consequently went through my usual quantity of reading then and this afternoon I thought for once I would break through my determination - as I felt so particularly like having something to do with you. Thee this will be my last letter but one which I intend sending this coming Thursday - only three weeks now before we meet, tis a very short time, I will of course be delighted to see you but then again I do dread the time, and only wish <u>darling</u> that it was all up with me and I had died game. Some times I feel anxious for fear that all your anticipation will be not realized in erring Mittie. but do you not remember once you told me, "Mittie if you will only love me that is all I ask." Thee I <u>know I love you</u> much more positively than I ever did before, now that the time is fading away that I will be without you. I know that you are the only person who could ever suit me and I put every confidence in you, knowing

Chapter VII

my happiness will be secure in your keeping, oh dear Thee love me always tenderly - and we will not fail to be happy together.

Dear me, how grave I have been, I must immediately descend to a common place - to ballence the last. <u>Please, do dont</u> have the same gold watch chain you had while in Roswell. I do not wish you to get another as I like a great deal better than anything else a black ribbon the kind used for such purposes, worn around the neck - will Thee try and get this. Because I write this don't think I did not mean what I wrote before. I mean both.

I must stop now and finish tomorrow, as it is time for me to go to walk with Sister. Miss Rees who is here now with us has been very kind to me when I have been sick, I particularly want you to be very polite to her when you are here. Thee when you answer this please let me know when you wish me to be ready for returning to New York - dearie don't forget as it makes quite a difference in my arrangements.

Dec 5th I received your letter today and the invitations are to be sent in the envelope with this letter, they should have been sent earlier but Sister arrived only on saturday and she brought the materials with her, and this is the first mail since she has come, I send an invitation to Julia, you did not mention her, but I thought as Anna and I had become acquainted with her, she might expect one, however there may be others who you might think just if not more important to invite, so you may send it or not as you please, I would like it sent. I liked Julia -

So you should have liked very much to have [had me] heard the sermon, you think I am quite dificient in proper ideas about my duties - well, Thee I expect I am, but I do not think such a sermon would have had a happy effect upon me - anything of the kind generally makes me a [- - - -], Thee now that the day has been changed, you must not arrive in Roswell till

<u>the day before the wedding</u> - this will just suit your being in Charleston you can perfectly well leave on Tuesday-and get here on Wednesday <u>not before three oclock</u>. 'Twill seriously inconvenience us if you do otherwise, and I shall not be half so glad to see you. We were delighted to see Sister and Mr West on Saturday - we are expecting Anna in a day or two. I have missed her most sadly and do not know how I could have stood it, if it had not been that Tillie (Miss Rees) was with me. I am writing so very hurriedly. I have been so extremely busy all the morning and this afternoon paying visits, and this evening we are all of us going to get the invitations ready as it is time for them to be out now. So you see I am scribbling this while they are bringing in tea in my lap on the cover of a box. Do you not pity me? Will it not be exciting when we meet? I will be very <u>very</u> glad to be near Thee again, but tho' I am engaged I still should like to dance with who ever I pleased, but ----- Thee I have so much to say I cannot write, never mind I will talk to you all my life (except sometimes) after these few short weeks which are passing so rapidly away. On my wedding night I want you particularly to notice my dress as it is very beautiful, I tell you this now as I may not remember when you arrive - as we will have so much else to think and speak about - I must stop - every body is at tea except myself. Thee will I ever be able to break myself of always being late. No never - I expect you think I am in a dreadful mood, I know I am in a loving mood.

Mittie Bulloch

The Roosevelts began the month traveling toward Roswell. While Thee stopped in Charleston to visit with the Morris family, Cornelius and Margaret enjoyed a brief visit to the southern home of Miss Eliza Clay at Richmond-on-

Chapter VII

Ogeechee Plantation in Bryan County.[78] Margaret wrote to Thee from there in early December.

Richmond Bryan County [Georgia]
Dec 8th 1853

Dear Thee

We have received your letter, telling of the change in the day appointed, and I have just written to Mrs. Bulloch to say we shall not leave Savannah until Monday, and shall arrive at her house on Tuesday, father begs me to write to you, to tell you not to leave it later, there is such risk of accident or detention on the road, if you leave Charleston on Monday we shall meet at Atlanta. I have a great deal to say but as there is some danger of your not receiving this I shall be brief. I hear now frequently of Mittie's beauty, and loveliness, everyone says the girls made such a pleasant impression here last winter. I have made two discoveries without seeking to do so, who Dr. Morris fancies (I saw her at the Mann farm and admired her too) and Mittie's [___]. Latrobe was so kind and attentive to us, he gave us his time, and carriage, his man, and buggy, and horse he took us all about, and really made our day very pleasant. I find we have a namesake here, one of Miss Eliza's favorite servants has called her baby Roosevelt, after Miss Eliza's friend. I am enjoying myself and feel much better. Goodbye Sweetest. I long to see you, but feel so glad you have all been together so much,

Father sends love Your affectionate Mother

Brides appear to abound, we have had three as traveling companions at different stages, and we saw the merriest party of boys going to a wedding at Petersburg, Virginia

The Mann farm to which Mrs. Roosevelt refers would have been the plantation of John Elliott Mann. Named for Martha Stewart Elliot Bulloch's first husband, John Mann would have known the Bulloch family as well. Considered a small plantation, the Mann family resided near Flemington in Liberty County and attended the Midway Church.[79]

The Wedding

Mittie and Thee's long anticipated wedding day finally arrived, Thursday, 22 December 1853. For of all the careful planning done by Mittie and her mother, the weather proved uncooperative. That cold dark night heavy rain fell, and dropping temperatures threatened the change to snow. One guest, Jane Camp, described the day as so rainy and bad she had to wear her overshoes for the walk from her home, Primrose Cottage. Unfortunately, we cannot list the other family and friends who attended the ceremony, as no such account is known to exist. The only first person accounts are from interviews dated at least 50 years after the wedding so the stories vary widely. We do know that Thee's parents, Margaret and Cornelius attended as well as his younger brother Cornelius. Bulloch family members, Susan and Hilborne West and Daniel Elliott, arrived in plenty of time to enjoy the festivities.[80] Jane Camp wrote to Elisabeth Hitchcock Camp in January of 1854:

> Miss M Bullochs wedding that has been so long talked of came off on the 22nd. It was a grand affair. The entertainment was splendid. There was so few there to enjoy it, was really too bad. The only persons from abroad were Mr & Mrs Roosevelt & son, parents &

Chapter VII

brother of the groom. They left on Friday last for New York.[81]

The wedding would be the social event of the season in Roswell. Mittie's village friends held parties that week to decorate cakes for the wedding feast. Mrs. Bulloch, anxious to serve something special ordered ice from Savannah. The slaves made ice cream, a rare treat in the South in 1853, to be served with the cakes. *Daddy* William and his helpers decorated the majestic white house on the hill with ribbons and greens. They readied every inch of the house. Lamps were cleaned and lighted, and that evening fresh candlelight glowed from every window. Carriages lined the muddy heart-shaped drive. As the guests descended from their carriages dressed in their finest, the family welcomed them at the door and escorted each guest into the parlor. Delicious aromas floated from the kitchen below where *Maum* Rose and her helpers finished preparations for the feast to follow. The closed pocket doors leading to the dining room increased the sense of anticipation.

From her "many friends" Mittie finally settled on four attendants with her sister Anna as first bridesmaid. Then she chose her long-time friends Julia Hand, Mary Stiles, and from next door at Barrington Hall, Evelyn King. With consultation from Mittie, Thee chose his brother Cornelius as first groomsman and next Mittie's brother, Daniel Elliott, his friend, George Morris, and Tom King. However, at the last moment, George could not attend so Ralph King stepped up to fill in. Evelyn King (Baker) remembered many years later that Cornelius stood with Anna, Tom King with Mary, Ralph King with Julia, and Daniel with her.

Mittie in white satin and her bridesmaids in white muslin descended the long staircase. Thee and his groomsmen waited anxiously for their appearance. Those waiting in the parlor watched as the doors opened revealing the wedding party. Guests, knowing Mittie's love of drama, were not surprised to see them standing arranged as a tableau.

Mittie's gown glistened in the candlelight as she stood by the love of her life, her tall, blue-eyed groom. Reverend James Bulloch Dunwoody, Mittie's cousin, stepped forward to perform the ceremony.[82] (He also later described the weather that evening as inclement in the extreme.) Mittie wanted music for the evening and persuaded her brother Daniel to play the flute.[83] At the conclusion of the ceremony, an elaborate feast was served and dancing began. Jane Camp was embarrassed when she realized she was still wearing her boots during the first waltz. The newlyweds remained in Roswell for a week attending parties held in their honor before leaving for New York City. A new home, a gift from the Roosevelts, was under construction for the young couple. They planned to live with Thee's parents until the new home could be completed.

The ceremony that December night served as the beginning of a long marriage and the continuation the couple's intimate relationship. This timeless, enduring love story carries on in many, many Bulloch and Roosevelt letters.

Endnotes

1. George White, Historical Collections of Georgia: Containing the Most Interesting Facts, Traditions, Biographical Sketches, Anecdotes, Etc. Relating to the History and Antiquities, From Its First Settlement to the Present Time (New York: Pudney & Russell, Publishers, 1855), 353-364: Rebecca McLeod, "The Loss of the Steamer Pulaski," *The Georgia Historical Quarterly* 3, no. 2 (1919): 88.
2. Walter E. Wilson and Gary L. McKay, James D. Bulloch: Secret Agent and Mastermind of the Confederate Navy (Jefferson, North Carolina and London: McFarland & Company, Inc. Publishers, 2012),16-17.
3. James Holmes, MD, "Dr. Bullie's" Notes: Reminiscences of Early Georgia and of Philadelphia and New Haven In The 1800s (Atlanta: Cherokee Publishing Company, 1976).
4. *Darien Gazette*, 22 September 1821.
5. Susan Ann Elliott, born 6 August 1820; Georgia Amanda Elliott, born 14 June 1822, and Daniel Stewart, born 20 November 1826.
6. *Savannah Georgian*, 15 August 1827.
7. *Savannah Georgian*, 11 September 1827. Obituary reads in part, "On the 8th inst. Charles Williams, son of the late John Elliott, age three." The "Savannah Georgia Select Board of Health and Health Department Records 1824-1864" listed his interment as 8 October rather than his death.
8. *Savannah Georgian*, 3 May 1828.
9. *Daily Georgian*, 3 June 1829.
10. *Savannah Daily Georgian*, 1831.
11. In the antebellum period, a sister-in-law or brother-in-law was considered a brother or sister. Mary Telfair wrote of Martha and James' relationship as it would have been recognized by the social community. BettyWood (editor),

Mary Telfair to Mary Few: Selected Letters 1802-1844 (Athens: The University of Georgia Press, 2007),106-10:

12. Betty Wood (editor), Mary Telfair to Mary Few: Selected Letters 1802-1844 (Athens: The University of Georgia Press, 2007),106-10: Charles Johnson, Jr., Mary Telfair: The Life And Legacy of a Nineteenth-Century Woman (Savannah, Georgia: Frederic C. Beil Publisher, 2002), 93-94.
13. Ibid., 93-94.
14. Wood, 107.
15. Roswell King and his son, Barrington King, established a cotton mill at Vickery Creek in upland Georgia in the mid-1830s. Roswell invited investors to his "Colony of Roswell" so as to establish a town with the social and religious values so desired by his social and economic status. By 1839, a number of prominent Savannah and Liberty County families had accepted King's offer and relocated to the village. A number of books on the subject can be found including Paulette Snoby's *Georgia's Colony of Roswell: One Man's Dream and the People Who Lived It,* published in 2015 by Interpreting Time's Past, LLC.
16. Southern slave-holding families often gave honorary titles to their beloved house slaves, such as *Maum* for Mama and *Daddy*. The slaves mentioned here were called by these titles in everyday speech and family letters by the Bulloch women.
17. Bulloch Hall is currently a house museum, owned by the City of Roswell, and funded in part by the Friends of Bulloch, Inc., 501(c)3.
18. Mimosa Hall is a privately-owned residence.
19. Christie Anna Farnham, The Education of the Southern Belle: Higher Education and Student Socialization in the Antebellum South (New York: New York University Press, 1994), 65-67.
20. Mrs. I.M.E. Blandin, History of Higher Education of Women in the South, Prior to 1860. (New York: The Neale Publishing Company, 1909), 260-263.

21. Lynn Salsi and Margaret Sims, Columbia: History of a Southern Capital (Charleston, SC: Arcadia Publishing, 2003), 41-42.
22. John Hammond Moore, Columbia and Richmond County: A South Carolina Community, 1740-1990 (Columbia: University of South Carolina Press, 1992),111.
23. Kennesaw Seminary was founded in 1845 under the auspices of the St. James's Episcopal Church, beginning in 1846. Sarah's father, Benjamin Green, served as the school's director from 1850 to 1858 when it closed. Sarah's sister, Jane Eliza, also attended the seminary. From Robert Manson Myers, The Children of Pride: A True Story of Georgia and the Civil War (New Haven and London: Yale University Press, 1972),1534. During this period *seminary* denoted a school not for the teaching of religion but simply a church connection.
24. Betty Boyd Caroli, The Roosevelt Women (New York: Basic Books, 1998), ii and iii.
25. Joseph Bucklin Bishop, Theodore Roosevelt and His Time Shown in His Own Letters - Book I (New York: Charles Scribner's Son's, 1920), 3.
26. Corinne Roosevelt Robinson, My Brother Theodore Roosevelt (New York: Scribner's Sons, 1921), 3.
27. National Archives and Records Administration (NARA); Washington D.C.; NARA Series: Passport Applications, 1795-1905; Roll #: 36; Volume #: Roll 036 - 07 Apr 1851- 22 May 1851.
28. Robinson, 13.
29. *Savannah Republican*, 15 February 1851.
30. Hermann Hagedorn, The Boys' Life of Theodore Roosevelt (New York: Harper & Brothers Publishers, 1918), 8.
31. New York Circuses - Circopedia. http://www.circopedia.org/New_York_circuses (accessed 14 April 2015).
32. Baroness Jemima Montgomery Tautphoeus. http://www.goodreads.com/author/show/4513662_Jemima_Montgomery_Baroness_von_tautphoeus (accessed 14 April 2015).

Endnotes

33. Putnam's Monthly Magazine and Its Successors. http://www.bartleby.com/227/1212.html (accessed 14 April 2015): "George William Curtis," www.britannica.com (accessed 15 April 2015).
34. Joan Severa, Dressed for the Photographer: Ordinary Americans & Fashion, 1840-1900 (Kent, Ohio: The Kent State University Press, 1995), 1-2.
35. Wilson and McKay, 16-17.
36. Aaron Lake, "White Sulphur Springs." www.chattahoocheeheritage.org/2013/12/white_sulphur_springs/ (accessed 17 April 2015): Bates, Ashley. "White Sulphur community was home to resort for wealthy." www.gainesvilletimes.com/archives/23706/ (accessed 17 April 2015).
37. Spas: Pleasure or Penance? http://www.historytoday.com/pamela-steen/spas-pleasure-or-penance#sthash.mlESS66s.dpuf. (accessed 17 April 2015).
38. Charles Hirschfield, America on Exhibition: The New York Crystal Palace, *American Quarterly* 9, no. 2, Part 1 (Summer 1957):101-116: New York Crystal Palace. en.m.wikipedia.org/wiki/New_York_Crystal_Palace (accessed 17 April 2015).
39. Schooley's Mountain, New Jersey http://wtpl.org/download/WTHistoryScans/ThisIsWT.pdf (accessed 15 August 2015): Henry Charlton Beck, The Roads of Home: Lanes and Legends of New Jersey (New Brunswick, New Jersey: Rutgers University Press, 1982), 48-62.
40. Harriet Beecher Stowe Center, https://www.harrietbeecherstowecenter.org/utc/ (accessed 24 April 2015)
41. Charles Lamb: British author, www.britannica.com. (accessed 17 April 2015)
42. Robie S. Lange, "National Register of Historic Places Registration: Croton Aqueduct" (October 1991, PDF). National Park Service. and Accompanying 20 photos and drawings, from 1978 and 1843.
43. Tallulah Gorge is now Tallulah Gorge State Park. The Toccoa Falls waterfall, with a vertical drop of 186 feet (57

m), is located on the campus of Toccoa Falls College in Stephens County, Georgia. Toccoa is the Cherokee word for "beautiful".
44. Samuel Warren Dunlap, C. R. B., A Victorian Law and Literature Practitioner, *Cardozo Studies in Law and Literature* 12, no. 2. (Autumn-Winter 2000): 265-291.
45. 1850's Men's Fashion, www.gentlemansemporium.com/1850-victorian-phopo-gallery.php, (accessed 24 April 2015): Joan Severa, Dressed for the Photographer: Ordinary Americans & Fashion, 1840-1900, (Kent, Ohio: The Kent State University Press, 1995), 84-106.
46. Wilson and McKay, 16-17.
47. Punch (magazine), en.m.wikipedia.org/wiki/Punch_(magazine) (accessed 24 April 2015).
48. Dinah Maria Mulock Craik, www.goodreads.com/author/show/16852: Dinah_Maria_Mulock_Craik: en.m.wikipedia.org/wiki/Dinah_Craik. (accessed 24 April 2015).
49. Charles Hoffmann and Tess Hoffmann, North by South: The Two Lives of Richard James Arnold. (Athens, Georgia: University of Georgia Press, 2009) xix.
50. *Punch*, Volume XXV:72.
51. *Punch*, Volume XXIV:189.
52. Barbara Hofland, en.m.wikipedia.org/wiki/Barbara_Hofland, (accessed 3 May 2015).
53. *The Literary Gazette; and Journal of Belles Lettres, Arts, Sciences, &c. for the Year 1829* (London: 1829), 708.
54. Connie M. Cox and Darlene M. Walsh, Providence: Selected Correspondence of George Hull Camp 1837-1907, Son of the North, Citizen of the South (Macon, Georgia: Indigo Publishing Group, 2008), 62-63.
55. *Stone Mountain History*. http://www.stonemountainpark.org/5.%20Explore/Text/History/Stone%20Mountain%20History.pdf, (accessed 3 May 2015).
56. Ibid.
57. Ibid.

Endnotes

58. *Savannah Daily Georgian*, 17 June 1829: Darlene M. Walsh, Roswell A Pictorial History (Roswell, Georgia: Roswell Historical Society, 1994, second edition), 39.
59. Ibid. Document is stored in the History Room of the Roswell Presbyterian Church.
60. Ibid.
61. "Henry Wadsworth Longfellow" A Maine Historical Society Website, www.hwlongfellow.org/ (accessed 3 May 2015).
62. Jonathan Aitken, John Newton: From Disgrace to Amazing Grace, (Wheaton, Illinois: Crossway Books, 2007): "John Dunn, A Biography of John Newton (New Creation Teaching Ministry, 1994). PDF available online at New Creation Teaching Ministry.
63. Ibid. Although Newton continued to serve in the slave trade, Newton began a deep study of the Bible and the doctrines of his new religion. He avoided profanity, gambling, and drinking while developing a deep sympathy for the people they enslaved. He rose to the rank of captain and made several runs in the Triangle Trade out of Liverpool before suffering a severe stroke in 1754. At this time Newton removed himself from the seafaring life and settled in Liverpool with his wife of four years. Working as a tax collector, Newton began a serious study of Greek, Hebrew, and Syriac while becoming a well-known evangelical lay minister. He applied to the Church of England to become a priest, but had to wait seven years for acceptance. In 1764, Newton received deacon's orders and was ordained as a priest. As curate of Olney, Buckinghamshire, Newton became well known for his pastoral care and as a popular preacher. He spent 16 years at this post before accepting the post of Rector of St. Mary Woolnoth in London. It was during his time at Olney that Newton wrote the hymn we now know as *Amazing Grace*. In 1788, Newton wrote his *Thoughts Upon the Slave Trade*, where he described the horrible conditions aboard the slave ships during the Middle Passage. He apologized and confessed for his role in the slave trade. Newton sent copies of the pamphlet to every member

of Parliament. The pamphlet sold so swiftly that it required several reprints. Newton worked with William Wilberforce, the leader of the Parliamentary campaign to abolish the African slave trade and lived to see passage of the British Slave Trade Act of 1807.

64. See August 30th letter for info on *Agatha's Husband*.
65. A Brief History of the Sewing Machine, www.ismacs.net/sewing_machine_history.html, (accessed 5 May 2015).
66. Herbert, William Henry, www.ulib/niu.edu/badndp/herbert_henry.html, (accessed 5 May 2015): Henry William Herbert, en.m.wikipedia.org/wiki/Henry_William_Herbert, (accessed 5 May 2015).
67. Internet Broadway Database, www.ibdb.com/mobile/venue.php?id=1320, (accessed 5 May 2015): Daytonian in Manhattan, www.daytoninmanhattan.blogspot.com/61-wallacks-theatre-broadway.html (accessed 5 May 2015).
68. Ibid.
69. *Putnam's Monthly*, Vol. 3 No. 14 (February 1854). G. P. Putnam & Co., New York:151. Online at HathiTrust Digital Library, (accessed 5 May 2015).
70. Lafayette Cemetery Research Project, New Orleans, "The Yellow Fever Epidemic in New Orleans - 1853," www.lafayettecemetery.org/yellowfever1853_page1, (accessed 5 May 2015).
71. American Waldensian Society, www.waldensian.org, (accessed 5 May 2015): Emilo Comba, History of the Waldenses of Italy, from their origin to the Reformation, (New York: AMS Press, 1978).
72. Ibid.
73. Nicholas Murray, www.en.m.wikipedia.org/wiki/Nicholas_Murray, (accessed 5 May 2015).
74. A grave memorial for Julian Taylor, who died 16 December 1852 in Paris, France, was located using Find A Grave.com in an Alexandria City, Virginia cemetery. However, at the time of printing, the family has not been further identified.
75. *Home Journal*, 5 November 1853: Vera Brodsky Lawrence, Strong on Music: The New York Music Scene in the Days of

Endnotes

George Templeton Strong, Volume 2: Reverberations, 1850-1856, (Chicago: University of Chicago Press, 1995).
76. *Gleason's Pictorial Drawing-Room Companion*, Vol. 4, No. 20. (Boston: Published 14 May 1853).
77. An additional reference to Daniel's character is one brief line from George Hull Camp to Jane Atwood Camp, 6 February 1851, ". . .as Dan is nothing in my estimation better than a brute. . ." as seen in Cox and Walsh, 202.
78. Myers, 1491.
79. Myers, 1616.
80. Florence L. Tucker, "Girl-Hood Chum, Bridesmaid of Roosevelt's Mother, Gives First True Account of Marriage," *The Sunny South*, Week Ending December 26, 1903: Peggy Mitchell, "Bridesmaid of 87 Recalls Mittie Roosevelt's Wedding," *The Atlanta Journal*, 10 June 1923: Leleah Georgianna Dunwoody Waddell, "Reminiscences of the Dunwody-Bulloch Families," Dated October 1905. Typewritten copy on file at Bulloch Hall, Roswell, Georgia. Original source unknown.
81. Cox and Walsh, 295.
82. Several early twentieth century newspaper accounts list the Rev. Nathaniel Pratt as performing the ceremony. However, the New York Evening Post, Thursday, December 29, 1853, Marriage Notices: reads "Roswell Ga. 22nd Rev. James Dunwoody, Theodore Roosevelt of NY to Martha dau of late James J Bullock of former place."
83. Cox and Walsh, 292. Tom King writing to Walter Bicker Camp praised Daniel's musical ability.

Bibliography

Aitken, Jonathon. *John Newton: From Disgrace to Amazing Grace.* Wheaton, Illinois: Crossway Books, 2007.

Beck, Henry Charlton. *The Roads of Home: Lanes and Legends of New Jersey.*, New Brunswick, NJ: Rutgers University Press. 1982

Bishop, Joseph Bucklin. *Theodore Roosevelt and His Time Shown in His Own Letters - Book I.* New York: Charles Scribner's Sons, 1920.

Blandin, Mrs. I.M.E. *History of Higher Education of Women in the South, Prior to 1860.* New York: The Neale Publishing Company, 1909.

Caroli, Betty Boyd. *The Roosevelt Women.* New York: Basic Books, 1998.

Cox, Connie M. and Darlene M. Walsh. *Providence: Selected Correspondence of George Hull Camp 1837-1907, Son of the North, Citizen of the South.* Macon, GA: Indigo Publishing Group, 2008

Dunlap, C. R. B. Samuel Warren: A Victorian Law and Literature Practitioner. *Cardozo Studies in Law and Literature* Vol. 12, No. 2. (Autumn-Winter 2000): 265-291.

Dunn, John. *A Biography of John Newton.* New Creation Teaching Ministry. PDF available online at New Creation Teaching Ministry. 1994.

Farnham, Christie Anna. *The Education of the Southern Belle: Higher Education and Student Socialization in the Antebellum South.* New York: New York University Press, 1994.

Gleason, Frederick, (editor). *Gleason's Pictorial Drawing-Room Companion*, Vol. 4, No. 20. Published 14 May 1853, Boston.

Hagedorn, Hermann. *The Boys' Life of Theodore Roosevelt.* New York: Harper & Brothers Publishers, 1918.

Hirschfield, Charles. "America on Exhibition: The New York Crystal Palace." *American Quarterly* Vol. 9, No. 2, Part 1 (Summer 1957), 101-116.

Hoffmann, Charles and Tess Hoffmann. *North by South: The Two Lives of Richard James Arnold.* Athens, GA. University of Georgia Press, 2009.

Holmes, James, MD. *"Dr. Bullie's" Notes: Reminiscences of Early Georgia and of Philadelphia and New Haven In The 1800s.* Atlanta: Cherokee Publishing Company, 1976.

Johnson, Jr., Charles J. *Mary Telfair: The Life And Legacy of a Nineteenth-Century Woman.* Savannah, GA: Frederic C. Beil Publisher, 2002.

Lange, Robie S. "National Register of Historic Places Registration: Croton Aqueduct." National Park Service and Accompanying 20 photos and drawings, from 1978 and 1843. 1991.

Lawrence, Vera Brodsky. *Strong on Music: The New York Music Scene in the Days of George Templeton Strong, Volume 2: Reverberations, 1850-1856.* Chicago: University of Chicago Press, 1995.

McLeod, Rebecca. "The Loss of the Steamer Pulaski," *The Georgia Historical Quarterly* 3, no. 2 (1919): 63-95.

Moore, John Hammond. *Columbia and Richmond County: A South Carolina Community, 1740-1990.* Columbia, SC: University of South Carolina Press, 1992.

Myers, Robert Manson. *The Children of Pride: A True Story of Georgia and the Civil War.* New Haven and London: Yale University Press, 1972.

Robinson, Corinne Roosevelt. *My Brother Theodore Roosevelt.* New Haven and London: Charles Scribner's Sons, New York. 1921.

Salsi, Lynn and Margaret Sims. *Columbia: History of a Southern Capital.* Charleston, SC: Arcadia Publishing, 2003.

Severa, Joan. *Dressed for the Photographer: Ordinary Americans & Fashion, 1840-1900.* Kent, OH: The Kent State University Press, 1995.

The Literary Gazette; and Journal of Belles Lettres, Arts, Sciences, &c. for the Year 1829. London: Moyes, 1929.

White, George. *Historical Collections of Georgia: Containing the Most Interesting Facts, Traditions, Biographical Sketches, Anecdotes, Etc. Relating to the History and Antiquities, From Its First Settlement to the Present Time.* New York: Pudney & Russell, Publishiers, 1855.

Wilson, Walter E. and Gary L. McKay. *James D. Bulloch: Secret Agent and Mastermind of the Confederate Navy.* Jefferson, NC and London: McFarland & Company, Inc. Publishers, 2012.

Wood, Betty (editor). *Mary Telfair to Mary Few: Selected Letters 1802-1844.* Athens, GA: The University of Georgia Press, 2007.

Newspapers and Magazines:
Darien Gazette (Georgia)
Daily Georgian
Harper's New Monthly Magazine
Home Journal (magazine)
New York Evening Post
Punch (magazine)
Putnam's Monthly (magazine)
Savannah Daily Georgian
Savannah Georgian
Savannah Republican
The Atlanta Journal (newspaper)
The Sunny South (newspaper)

Bibliography

Images:

p. ii - **Martha "Mittie" Bulloch Roosevelt,** Theodore Roosevelt Collection, Houghton Library, Harvard University, **Theodore Roosevelt**, Theodore Roosevelt Collection, Houghton Library, Harvard University.

p. xv - **1853 Map of Roswell**, Interpreting Time's Past, LLC after original by Michael Hitt.

p. xvi - **Roosevelt Family Tree by 1853**, Interpreting Time's Past, LLC.

p. xvii - **Bulloch Family Tree by 1853**, Interpreting Time's Past, LLC.

p. 27 - **Franconi's Hippodrome (New York City)** from *Gleason's Pictorial* (Boston) Vol. 4, No. 25, June 18, 1853.

p. 70 - **New York's Crystal Palace**, by Karl Gildemeister, Frontispiece to New York Crystal Palace: illustrated description of the building by Geo. Carstensen & Chs. Gildemeister, architects of the building ; with an oil-color exterior view, and six large plates containing plans, elevations, sections, and details, from the working drawings of the architects (New York: Riker, Thorne & Co., 1854)

p. 85 - **Croton River Dam, 1843 Engraving**, by F. B. Tower, *Illustrations of the Croton Aqueduct*, New York, Wiley and Putnam, 1843.

p. 86 - **Croton Reservoir in Manhattan, erected in 1842**, *Valentine's Manual of Old New York*, No. 7, p.151.

p. 110 - **Uncomfortable Position of Mr. Jones During a Table-Turning Experiment**, *Punch*, Volume XXIV:189.

p. 129 - **Singer Sewing Company Advertisement, 1851**.

p. 134 - **The Death of Virginia** by Guillaume-Guillon Lethière circa 1800.

p. 179 - *Harper's New Monthly Magazine's* **Bridal Fashion**, September, 1853

p. 187 - **Interior of Opera House at Niblo's Garden**, *Gleason's Pictoral Drawing-Room Companion*, Vol. 4, No. 20, 1853, (Boston).

p. 242 - **The Spectre Cow** by Daniel Stewart Elliott, Theodore Roosevetl Collection, Houghton Library, Harvard University.

List of Persons

Each is described as to their status in 1853. Additionally their 1853 relationship to Mittie Bulloch or Thee Roosevelt is noted.

Adams, Theodore Dwight (1829-1901): storekeeper at the Roswell Manufacturing Company and assistant postmaster, Mittie's acquaintance.

Atwood, Sarah Alice (1832-unknown): sister of Ruth Ann Atwood Dunwoody and Jane Margaret Camp, resident of McIntosh County, Georgia, Mittie's friend.

Bayard, Florida (1834-1917): daughter of Nicholas Bayard and step-daughter of Eliza King Hand, residents of Primrose Cottage, Mittie's friend.

Bulloch, Anna Louise (1833-1893): daughter of Martha and James Stephens Bulloch, Mittie's sister.

Bulloch, Elizabeth "Lizzie" Euphemia Caskie (1831-1854): of Richmond, Virginia, sister to Mary Edmonia Caskie, (second wife to Robert Hutchison) married James Dunwoody Bulloch in 1851, Mittie's half-sister-in-law.

Bulloch, Irvine Stephens (1842-1898): son of Martha and James Stephens Bulloch, Mittie's brother.

Bulloch, James Dunwoody (1823-1901): son of Hester and James Stephens Bulloch, married Lizzie Caskie in 1851. Often referred to as "brother Jimmie," Mittie's half-brother.

List of Persons

Bulloch, James Stephens, Major (1793-1849): grandson of Georgia's first governor, Archibald Bulloch, veteran of the War of 1812, invested in Roswell Manufacturing Company, built Bulloch Hall. Married first to Hester Amarantha Elliott (1797-1831) in 1817, one son James Dunwoody Bulloch (1823-1901) lived to maturity. Second marriage to his stepmother-in-law, Martha Stewart Elliott in 1832, children include Anna (1833-1893), Martha "Mittie" (1835-1884), Charles Irvine (1838-1841) and Irvine Stephens (1842-1898), Mittie's father.

Bulloch, Martha (1835-1884): daughter of Martha and James Stephens Bulloch, known as *Mittie*, mother of the future president.

Bulloch, Martha Stewart Elliott (1799-1864): daughter of American Revolutionary General Daniel Stewart. Married first John Elliott in 1818, children include John Whitehead (1818-1820), Susan Ann (1820-1895), Georgia Amanda (1822-1848), Charles William (1824-1827), and Daniel Stewart (1826-1862). Second marriage in 1832 to James Stephens Bulloch (her step-son-in-law), children include Anna (1833-1893), Martha "Mittie" (1835-1884), Charles Irvine (1838-1841) and Irvine Stephens (1842-1898), Mittie's mother.

Bulloch, Mary Eliza Adams Lewis (1828-1902): wife of Dr. William Gaston Bulloch, Mittie's cousin-in-law.

Bulloch, William Gaston, Dr. (1815-1885): cousin to James Stephens Bulloch, resident of Savannah, Mittie's second cousin.

Camp, George Hull (1817-1907) : New Yorker who moved to Roswell for his health and a position with the Roswell Manufacturing Company. He is assistant agent for the company in 1853 as well as Roswell's postmaster, Mittie's acquaintance.

Camp, Jane Margaret (1826-1911): daughter of Henry Skelton Atwood of McIntosh County, Georgia, and Ann Margaret

McIntosh whose ancestors came to Georgia with General Oglethorpe, married George Camp in 1850, Mittie's friend.

Caskie, Ellen Laura (1836-1858): resident of Richmond, Virginia, first cousin to Robert Hutchison's second wife and Lizzie Bulloch, Mittie's acquaintance.

Clapp, Nathaniel Bowditch (1832-1903): originally from Boston, Mittie's friend (based on Cox and Walsh 2008).

Clapp, Julia Hall (1828-1884): married Roger Derastus Clapp in 1847, one son before Roger's death in 1849, Mittie's friend.

Clay, Eliza Caroline (1809-1895): Bryan County, Georgia resident, daughter of Hon. Joseph Clay and Mary Ann Savage, raised in Boston, never married but raised her brother's children, Martha's acquaintance and a friend of the Roosevelt family.

Although most Dunwoody family documents from this period use only one "o" in the name, we have used the more familiar Dunwoody spelling for consistency.

Dunwoody, Charles Archibald Alexander (1828-1905): son of John Dunwoody, married Ellen Rice (1827-1895) in 1852, Mittie's cousin.

Dunwoody, Ellen Rice (1827-1895): married Charles Dunwoody in 1852, Mittie's cousin by marriage.

Dunwoody, Henry Macon (1826-1863): fourth child of John and Jane Dunwoody, Mittie's cousin.

Dunwoody, Jane Irvine Bulloch (1788-1856): wife of John Dunwoody of Roswell, sister to James Stephens Bulloch, Mittie's aunt.

List of Persons

Dunwoody, John (1786-1858): planter in Liberty County, Georgia, before moving to Roswell, Georgia, married Jane Bulloch in 1808, brother-in-law to Martha Bulloch, Mittie's uncle.

Dunwoody, John Franklin (1829-1916): son of James Bulloch and Elizabeth Dunwoody of McIntosh County, Georgia, Mittie's second cousin

Dunwoody, James Bulloch (1816-1902): son of John and Jane Dunwoody. A Presbyterian minister who served from 1845 to 1855 in Pocotaligo, South Carolina. Married Laleah Georgianna Wood Pratt (1823 to 1853) who died about 1 October giving birth to a son. Mittie's cousin.

Dunwoody, Laleah "Lilly" Georgianna (1844-1919): daughter of Reverend James and Laleah Dunwoody. She attended Mittie's wedding with her father. Mittie's second cousin.

Dunwoody, Marion (1821-1885): fifth child of John and Jane Dunwoody, married for second time in 1851 to William Glen, Mittie's cousin.

Dunwoody, Rosaline M. (1853 - unknown): daughter of Charles and Ellen Dunwoody, Mittie's second cousin.

Dunwoody, Ruth Ann Atwood (1826-1899): married to Dr. William Elliott Dunwoody, mother of three children by 1853, Mittie's cousin by marriage.

Dunwoody, William Elliott, Sr. Dr. (1823-1891): son of John and Jane Dunwoody, Mittie's cousin.

Elliott, Daniel Stewart (1826-1862): son of Martha Stewart and John Elliott, often referred to as "Brother Dan," Mittie's half brother.

Elliott, John (1773-1827): planter, lawyer, and U.S. Senator. Married in 1795 to Esther Dunwoody (d. 1815), children included Caroline Matilda (1796-before1829), Esther (or Hester) Amarantha (1797-1831), John (1801-1803), Rebecca Jane (1803-1804), John (1807-1813), Jane Elizabeth (1809-1829), Corinne Louisa (1813-1838) and Charles James (1815-1817). Second marriage to Martha Stewart in 1818, children included John Whitehead (1818-1820), Susan Ann (1820-1895), Georgia Amanda (1822-1848), Charles William (1824-1827), and Daniel Stewart (1826-1862), father of Mittie's half-siblings Susan, Georgia, and Daniel.

Emlen, George (1814-1853): resident and wealthy merchant in Philadelphia, brother-in-law to James Alfred Roosevelt, Thee's acquaintance.

Emlen, Sarah (1832-unknown): sister to George and Elizabeth Norris Emlen. (Note: their mother was Mary Parker Norris.) Resident of Philadelphia, Thee's acquaintance.

Green, Elizabeth Sarah (1835-1916): student at Kennesaw Female Seminary in Marietta, Mittie's friend (Myers 1972:1534)

Habersham, Ann Wylly Adams (1795-1876): wife of Dr. Joseph Clay Habersham, Sr., of Savannah, frequent visitor to Roswell, Mittie's acquaintance.

Habersham, Joseph Clay, Jr., Dr. (1829-1881): resident of Savannah, married Mary Ann Stiles in 1851, Mittie's acquaintance.

Habersham, Mary Ann Stiles (1834-unknown): wife of Dr. Joseph Clay Habersham, Jr. of Savannah, Mittie's acquaintance.

Hand, Julia Isabella (1834-1911): younger daughter of Eliza Barrington King Bayard and Bayard Hand, granddaughter of Roswell King, lived in Primrose Cottage, Mittie's friend.

Harrison, Nannie Euphemia Caskie (1824-1857). Sister of James Dunwoody Bulloch's wife Lizzie Caskie. She married Samuel Jordan Harrison in 1845. The census of 1850 shows the Harrison's living with the Caskies in Richmond.

Hodgson, Margaret Cairns Telfair (1797-1874): Savannah resident, sister of Mary Telfair, daughter of Governor Edward Telfair, also lived in New York City, married Dr. William Brown Hodgson.

Hutchison, Robert (1802-1861): Scottish born, wealthy Savannah merchant, married first in 1832 Corinne Louisa Elliott, Martha Bulloch's stepdaughter. Corinne and their two daughters died in the sinking of the Steamship *Pulaski* in 1838. Hutchison married his second wife, Mary Edmonia Caskie of Virginia in 1848. Mary died of consumption in 1852. Hutchison remained a friend of the family and was executor of James Stephens Bulloch's estate. Mittie's stepbrother-in law.

King, Catherine Evelyn "Eva" (1837-1923): only daughter of Barrington and Catherine King, granddaughter of Roswell King (Roswell's founder), lived at Barrington Hall, Mittie's friend.

King, Ralph Browne (1835-1900): son of Barrington and Catherine King, grandson of Roswell King (Roswell's founder), lived at Barrington Hall, Mittie's friend.

King, Thomas Edward "Tom" (1829-1863): son of Barrington and Catherine King, grandson of Roswell King (Roswell's founder), lived at Barrington Hall, Mittie's friend.

King, William Nephew, Dr. (1825-1894): son of Barrington and Catherine King, grandson of Roswell King (Roswell's founder), lived at Barrington Hall, Mittie's friend.

Lachenour, Julia Augusta (1834-1915): daughter of Sarah Barnhill Miller, resident of Easton, Pennsylvania, Thee's cousin.

List of Persons

McAllister, Joseph Longworth (1820-1864): Bryan County lawyer and planter, (Note, he was related to Georgia's Clay family on his mother's side.) Mittie's acquaintance.

McGill, Charles Arthur (1817-1884): brother of Elizabeth Pye Magill Merrell (Mrs. Henry Merrill), educated as a physician and lawyer, Mittie's acquaintance.

Mackey, Robert (1813-1857): resident of Savannah, Mittie's acquaintance.

Mann, John Elliott (1813-1888): Bryan County, Georgia, planter.

Merrell, Henry (1816-1883): born in Connecticut, employed by the Roswell Manufacturing Company, first as assistant agent and later as agent, Mittie's acquaintance.

Morris, George Dr. (unknown): resident of South Carolina whom Thee met while on his trip to Europe.

Nesbitt, Martha Deloney Berrien (1818-1896), wife of Dr. Hugh O'Keefe Nesbitt, moved to Marietta in 1851, stepsister of Richard Deloney Bolling Taylor, Mittie's friend.

Pratt, Horace Alpheus (1830-1870): son of Rev. Nathaniel and Catherine Pratt, resident of Roswell, married Lilias Logan, Mittie's friend.

Pratt, Reverend Nathaniel Alpheus (1796-1879): first minister of the Roswell Presbyterian Church and schoolmaster, married Catherine Barrington King in 1830, Mittie's pastor.

Pratt, Nathaniel Alpheus, Jr. (1833-1906) son of Reverend Nathaniel and Catherine Pratt, Mittie's friend.

List of Persons

Rice, Rosaline M. Jackson (unknown): resident of Charleston, S.C., mother of Ellen Rice wife of Charles Archibald Alexander Dunwoody, Mittie's acquaintance. (based on Cox and Walsh 2008)

Roosevelt, Caroline Van Ness (1810-1876): wife of John James Roosevelt, mother of James Nicholas Roosevelt. Thee's aunt.

Roosevelt, Cornelius Van Schaak (1794-1871): married Margaret Barnhill (1790-1861) in 1821, Thee's father.

Roosevelt, Cornelius Van Schaak, Jr. (1827-1887): married Laura H. Porter (1833-1900) in 1854, Thee's brother.

Roosevelt, Elizabeth "Lizzie" Thorne Ellis (1833-1877): married to Robert Barnhill Roosevelt, Thee's sister-in-law.

Roosevelt, Elizabeth "Lizzie" Norris Emlen (1825-1912): married James Alfred Roosevelt in 1847, Thee's sister-in-law.

Roosevelt, Henry Latrobe (1812-1884): part owner of Roosevelt Hyde & Clarke, a hardware, cutlery, and guns company in Charleston, S.C., son of Nicholas Roosevelt and Lydia Marie Latrobe, Thee's first cousin.

Roosevelt, James Alfred (1825-1898): married Elizabeth Norris Emlen (1825-1912) in 1847, often called Jim, Thee's brother.

Roosevelt, James John (1795-1875): judge, Justice of New York's Supreme Court, married Caroline Van Ness in 1831, brother of Cornelius Sr. and Thee's uncle.

Roosevelt, James Nicholas (1836-1856): son of James John Roosevelt, Thee's cousin.

Roosevelt, John Ellis (1853-1939): first child of Robert and Lizzie Roosevelt, Thee's nephew.

List of Persons

Roosevelt, Margaret Barnhill (1799-1861): married Cornelius Van Schaak Roosevetl in 1821, Thee's mother.

Roosevelt, Margaret Barnhill (1851-1927): daughter of Robert and Lizzie Ellis, Thee's niece.

Roosevelt, Mary West (1823-1877): wife of Silas Weir Roosevelt, Mittie's acquaintance and Thee's sister-in-law.

Roosevelt, Robert Barnhill (1829-1908): married "Lizzie" Ellis in 1850, Thee's brother.

Roosevelt, Silas Weir (1823-1870): married Mary West in 1845, Thee's brother.

Roosevelt, Theodore (1831-1878): married Mittie Bulloch in 1853, father of the future president.

Shackleford, Caroline "Carrie" Matilda Elizabeth (1835-1927): daughter of Francis Robert Shackleford and Caroline Seymour Dunwoody, cousin to the Dunwoody children, frequent visitor to Roswell, and Mittie's friend.

Smith, Ann Magill (1807-1887): resident of Roswell, married to Archibald Smith, Bulloch family friend.

Smith, Archibald (1801-1886): resident of Roswell married to Ann Magill, Bulloch family friend.

Smith, Archibald, "Archie" (1844-1923): youngest child of Archibald and Ann Smith, resident of Roswell, Bulloch family friend.

Smith, Elizabeth Anne "Lizzie" (1831-1915): eldest child of Archibald and Ann Smith, resident of Roswell, Mittie's friend.

List of Persons

Smith, Helen Zubly (1841-1896): third child of Archibald and Ann Smith, resident of Roswell, Mittie's friend.

Smith, William Seagrove "Willie" (1834-1865): second child of Archibald and Ann Smith, resident of Roswell, Mittie's friend.

Stiles, Mary Cowper (1832-1863): sister of William Henry Stiles II, daughter of William Henry and Eliza Anne Stiles of Savannah, Mittie's friend.

Stiles, William Henry II (1834-1878): brother of Mary Cowper Stiles, son of William Henry and Eliza Anne Stiles of Savannah, Mittie's friend.

Taylor, Richard "Dick" Deloney Bolling (1830-1864): stepbrother of Martha Deloney Berrien Nesbitt, resident of Athens, Georgia, married Sara Jane Billups in 1853, Mittie's friend.

Terrell, Lucy (1833-1910): daughter of Dr. William and Sarah Terrell of Sparta, Georgia, Daniel Stewart Elliott's love-interest.

West, Hilborne, Dr. (1818-1907): of Philadelphia, married Susan Ann Elliott in 1849, Mittie's stepbrother-in-law and Thee's acquaintance.

West, Lewis "Lew" (1829-1867): of Philadelphia, officer in the U.S. Navy, younger brother of Hilborne and Mary West, Thee's acquaintance.

West, Susan Ann Elliott (1820-1895): daughter of Martha Stewart and John Elliott, married Hilborne West in 1849, Mittie's half-sister.

List of Persons

List of Bulloch Slaves Named in 1853 Letters and Text:

Bachus - driver
Bess - Mittie and Anna's personal maid
Maum Charlotte
Maum Grace
Henry - young male slave
Daddy Luke Moumar
Monroe
Maum Rose
Sally - at Bulloch Hall or Phoenix Hall (Dunwoody home)
Sarah - described as "the little girl about the house" in Mittie's
    Sept 14th letter
Daddy Stephen
Daddy William

Additional Notes:

Miss Mary Telfair (p. 154): Possibilities include, Margaret Long Telfair (b.1816) and Mary Eliza Telfair (b.1813); both are nieces of Mary Telfair. However, given their age, the Miss Telfair referenced is most likely an unknown descendant of William Telfair (Mary's uncle).

Appendix A: The Chronicles of Roswell by Daniel Stewart Elliott

For Mitty

A Chapter
from
the
Chronicles of Roswell.

24th Chapter
of the
Chronicles of Roswell.

And it came to pass in the fourth year of the reign of King Polk that there was a mighty man in Roswell, an exceeding great Captain feirce and terrible in battle, and his name was King.

Appendix A

2   Moreover he was a tiller of the ground and ruler over much people who wove and spun scarlet and fine linen, - dextrous and cunning workmen were they, and of much craft.

3   And prosperity encamped round about him and his farms overflowed with corn, and he gathered to him manservants and maidservants, oxen, and asses, and he built him a house fair and goodly to the sight.

4   Howbeit his heart was not right, and as riches gathered around him he waxed proud and stiff-necked, and did much evil in the sight of the people of that land.

5   Now it came to pass that over against the orchard of Bulloch (who was a great captain, and a mighty man of valour) there stood a hill, fair and lovely to the sight, insomuch that it was called Pleasant,

6   And on it grew the olive and the vine, the myrtle and the cedar, and the beasts of the forest, the hart and the roe did rest upon it, and in the branches of the trees thereof the birds of the air did build their nests, and the voice of the turtle was heard therein.

7   Now when King did cast his eyes upon that hill, and did see that it was fair and goodly to the eye his heart became wicked and he did covet it insomuch that he was sorely vexed by day, and slumber came not to his eyelids because he owned it not.

8   And he arose and took his staff, and girded his loins, and gat him over to the other side of the river called Chattahoochie to the tent of one Samauel who owned that hill, and he opened his mouth and said,

9 Oh, Samuel behold I have come, and with me are fifty shekels of silver,

10 I pray thee let me have the hill called Pleasant which standeth in the valley of Smith over against the land of Bulloch, and lo! I will give unto thee the fifty shekels of silver.

11 And Samuel's heart smote him, for he loved that hill, but he was exceeding poor, and the money was exceeding bright; so he took the silver, and gave unto him the land.

12 And the heart of King was glad mightily, and he went on his way rejoicing.

13 And when he was come unto his own house, he called unto him his messengers swift of foot, and said unto them,

14 Behold this day have I bought the hill, called Pleasant, which lyeth in the valley of Smith which is by the land of Bulloch; And now go ye throughout all the land, and gather unto me workmen such as are of exceeding craft & cunning, and cutters of wood a great company.

15 And they departed and did as King had commanded them.

16 And it came to pass, the third day after that King had spoken, a mighty multitude was gathered together before his house.

17 And these were men of every craft and trade & calling; both masons from the land of Uz, and layers of stone, and carpenters, and hewers, from the plains of Buzz & Zuzz;

Appendix A

18   And they were gathered before the house of King as he had commanded.

19   And when King saw them his heart was light within him, and he called upon him his Steward, whose name was Brown, and he spake unto him and said;

20   Get thee unto the multitude, and speak unto them thus,

21   Thus saith my Lord: go ye unto the hill which is called Pleasant, and cut me down the trees there of, and all the brushes and underwood thereon, spare not olive nor cedar, nor yet the vine nor the young grapes therein,

22   And let the masons and the carpenters, the stone layers and the hewers build thereon a house for the threshing of my grain, the height where of shall be fourteen cubits, and the width thereof six cubits, and the length thereof twenty cubits: so let it be built.

23   So the masons and the carpenters, and the hewers of wood and of stone, departed from the sight of the Steward, and did even as King had commanded them.

24   And they cut down the groves of myrtle and of fir, and of cedar, and they laid bare the surface of the land so that the hart and the roe fled from that hill, and the birds of the air forsook their young, and the voice of the turtle was heard no more therein.

25   And they erected the house as King had commanded; fourteen cubits was it high, and six cubits broad, and twenty cubits was it long.

26 Now when Bulloch saw this, his heart was troubled, and his countenance fell, nevertheless he complained not; yet neither spake he.

27 But when, by reason of the exceeding noise, and the cloud of dust which arose from the threshing of the grain, he could gain no rest by day or by night, neither he, nor any of his house, he was wroth, and he tore his pants, and he cut off the straps thereof, and he put ashes on his head.

28 And he arose and said, I will go even to the house of King, peradventure I may persuade him to destroy this house, and if he refuse to do justice unto me verily I will avenge my wrong.

29 So he combed the ashes from his head, and he mended his straps, and he girded on his sword and departed.

30 And when he was come unto the house of King, even unto his presence, he opened his mouth and spoke;

31 Oh! King, live forever! Why hath Satan tempted thee to lay waste the hill called Pleasant, and thereon to build a house?

32 Behold! even how the noise of thy threshing disturbeth me and my house, and the dust thereof hath greivously afflicted my servants and mine handmaidens.

33 Destroy this house O! King, and I will repay thee, yea! fourfold what it hath cost thee, for I have no rest by day, nor slumber in the night.

34 But the heart of King waxed haughty, and he laughed him to scorn.

Appendix A

35 Then Bulloch arose in wrath, and he fell upon him, and he smote him under the fifth rib with his sword, and he shed his bowels on the ground.

36 At the same time a mighty East wind arose, and it prevailed over the house of King, and the house of his threshing also, insomuch that they fell, and were destroyed.

37 But Bulloch returned to his house in peace.

Appendix B
The Spectre Cow
by
Daniel Stewart Elliott

The Spectre Cow

A Legend of Roswell

It was a dark and stormy night. The moon which but an hour before had shed her silver flood over the still deep forest and illuminated even the awful abyss of the dry well, was covered with a thick pall of cloud. The wind moaned dismally through the leafless trees, the rain fell in those big, far-apart drops which always denote the coming of a tempest—while the deep-toned thunder reechoed from east to west, and the lightning rent the jetty sky with its vivid jagged line. It was a night when all animated nature by laying shuddering at the fearful convulsions of the elements; when men pulled the bed-clothes so far over their horror-struck eyes as to leave their naked legs exposed, and when the beasts of prey all, save one, crouched and cowered in their mountain caves.
It was on such a night that in the piazza of the lordly castle of the great Baron James Stephens Bullocho von Clifton two figures enveloped in cloaks might have been seen leaning aginst the centre pillar, and conversing in a low earnest tone.

Appendix B

The most remarkable of these two individuals was a female of perhaps some forty years of age. In appearance she was portly & commanding, and by occasional flashes of lightning one might see majesty, revenge, and deep determination written on her lowering brow, and flashing from her eye. Her raven hair was loose and floating in the midnight gale, & a long sharp dagger glittered in her hand. She was the noble & beautiful Baroness Martheria Stephens Bullucho von Clifton. The other individual from his humble dress and swarthy hue might easily be recognized as a peasant. He was the faithful henchman of the Baron, and answered to the name of Henrique. In one hand he bore a lasso, and in the other a brickbat. The Castle Clock stuck twelve.

"It is the hour," said the Baroness in a deep low whisper, "when the Spectre Cow is wont to appear in our Court: Thou remember Henrique, at this very time last night - Bristerio saw it appear & by my halidom the scurvy knave was so terrified that he cowered behind the battlements unable to stir until after it had eaten more than half my plants. When he did rush upon it the Monster only gazed upon him for a moment, shook its head, elevated its tail, & disappeared in a blue flash lightning, leaving behind a strong sulfureous smell; Methinks that the slave was drunk, and coined this marvelous lie"—

"Hist! Hist!! My lady, see what a strange light has spread over the woods behind the walls. And now the Virgin protect us, for by our Lady I see two eyes like balls of fire far up the Castle road. Seest them not? It is the Spectre Cow! Mark you the fires which play around two tips of her horns & tail."

Scarcely had Henrique spoken these words were the two fireballs were seen to rise above the wall, and then quickly to descend. The Spectre had leaped the draw bridge, moat, and walls, and in a moment more stood within twenty yards of where the two lay concealed. The heart of the Baroness beat quickly, but her courage soon rallied.

"Henrique" she exclaimed in a tone of authority —"here are sacred relics which will keep you from all harm, the great-toe-nail of St John Smith, the moustache of St Dandy Marx, and a hair from the tail of Father Mathews horse; Go, my brave henchman, they will preserve you in safety from all harm. Capture me yon scurrilous fiend, and by Our Lady a thousand marks shall be your meed."

"By the little finger of St. Ursula" — she exclaimed impatiently as the Spectre with its cavernous mouth bit off nearly four feet of a bulbous root —"this is unbearable. Hie thee quickly my good villain, or my plants are gone. Remember! A thousand marks!!"

"Not for ten times the sum my Lady: Oh holy Virgin what shall I do?" exclaimed the poor henchman trembling like aspen.

"Out on thee!! dastardly slave" said the Baroness, her eyes flashing fire, fury & contempt. Give *me* the weapons, I'll go myself."

"Heaven forefend!! It was but a momentary fear. All's right now my Lady, I go! St. Pratt protect me"—and he leaped from the piazza to the ground. Poising the fearful brickbat for one moment in his hand, he hurled the missile with all the force of his brawny arm full at the forehead of the Spectre. The fearful beast merely bowed her head as if in derision, and the next moment—the terror stricken henchman saw the brick-bat spinning on the tip end of her right horn. At the same time she shut one eye and winked the other slowly at him. Henrique's knees smote together and he suddenly found difficulty in swallowing, but recovering his presence of mind he flung his lasso with unerring aim. Just then the Spectre wheeled, and the noose fell directly over its uplifted tail. Henrique drew the knot tight, and with a snort — which might be heard a mile the Monster took for the Castle wall. Henrique unable to extricate himself, with the lasso tied around his wrist—was obilged to follow, & before the Baroness could recover her

Appendix B

senses all that could be seen of Henrique was the end of his coat-tails as he and the deamon cleared the Castle Wall.

Nothing more was heard of the unfortunate henchman, although one thing may throw light upon his mysterious fate. As a celebrated botanist in a sack coat & yellow leggins was roaming through the trackless forest near the Castle of Bullocho von Clifton he was surprised to find a skeleton at the foot of that awful precipice called Lover's Rock; in its right hand was the remnant of a rotten rope and in its wide extended jaws a brick bat.— On turning to leave the spot he chanced to observe aloud. "I do wonder who met this awful fate" when a screech owl yelled from a blasted pine "Henrique" "Henrique".

Daniel Elliott's Spectre Cow illustration

Index

Adams, Theodore Dwight 177
Atwood, Sarah Alice 166

Ball, Willis 10
Barham, Jane 11
Barhamville, South Carolina 11, 134
Bayard, Florida121
Beman, Miss 44
Brush Mountain, Georgia 44, 46, 56
Bryant, William Cullen 118
Bulloch, Anna "Annie" 2, 9-12, 13-15, 18-20, 24, 29, 35, 37-38, 40, 44-45, 49, 50, 52, 60, 63, 72-73, 76, 79-80, 82, 86-87, 93-94, 96-97, 100-102, 106, 108, 111-113, 117, 120, 123-124, 128, 130-131, 133, 136, 138, 141, 143, 148-153, 155, 157, 160-162, 164-165, 168-170, 176-178, 186, 188-189, 192-194, 197-199, 202-203, 206
Bulloch, Archibald 3
Bulloch, Charles Irvine 10
Bulloch, Elizabeth "Lizzie" Caskie 24, 29, 34, 48- 49, 82, 92, 144, 152-153, 154, 168
Bulloch Enslaved Persons:
    Bachus 54
    Bess 193
    Maum Charlotte 9, 112, 163, 176, 199
    Maum Grace 9
    Henry 71, 73, 155, 163
    Daddy Luke Moumar 9
    Monroe 45
    Maum Rose 9, 206
    Sally 71, 80

Index

Sarah 62, 120, 127,154-155, 194
Daddy Stephen 9
Daddy William 9, 206
Bulloch, Georgia Amanda 1, 4
Bulloch, Hester "Hettie" Amarantha Elliott 1-5, 7
Bulloch, Irvine Stephens 10, 71-73, 80, 92, 101, 131, 147, 178, 194, 197, 199
Bulloch, James Dunwoody 1, 3, 7, 9, 12, 24, 29, 33-34, 49, 82, 84, 90-92, 99, 103, 153-154, 157, 160, 178,
Bulloch, James Stephens xi, 115, 7, 9, 10,
Bulloch, John Elliott 3
Bulloch, Martha Stewart Elliott (includes references to "Mother") xi, 1-12, 15, 23-24, 28, 31-32, 38, 40, 44, 48-49, 51-52, 55, 57-58, 63-65, 71-73, 78-79, 86, 89, 91-92, 97, 100, 102, 111-112, 117, 120-121, 123, 127-128, 130-133, 136, 141-142, 148-149, 152-157, 159-162, 165-168, 171, 174-176, 178, 180, 185-186, 189, 192-193, 197-199, 200, 204,
Bulloch, Mary Eliza Adams Lewis 106
Burke County, Georgia 3

Camp, George Hull 114, 177
Camp, Jane Margaret 205, 207
Carstensen, Georg 70
Caskie, Ellen Laura 48
Charleston, South Carolina 6-7, 21, 38, 46-47, 61, 64, 87, 92, 173, 195, 197, 200, 203-204
Clapp, Julia Hall 45
Clapp, Nathaniel Bowditch 44, 50, 52
Clay, Eliza Caroline 144, 158-159, 192, 199, 203
Cloud, Aaron 114
Cobb County, Georgia 46
Craik, George Lillie 102
Crystal Palace 69-70, 127, 135, 158, 170, 172, 184
Cumming, Georgia 62
Curtis, George William 27

DeWitt, Miss 98-99, 111, 159
DeWitt, Dr. Thomas 99, 164-165
Dickens, Charles 21, 58, 105
Dunwoody, Charles Archibald 52, 55, 62, 71, 73, 79-80, 88
Dunwoody, Ellen Rice 52, 55, 71, 73-74, 79-80
Dunwoody, Henry Macon 73, 89
Dunwoody, James Bulloch 181, 207
Dunwoody, Jane Irvine Bulloch 71, 79, 112, 161
Dunwoody, John 10, 71, 79, 112, 195
Dunwoody, John Franklin 111, 132
Dunwoody, Marion 71, 80
Dunwoody, Rosaline "Rosa" 71, 79-80
Dunwoody, Ruth Ann Atwood 166

Elliott, Caroline Matilda 4
Elliott, Charles William 4, 5
Elliott, Daniel Stewart 4-5, 9, 90-91, 126, 128, 132, 135-137, 141-142, 144-145, 147, 151-152, 154, 156, 159, 163, 166, 173, 175, 190-191, 199, 201, 205-207
Elliott, Jane Elizabeth 4-6
Elliott, John 2-5, 8
Elliott, John Whitehead 4
Emlen, George 36
Emlen, Sarah 163-164, 170-171

Franconi, Henri Narcisse 26
Franconi's Hippodrome 25, 26
Few, Mary 7
Fisher, John 128

Gainsville, Georgia 55, 61, 87
Gildemeister, Charles 70
Green, Martha E. Marvin 13
Green, Sarah Elizabeth 12, 156, 161

Habersham County, Georgia 87
Habersham, Ann Wylly Adams 44?, 101

Index

Habersham, Mary Ann Stiles 44, 80, 91, 93, 132, 144, 156, 177
Hagedorn, Herman 19
Hall County, Georgia 55
Hand, Julia Isabella 166, 206
Hander, Noble 19
Harrison, Nannie Euphemia Caskie 25
Hartford, Connecticut 9, 84
Henry, Patrick 49
Herbert, Henry William 137
Hodge, James 19
Hodgson, Margaret Telfair 135
Hofland, Barbara 113
Hofland, Thomas 113
Holmes, Oliver Wendell, Sr. 117-118
Hoole, T. Bradshawe 113
Howe, Elias 128-129
Huger, Daniel Elliott 20
Huger, Isabella 20
Hutchison, Corinne Louisa Elliott 1, 7-8
Hutchison, Robert 1, 7, 24, 34, 90, 91, 94

Kennesaw Female Seminary 12, 15
Kennesaw, Georgia 46
King, Barrington 9-10
King, Catherine Evelyn 206
King, Ralph Browne 206
King, Roswell 9
King, Thomas Edward "Tom" 35, 39, 44, 63, 80, 91, 93, 111, 128, 132, 141, 147, 151, 163, 166, 168, 173-174, 178, 181, 184, 189, 194, 206
King, Dr. William Nephew 198

Lachenour, Julia Augusta 171, 190
Lamb, Charles 85
Lamb, Mary 85
Lathrop, Nellie 192, 198

Law, John Stevens 6
Liberty County, Georgia 2-4, 6, 9, 71, 205
Livingstone, Fannie 19
Longfellow, Henry Wadsworth 117-118
Lowell, James Russell 118

McAllister, Joseph Longworth, 144
McGill, Dr. Charles Arthur 44-45
Mackey, Robert 156
Mann, John Elliott 204-205
Marietta, Georgia 12, 21, 28, 71, 79, 130, 156
Marks, Dr. Humphrey 11
Midway Congregational Church 3, 205
Morris, Fanny 183
Morris, Dr. George 37, 68-69, 83, 96, 108, 116, 123, 143,
    147-148, 151, 160, 166, 168, 174, 180, 184-185, 189,
    193, 195, 197, 203, 204, 206
Mulock, Dinah Maria 102
Murray, Nicholas 172

Nesbitt, Martha Deloney Berrien 192, 199
Newton, John 120-122, 135
Niblo, William 186

Palmetto Bluff, South Carolina 1
Philadelphia, Pennsylvania 3-4, 18-19, 24, 30 36, 38, 106,
    108, 124, 126, 143, 148, 163, 194, 201
Phoenix Hall 11
Pratt, Horace Alpheus 14, 156
Pratt, Reverend Nathaniel Alpheus 51, 80. 87. 181
Pratt, Nathaniel Alpheus, Jr. 45
Putnam, George Palmer 27

Rabun County, Georgia 90
Rees, Elizabeth "Lizzie" 188? 190? 202?
Rees, Mary Dews Rice 190
Rees, Matilda 188? 190? 202?, 203

Index

Rice, Rosaline M. Jackson 71
Richmond, Bryan County, Georgia 203-204
Richmond, Virginia 45-46, 65, 72
Robinson, Corinne Roosevelt 17-19
Roosevelt & Son 15, 24
Roosevelt, Caroline Van Ness 32, 104, 148, 150? 184, 195-196
Roosevelt, Cornelius Van Schaak 15, 22, 40
Roosevelt, Cornelius Van Schaak , Jr.15, 39, 77
Roosevelt, Elizabeth "Lizzie" Ellis 24, 61, 66, 76-77, 170? 183
Roosevelt, Elizabeth "Lizzie" Norris Emlen 30, 36, 38, 53, 96, 104, 148, 150, 170? 183, 191
Roosevelt, Henry Latrobe 173, 197
Roosevelt Hyde & Clarke 195, 197
Roosevelt, James "Jim" Alfred 15, 36-37, 51, 68, 74, 76, 104, 157, 163, 171, 195
Roosevelt, Judge James John 104, 106, 184, 197
Roosevelt, James Nicholas 104, 106
Roosevelt, John (child) 61, 76-78
Roosevelt, Margaret Barnhill (includes references to "Mother") 15, 17, 26, 29, 32, 35, 39-41, 46, 50, 53, 60, 63-64, 67, 74, 76, 83, 88-89, 92, 95, 102, 112-113, 120, 131, 133, 149, 152, 154-155, 158, 166-169, 171, 174-176, 178, 180, 182, 190, 193, 195, 199- 200, 203-206
Roosevelt, Margaret Barnhill (child) 76-77
Roosevelt, Mary West 8, 19, 24-25, 30-31, 37, 39-40, 53, 69, 76, 81, 93, 108, 116, 163, 176, 192
Roosevelt, Robert "Rob" Barnhill 15, 17, 36, 61, 76-77, 108, 124, 127, 129, 183
Roosevelt, Silas Weir 15, 18-19, 74, 77, 93, 105, 108, 117, 123, 127, 136
Roosevelt, President Theodore 15, 114
Roosevelt servant
    William (escaped slave) 76-79, 95
Roswell Manufacturing Company 9, 20

Savannah, Georgia 3-5, 7, 9, 19, 21, 24, 47, 94, 116, 131, 156, 161, 177, 190, 204, 206

Index

Schooley's Mountain, New Jersey 77-78
Scriven, Barbaree 71
Shackleford, Carrie 13-14, 63, 111, 130, 160, 162
Singer, Isaac Merritt 128-129
Smith, Archibald (also "the Smiths) 10, 35, 80
Smith, Archibald "Archie" 44?
Smith, Elizabeth Ann "Lizzie" 35? 44-45
Smith, Helen Zubly 35?
Smith, William "Willie" 80, 133
Staten Island, New York 30, 36, 38, 40, 50, 53-54, 70, 94
SS *Arctic* 15
SS *Black Warrior* 82, 84, 91
SS *Georgia* 1, 84
SS *Pulaski* 1
Stewart, Daniel 2, 6
Stiles, William Henry, II 45, 80, 132, 155
Stiles, Mary Cowper 141, 148, 161, 166, 189, 198, 206
Stone Mountain, Georgia 111, 114, 119
Stowe, Harriet Beecher 83-85

Tallulah, Georgia 87, 89-90
Tautphoeus, Jemima Montgomery 27
Taylor, Richard "Dick" Deloney Boling 199
Telfair, Mary (Mrs.) 7-8
Telfair, Mary (Miss) 154
Terrell, Lucy 135-136
Tittlebat Titmouse 87, 90
Toccoa, Georgia 87, 89-90

Wallack, James W. 142, 145-146
Wallack, Lester 145
Warren, Samuel 90
West, Hilborne 1, 18-19, 23, 30, 89, 93, 100, 103,
    136, 143, 153, 174, 189, 193, 201, 203, 205
West, Lewis "Lew" 53, 57, 60, 74, 102, 157, 163, 193,
West, Susan Ann Elliott 1, 4, 9, 18-19, 23-24, 33, 79, 89, 93,
    104, 174, 189, 193, 201, 203, 205

Index

West Point, New York 39, 82
White Sulphur Springs, Georgia 55, 90
Whittier, John Greenleaf 118
Wilmington, North Carolina 47

The Authors

Connie M. Huddleston, a professional historian and historic preservation consultant, has researched the Bulloch family for more than ten years. This is her first book on the Bulloch family, however, three more are in progress. She lives in a log cabin in rural Kentucky and continues to work on the Bulloch/Roosevelt letters along with her historical fiction series for middle graders.

Born in New York's beautiful Finger Lakes Region, **Gwendolyn I. Koehler** now resides near Roswell, Georgia. She is the Education Coordinator at Bulloch Hall, Mittie's girlhood home. Gwen's passion for these letters and the Bulloch family stories inspired the collaboration that brought these letters to print.

Rowill, June 22nd.

My dear the

Your letter came to me this morning, and at the same time is being me to Bratton from his Bro and it is still uncertain with regard to this return to this country, as the many conclude to spend some time in England and Scotland. It is most probable James and he will come home about the end of September. Mrs Bratton had no previous knowledge of James's engagement, hinting say it is almost impossible for James to decide it— so she says...

Made in the USA
Columbia, SC
15 October 2021